THE
NATIONAL
QUIZ TEAM

presents

THE *ONLY*
QUIZ BOOK
YOU WILL
EVER NEED

THE NATIONAL QUIZ TEAM

presents

THE *ONLY* QUIZ BOOK YOU WILL EVER NEED

CENTURY

Published by Century 2014

2 4 6 8 10 9 7 5 3 1

First published in Great Britain in 2014 by
Century
Random House, 20 Vauxhall Bridge Road,
London SW1V 2SA

www.randomhouse.co.uk

Addresses for companies within The Random House Group Limited can be found at:
www.randomhouse.co.uk

The Random House Group Limited Reg. No. 954009

A CIP catalogue record for this book
is available from the British Library

ISBN 9781780893693

The Random House Group Limited supports The Forest Stewardship Council® (FSC®), the leading international forest-certification organisation. Our books carrying the FSC label are printed on FSC®-certified paper. FSC is the only forest-certification scheme supported by the leading environmental organisations, including Greenpeace. Our paper procurement policy can be found at www.randomhouse.co.uk/environment

MIX
Paper from responsible sources
FSC® C016897

Typeset in Sabon 12/15 pt by Palimpsest Book Production Limited,
Falkirk, Stirlingshire

Printed and bound in Great Britain by Clays Ltd, St Ives plc

Contents

Foreword

Welcome to *The Only Quiz Book You Will Ever Need*, written by the four of us – who have all represented England at quizzing.

You probably weren't even aware that there is a national quiz team. Each November some of Europe's strongest general knowledge experts gather together to take part in the European Quizzing Championships (EQC). The first EQC took place ten years ago, in the Belgian city of Ghent, and in November 2014 we will be travelling to Bucharest in Romania, one of quizzing's up-and-coming nations, which is hosting the event for the first time.

One of the most important events at the EQC is the national team quizzing championships, competed for by teams of four representing the leading European quizzing nations and facing some pretty difficult general knowledge questions. England has won six times in the ten years the event has been running, and has reached the final in three of the other four years, so we have a good claim to be the strongest quizzing nation in Europe.

Kevin Ashman and Pat Gibson have played on all six of those winning teams. Kevin and Pat are both members of the formidable Eggheads on the BBC quiz show of that name. Kevin has won four World Quizzing Championships (WQCs) and six EQC individual titles, and holds a host of quiz records including the highest ever scores on *Mastermind* and *Brain of Britain*. Pat has also won four WQC titles and *Brain of Britain*, he is one of five people to win the top prize on the UK version of *Who Wants To Be A Millionaire*, and in 2010 won the *Mastermind* champion of champions title.

Olav Bjortomt has been on four winning national quizzing championships teams. He sets questions for the quiz shows *The Chase* and *University Challenge*, as well as the weekday daily quiz in *Times2*. Olav has won one WQC and one EQC individual title and habitually finishes near the top in major international quiz competitions.

David Stainer has played on two winning national quizzing championships teams. Unlike the others, David is a part-time quizzer; he works full-time as a solicitor in the City of London. David has finished in the top ten at both the WQC and EQC, and is a member of the Crossworders, the reigning champions of champions on ultra-tough BBC quiz show *Only Connect*.

When putting this book together, we wanted to appeal to all ages and abilities. For the serious quizzer, it includes a selection of intentionally very challenging questions of the kind which get asked at the big international quiz events such as the WQC or EQC. As is the case with all serious quiz competitions, these questions require wide and deep reading across a variety of topics, recall of specific points of detail, and often top-quality lateral thinking. We hope that even if you're struggling with these ones, you'll find them interesting and be prompted to read more on the subjects. For all of us, one of the great aspects of quizzing is the ability to learn about stuff you've never heard of before.

As well as some very tough questions, we also include some more moderate ones of a similar difficulty to those you might expect in a typical quiz league or pub quiz, or on a serious quiz show on television. If you're doing well on these questions (or even the super-tough questions), you should consider getting involved in the UK quiz circuit! The British Quizzing Association (BQA) runs a monthly circuit of UK events, which tend to consist of an individual quiz paper and then a team event. You'll be competing with some of the brightest stars in the quiz firmament, so you shouldn't expect to win first time, but you'll soon get a sense of who your rivals are, and will look forward to doing battle every month. Just visit www.quizzing.co.uk for details of the next event.

Within this book you'll also find a broad selection of specialist rounds on a wide array of topics. We've certainly enjoyed being able to set questions on some of our favourite topics and hope you enjoy the questions we've written. We've tried to ensure that between them our specialist rounds cover most categories of general knowledge, so there should be something to please everyone.

Finally, we include something for the quizzers of the future: a selection of quizzes aimed at children. All of us first became interested in quizzing as children and we hope that our younger readers enjoy this book too.

Happy quizzing!

The National Quiz Team

General Knowledge:
Standard

1. Which well-known pair live at 6 West Wallaby Street, Wigan?
2. What is the sinister common name of *Amanita phalloides*, the most poisonous of British mushrooms, accounting for at least 90% of fungus-related fatalities?
3. Lowenbrau, Hofbrauhaus, Augustinerbrau, Paulaner, Hacker-Pschorr and Spaten are the 'Big Six' breweries in which city?
4. Which is England's largest landlocked county?
5. What one word links an arch-enemy of Bugs Bunny and a California National Park that receives over 3 million visitors a year?
6. How many Apollo missions landed men on the moon?
7. In arithmetic, what is the value of 4! i.e. 'four factorial'?
8. In Japan, who controls the so-called Nine Fingered Economy?
9. Who was Henry VIII's wife at the time of his death?
10. Noted for his large-scale nude shoots, who fears for the future of his art because of the withdrawal of the high speed 800 ASA films which enabled him to work at sunrise before cities got crowded?
11. Where on your body would you wear a fascinator?
12. Which Indian lost his world chess title to Magnus Carlsen in November 2013?
13. In which country will the 2018 Winter Olympics be held?
14. In a food context, according to Shirley Conran, 'Life's too short to stuff a . . .' what?
15. Which Dan Brown novel of 2013 shares its name with the first part of Dante Alighieri's 14th-century epic poem *Divine Comedy*?

1. Wallace and Gromit
2. Death cap
3. Munich
4. Shropshire
5. Yosemite (Yosemite Sam)
6. Six – 11, 12, 14, 15, 16 and 17
7. 24 – 4×3×2×1
8. The Yakuza – the names refers to a punishment/penitence practice within the organisation
9. Catherine Parr
10. Spencer Tunick
11. On the head
12. Viswanathan Anand
13. South Korea
14. Mushroom
15. *Inferno*

1. Under what name did Belgian-born Wally de Backer enjoy a worldwide hit with 'Somebody That I Used to Know' in 2012?

2. Played by hip hop recording artist Method Man, Cheese Wagstaff was the last on-screen death in which drama series?

3. As of 2014, which huge South Korean company, a sponsor of Chelsea FC and the main contractor for the Petronas Towers and Burj Khalifa skyscrapers, had over 20% of the world LCD TV market?

4. With 16 active volcanoes, which large Russian peninsula is considered the most volcanic area of the Eurasian content?

5. Sukarno, Suharto and Susilo Bambang Yudhoyono (or SBY) have held the office of President in which large nation?

6. Discovered in 1996, element number 112 in the periodic table, with the symbol Cn is named after which Polish astronomer?

7. Which commercially important food fish has types called bluefin, yellowfin and albacore?

8. What, generally weekly, activity was described by Prime Minister Harold Wilson as 'Going to see Mother'?

9. Derived from a profession/trade, what is the English equivalent of the German surname Fassbinder/Fassbender?

10. In which city will you find Michelangelo's famous 17-foot-tall marble sculpture *David*?

11. Robert (or Robin) Gunningham from Bristol is alleged by some to be which graffiti artist?

12. In which sport was Yani Tseng of Taiwan ranked world number one for 109 consecutive weeks from 2011 to 2013?

13. Of all the cities to host the Summer Olympic Games in the modern era, which comes last alphabetically?

14. Which children's character created by Jean de Brunhoff shares his name with one of the nicknames of Zahir-ud-din Muhammad, the founder of the Mughal dynasty in the Indian subcontinent?

15. Who played Jane Tennison in ITV's series *Prime Suspect* and Queen Elizabeth II in the 2006 film *The Queen*?

1. Gotye (featuring Kimbra)
2. *The Wire*
3. Samsung
4. Kamchatka
5. Indonesia
6. Copernicus
7. Tuna
8. The PM's audience with the Queen
9. Cooper (i.e. barrel-maker)
10. Florence
11. Banksy
12. Golf (women's)
13. Tokyo (1964)
14. Babar (the Elephant)
15. Helen Mirren

1. Ashley Butler won the TV show *Britain's Got Talent* in 2012 with an act featuring which dog?
2. Bela Fleck, the actor Steve Martin and the late Earl Scruggs are particularly associated with playing which musical instrument?
3. In 1985 France, Germany, Belgium, the Netherlands and Luxembourg signed a treaty to cut border checks. The treaty was signed on a boat on the River Moselle running through which namesake village in Luxembourg?
4. In January 2009, which brand temporarily renamed their Butter Pecan ice cream to 'Yes, Pecan!' in honour of newly elected US President Barack Obama?
5. Which large and frequently active volcano dominates the eastern portion of the island of Sicily?
6. Which is bigger . . . 3 squared or 2 cubed?
7. Who wrote the hugely influential book *On the Origin of Species*, first published in 1859?
8. In January 1989, which US President's penultimate diary entry was 'Tomorrow I stop being president'?
9. Commemorated in a G. K. Chesterton poem, which major naval battle of 1571 saw a coalition of southern European Catholic maritime states decisively defeat the main fleet of the Ottoman Empire off western Greece?
10. Born in Liverpool in 1724, which painter is noted for paintings of horses such as *Whistlejacket* and *Hambletonian*?
11. Nihonbashi is a famous bridge, used as the zero marker for all road distances in which country?
12. What nationality is Cadel Evans, the winner of the 2011 Tour de France?
13. Which 2012 World Snooker finalist is a qualified airline pilot, having the nickname 'The Captain' as a result?
14. Which author who died in 2014 wrote *The Queen and I* and *Queen Camilla*?
15. Which Yorkshireman was Poet Laureate from 1984 until 1998 and is noted for collections such as *The Hawk in the Rain*, *Birthday Letters* and *Tales from Ovid*?

Answers to General Knowledge: Standard Quiz 3

1. Pudsey
2. Banjo
3. Schengen
4. Ben & Jerry's
5. Mt Etna
6. 3 squared (9 as opposed to 8)
7. Charles Darwin
8. Ronald Reagan
9. Lepanto
10. George Stubbs
11. Japan – it is in central Tokyo and now has a roaring expressway suspended 10 metres above it
12. Australian
13. Ali Carter
14. Sue Townsend
15. Ted Hughes

1. Which word can refer both to a thick soup made from pureed seafood or vegetables or a handicapping mechanism used in croquet and real tennis?

2. In which city is the vast majority of the political drama *Borgen* set?

3. The album *Stainless Style* by Neon Neon is about the rise and fall of which auto industry figure?

4. Introduced to Paris from Italy in the 16th century by Queen Catherine de Medici, which cake/biscuit is most associated with the Parisian bakers Laduree?

5. Composed of two main islands and with its capital at Basseterre, which is the smallest nation in the Americas?

6. In 2012, Joyce Banda was sworn in as which African country's first female president?

7. Located in Cheshire, by what name is the Nuffield Radio Astronomy Laboratory better known?

8. In which US state is the country's largest Indian reservation?

9. *Dreams from My Father* and *The Audacity of Hope – Thoughts on Reclaiming the American Dream* were both written by which man?

10. In AD 828 the relics of St Mark were taken from which city to Venice and placed in the new basilica?

11. Home to *The Night Watch* amongst many other treasures, in which city did the Rijksmuseum reopen in 2013 after a massive 10-year restoration project?

12. In 1984, in accordance with his expressed wishes, what was played three times as Olympic swimmer Johnny Weismuller's coffin was lowered into the grave?

13. Phil Ivey, Antonio Esfandari and Gus Hansen are three of the world's top players in which game?

14. Who played the implacable policeman Javert in the 2013 film of *Les Miserables*?

15. At the end of World War II, upwards of 70 U-boats were escorted into Lisahally and at one stage 45 were moored, five-deep, along the jetty. Lisahally lies near which city in the British Isles?

Answers to General Knowledge: Standard Quiz 4

1. Bisque
2. Copenhagen
3. John DeLorean – DMC-12 had brushed stainless steel panels
4. Macaroons
5. St Kitts and Nevis
6. Malawi
7. Jodrell Bank
8. Arizona – Navajo Nation
9. Barack Obama
10. Alexandria
11. Amsterdam
12. His Tarzan call
13. Poker
14. Russell Crowe
15. Derry/Londonderry

1. Which BBC sitcom featured the Brockman family comprising parents Pete and Sue and their three children Jake, Ben and Karen?

2. Which Wiganer invented the Bully Proof Vest, the Soccamatic, the Tellyscope and the Autochef?

3. Billionaires Tadashi Yanai (Uniqlo), Chip Wilson (Lululemon) and Stefan Persson (H&M) are particularly associated with which industry?

4. Which EU capital city, the westernmost in mainland Europe, was almost completely destroyed by an earthquake in 1755?

5. In 2008, in which country was Fernando Lugo elected President ending 61 years of continuous rule by the Colorado party?

6. Which island in Indonesia has the largest population of any island in the world with an estimated 132 million inhabitants?

7. Which manufacturer makes the car models Qashqai, Juke and Note?

8. Which became the fifth nation to land on the Moon, after its Chandrayaan-1 unmanned probe landed successfully on 14 November 2008?

9. Which Viennese woman wrote about her abduction and long captivity in the 2010 autobiography *3,096 Days*?

10. Named after a national hero, Skandebeg Square is the main plaza in which European capital city?

11. Which comic strip created by Scott Adams features the title character, his Pointy-Haired Boss and colleagues including Alice, Wally and Asok?

12. With which team did Manchester United draw 5–5 in Sir Alex Ferguson's 1,500th and last game in charge?

13. Boris Becker contested consecutive Wimbledon men's singles finals in 1988, 1989 and 1990, winning in 1989. Who was his opponent in these three matches?

14. Who won the Best Supporting Oscar for his role in *No Country for Old Men* and played the villainous Raoul Silva in the Bond film *Skyfall*?

15. First staged in 1966, which Tom Stoppard play focuses on two minor characters from Shakespeare's *Hamlet*, the five-word title of the play being a direct quote from *Hamlet* Act V, Scene II, line 411?

Answers to General Knowledge: Standard Quiz 5

1. *Outnumbered*
2. Wallace (of Wallace and Gromit)
3. Fashion/Clothing
4. Lisbon
5. Paraguay
6. Java
7. Nissan
8. India
9. Natascha Kampusch
10. Tirana
11. *Dilbert*
12. West Bromwich Albion
13. Stefan Edberg
14. Javier Bardem
15. *Rosenkrantz and Guildenstern Are Dead*

1. Wigan law student John Whaite won which BBC TV contest in 2012?

2. Matt Bellamy is the lead singer with which big-selling rock band from Devon that has released albums including *Black Holes and Revelations* (2006) and *The Resistance* (2009)?

3. In which country is the accolade 'Vegas Finas Primeras' used to describe land on which the finest tobacco is grown?

4. With a peak elevation of 8,611 metres (28,251 feet), which is the highest point of the Karakoram Range and the highest point in Pakistan?

5. Which large lake on the Rhine has shores in Germany, Austria and Switzerland?

6. Which great English scientist, who worked initially as an assistant to Sir Humphrey Davy, was commemorated on the Bank of England £20 note from 1991 until 2001?

7. Which is both the longest venomous snake in Africa and the fastest snake in the world?

8. Deriving from the Italian for 'Red beard', what name was used by two Ottoman corsair brothers who dominated the Mediterranean in the early 16th century?

9. In 1860, which British High Commissioner in China ordered the looting and burning of Peking's Summer Palace?

10. From its completion in 1981, which British bridge was, for the next 16 years, the longest single-span suspension bridge in the world?

11. Serious competitors in which pursuit might train for long hours using the software package Zyzzyva?

12. Which male Ethiopian athlete holds both World and Olympic records in the 5,000 m and 10,000 m, winning both events at the Beijing Olympics in 2008 and the 10,000 m at the Athens Olympics in 2004?

13. Which Kenyan-born cyclist, riding for Team Sky, won the 2013 Tour de France?

14. Winning with *The Informer* (1935), *The Grapes of Wrath* (1940), *How Green Was My Valley* (1941) and *The Quiet Man* (1952), who is the only person to win four Best Director Oscars?

15. Which best-selling novel started the trilogy which continued with *Bring Up the Bodies* and will conclude with *The Mirror and the Light*?

1. *The Great British Bake Off*
2. Muse
3. Cuba – something like 'Appellation Contrôlée'
4. K2
5. Lake Constance or Bodensee
6. Michael Faraday
7. Black mamba – *Dendroaspis polylepis*
8. Barbarossa
9. Lord Elgin
10. Humber Bridge
11. Scrabble – it is a genus of tropical American weevil
12. Kenenisa Bekele
13. Chris Froome
14. John Ford
15. *Wolf Hall* (Hilary Mantel)

1. Which popular pet rodent, whose incisors never stop growing, comes in 24 different species, including the Syrian, the Russian dwarf Campbell and the Roborovski?

2. Hamad bin Isa Al Khalifa became King of which island-country in 2002? Previous rulers of this kingdom have used the titles Hakim and Emir.

3. Which artist's sculpture (1501–04) of David was created from a slab of marble abandoned 40 years earlier by Agostino di Duccio?

4. Who was the first US President to be assassinated?

5. Arranged by the 'Prime Minister of Jazz', Ferde Grofé, which 1924 composition by George Gershwin opens with a clarinet glissando made even more famous by its use in the opening of the Woody Allen film *Annie Hall*?

6. What is Poland's oldest institute of higher learning?

7. In 1889, the Frenchwoman Herminie Cadolle invented and patented what she initially called the 'corselet-gorge'. It has been called the first modern example of which undergarment?

8. In April 2014, which writer was called 'the greatest Colombian who ever lived' by Colombian President Juan Manuel Santos?

9. What is [the mother of director Rob] Estelle Reiner's only line in the film *When Harry Met Sally . . .* ?

10. Which 1988 film from director John Waters has become a Broadway musical featuring the songs 'Good Morning Baltimore', 'Welcome to the 60s' and 'You Can't Stop the Beat'?

11. In Arthurian legend, the Fisher King, who lives at the castle of Corbenic (or Corbin), is charged with keeping which cup?

12. On 9 June 1954, who was famously asked by army lawyer Joseph N. Welch: 'At long last, have you left no sense of decency?'

13. Which Asian country is ruled by the only remaining monarch in the world who reigns under the title of 'Emperor'?

14. Which detective is revealed in 'The Yellow Face' to occasionally use cocaine 'as a protest against the monotony of existence when cases were scanty and the papers uninteresting'?

15. Which city's 15 subway stations include St George's Cross, St Enoch, Kinning Park and Buchanan Street? They form the third-oldest underground metro system in the world.

Answers to General Knowledge: Standard Quiz 7

1. Hamster
2. Bahrain
3. Michelangelo
4. Abraham Lincoln
5. 'Rhapsody in Blue'
6. Jagiellonian University, Cracow
7. Bra/brassiere
8. Gabriel García Márquez, who died on 17 April 2014
9. 'I'll have what she's having'
10. *Hairspray*
11. The Holy Grail
12. Senator Joseph McCarthy
13. Japan
14. Sherlock Holmes
15. Glasgow – opened in 1896, after the London and Budapest systems

1. Which veteran British actor, who died in April 2014, played Nikita Khrushchev, Beria, Manuel Noriega, Pope John XXIII, Mussolini, J. Edgar Hoover and Winston Churchill?

2. 'I don't want a place to stay / Get your booty on the floor tonight, make my day' – lyrics from which Eurodance hit of 1989–90?

3. What are Olympus, Athos, Ossa, Giona and Parnassus?

4. Former CIA operative Bryan Mills wreaks havoc across Paris via the art of kicking major butt in which 2008 film?

5. The 16 November 1532 Battle of Cajamarca resulted in the defeat by 168 Spanish troops of an 80,000-strong army from which empire – the largest in pre-Columbian America?

6. Which US rapper was inspired by the artist Marina Abramović and her landmark MoMA piece *The Artist is Present* to create his own six-hour performance art piece *Picasso Baby* in 2013?

7. Regarded as the prestige dialect of Yue, which official language in Hong Kong and Macau is also known as Guangfuhua?

8. The herb *Nepeta cataria* attracts cats due to the organic compound nepetalactone. What is the plant's popular name?

9. J.K. Rowling was given a £1,500 advance by Bloomsbury editor Barry Cunningham for which novel?

10. The 2006 novel *I Want You* by Federico Moccia features a romantic scene at Rome's Milvian Bridge that is said to have inspired which global craze, blamed for a June 2014 parapet collapse on the Pont des Arts footbridge in Paris?

11. Flamengo, Botafogo, Fluminense and Vasco da Gama are known as the 'Big Four' football clubs of which Brazilian city?

12. Created by Jean Amic and Jean-Louis Sieuzac and released in 1977, which Yves Saint Laurent perfume shares its name with the dried latex obtained from *Papaver somniferum*?

13. Captured by a Gallic chief and put to death at Mark Antony's order, Decimus Brutus became, in 43 BC, the first of which man's assassins to be killed?

14. Jebediah, Shadrach, Marlon, Zak, Cain, Chas and Charity – members of which family in the TV soap *Emmerdale*?

15. Which two-word title links albums by Bruce Springsteen, Dead Confederate and Emmylou Harris and songs by Neil Young, Interpol, Gillian Welch and Miley Cyrus?

Answers to General Knowledge: Standard Quiz 8

1. Bob Hoskins
2. 'Pump up the Jam' by Technotronic
3. Greek mountains, with the prefix Mount
4. *Taken* – Mills is played by Liam Neeson
5. Inca Empire
6. Jay Z
7. Cantonese
8. Catnip (or catmint)
9. *Harry Potter and the Philosopher's Stone*
10. 'Love locks' – two lovers attaching a padlock inscribed with their names to a bridge then throwing the key in the river
11. Rio de Janeiro
12. Opium – *Papaver* . . . is the opium poppy
13. Julius Caesar
14. The Dingles
15. Wrecking Ball

1. Which Disney animated film features Olaf the Snowman?
2. Edith Cresson is the only woman to have held which office?
3. Wolverine World Wide manufacture boots and other footwear branded with the name of which company, the world's leading manufacturer of construction and mining equipment?
4. Which novella about the fisherman Santiago and his attempt to catch a marlin was singled out for particular recognition when Ernest Hemingway was awarded the Nobel Prize?
5. Which Austrian founder of psychoanalysis was nominated 32 times for the Nobel Prize in Medicine? The prize's committee engaged an expert who concluded that a further investigation was not necessary, since his work was of no proven scientific value.
6. Currently, it produces 5 million barrels per day and measures 174 miles by 19 miles. The world's largest oil field by far, Ghawar is in which country?
7. Which Nordic island-nation is the most sparsely populated country in Europe, with an average of 3 people per km²?
8. Which transvestite from Transsexual, Transylvania, was first played by Tim Curry in the 1973 London production of *The Rocky Horror Show*?
9. A Roman soldier who was martyred by decapitation in AD 303, who is the patron saint of Catalonia, Bulgaria, Egypt, Ethiopia, Greece, Portugal and Serbia, as well as leprosy, herpes and syphilis?
10. Which action star has been a *Kickboxer*, a *Hard Target*, a *Timecop* and a *Universal Soldier*?
11. On 1 January 1892, the 15-year-old Irish girl Annie Morris became the first ever person to pass through which immigration station?
12. 'The World's Biggest Tennis Racquet' is located in Barellan, New South Wales. It is a 13.8 metre-long replica of the racquet used by which two-time Wimbledon ladies' singles champion?
13. Which Sheffield rock band sold 12 million copies in the US of their 1987 album *Hysteria*?
14. *Salamandra salamandra* is perhaps Europe's best known salamander species. Coloured black with yellow dots or stripes, what is its common name?
15. Formerly called Saigon, the largest city in Vietnam is now named after which man, who was born Nguyễn Sinh Cung?

Answers to General Knowledge: Standard Quiz 9

1. *Frozen*
2. Prime Minister of France
3. Caterpillar
4. *The Old Man and the Sea*
5. Sigmund Freud
6. Saudi Arabia
7. Iceland
8. Dr Frank N. Furter
9. Saint George
10. Jean Claude van Damme
11. Ellis Island, New York City
12. Evonne Goolagong/Evonne Cawley – who was raised in the town
13. Def Leppard
14. Fire salamander
15. Ho Chi Minh

1. Launched on 23 November 1936, issue 1's motto was 'While there's _____, there's hope'. Which magazine's first cover was a photo of the Fort Peck Dam taken by Margaret Bourke-White?

2. Which film, starring Glenn Close as the perpetrator of the rabbit's gruesome fate, gave rise to the phrase 'bunny boiler'?

3. Which bloke from Stoke is the best-selling British solo musical artist in UK chart history, as well as the best-selling non-Latino artist in Latin America?

4. D.D. Palmer theorised that misalignment of the bones was the underlying cause of all 'dis-ease', and the majority of misalignments were in the spinal column. As a result, he founded which 'science of healing without drugs' in the 1890s?

5. Code-named Operation Dynamo, the mass wartime evacuation from which port-city features in the Ian McEwan novel *Atonement*?

6. Pisa's international airport is named after which 'father of modern science' and 'father of observational astronomy', who was born in the city in 1564?

7. Jonny Lee Miller plays Sherlock Holmes in which TV show?

8. Which sporting event was won by Australia on 7 June 2014?

9. The ad slogan 'You press the button, we do the rest' was coined by George Eastman, who founded which company in 1888?

10. Whose death at the age of 33 on 26 July 1952, was announced in a radio broadcast saying: 'The Press Secretary's Office of the Presidency of the Nation fulfils its very sad duty to inform the people of the Republic that at 20:25 hours Mrs _____ _____, Spiritual Leader of the Nation, died'?

11. Which 2000 memoir by US chef Anthony Bourdain is subtitled *Adventures in the Culinary Underbelly*?

12. Which film starred Will Ferrell as the evil fashion designer Mugatu, proud inventor of the piano key neck-tie?

13. Designed by architects Adolphe Willette and Édouard-Jean Niermans, which Paris cabaret at 82 boulevard de Clichy first opened on 6 October 1889?

14. In 1916, which Turin-based car company began building Europe's largest factory at Lingotto, along with a rooftop track for test driving?

15. Which US pop star and tabloid favourite is seen giving birth on a bearskin rug in a 2006 nude sculpture by Daniel Edwards?

1. *LIFE*
2. *Fatal Attraction*
3. Robbie Williams
4. Chiropractic
5. Dunkirk
6. Galileo Galilei
7. *Elementary*
8. Epsom Derby – Australia is a British-bred Irish-trained chestnut racehorse
9. Kodak
10. Eva Perón (aka Evita)
11. *Kitchen Confidential*
12. *Zoolander*
13. Moulin Rouge
14. Fiat
15. Britney Spears

1. Dedicated to his mother Joyce Barbara, the 2009 'Horn of Plenty' collection was created by which British fashion designer, whose previous clothing innovations included 'bumster' jeans?
2. In 1956, John Hunt retired from the army to run which award?
3. Complete the famous line that appeared in a *New York Sun* editorial in 1897: 'Yes, Virginia, there is . . .'?
4. Which actor starred alongside his mother Jill Balcon in the 2003 BBC radio play *Deadheading Roses*? He later dedicated his record-breaking third Oscar win to her memory.
5. Born Hakeem Seriki, which rapper had a hit with 'Ridin'?
6. While working at a London gallery in 1873, which Dutch artist is thought to have fallen in love with his landlady's daughter, Eugenie Loyer – a period of his life that was dramatised in a 2003 play by Nicholas Wright?
7. Which award statuette was once described by Billy Connolly as 'a death mask on a stick'?
8. Enoch Powell said: 'All political lives, unless they are cut off in midstream at a happy juncture, end in . . .' what?
9. Which item of clothing made its public debut on 5 July 1946, at a fashion show hosted by the Piscine Molitor, a popular swimming pool in the 16th arrondissement of Paris?
10. First staged at the National Theatre in 2013, *The Light Princess* is the first musical by which US musician, who topped the singles chart with a remix of her song 'Professional Widow'?
11. Which Kazakh reporter made fashion news headlines at the 2006 Cannes Film Festival when he modelled a fluorescent green mankini, a type of one-piece sling swimsuit for men?
12. Which Austrian was described by the pianist Glenn Gould as 'a bad composer who died too late rather than too early'?
13. The Yale University coach Walter Camp introduced the concept of 'downs' and 'yards gained' into which sport?
14. Which poet wrote the lyrics to the song 'Scots Wha Hae' in 1793?
15. Named after an extremely popular video game that came packaged with the Nintendo Game Boy, which 1992 one-hit wonder for Doctor Spin was co-written by Andrew Lloyd Webber?

1. Alexander McQueen or Lee McQueen
2. The Duke of Edinburgh's Award – Hunt led the first successful climb of Everest in 1953
3. '. . . a Santa Claus'
4. Daniel Day-Lewis
5. Chamillionaire – the 2006 no. 2 hit featured Krayzie Bone (of Bone Thugs-n-Harmony)
6. Vincent van Gogh – the play is *Vincent in Brixton*
7. BAFTA
8. '. . . failure'
9. Bikini – it was modelled by former nude dancer Micheline Bernardini
10. Tori Amos
11. Borat Sagdiyev (played by Sacha Baron Cohen)
12. Wolfgang Amadeus Mozart
13. American football or gridiron
14. Robert Burns
15. *Tetris*

General Knowledge: Standard Quiz 12

1. The special sauce in a McDonald's Big Mac is a variant of which salad dressing, whose name presumably comes from an archipelago in the St Lawrence River?
2. Kathleen Ni Houlihan is a female personification of what?
3. James Stewart played a photojournalist named Jeff who passes the time by watching neighbours like 'Miss Torso', 'Miss Lonelyhearts' and the suspicious-looking Lars Thorwald in which Hitchcock film?
4. Which of Henry VIII's wives was beheaded for committing adultery with her personal secretary Francis Dereham and Henry's favourite male courtier, Thomas Culpeper?
5. Which 1968 film, directed by Stanley Kubrick, had an LA premiere that Rock Hudson reputedly walked out of, saying: 'Will someone tell me what the hell this is about?'?
6. First released for Facebook in April 2012, which game features red jelly beans, orange lozenges, yellow lemon drops, green chiclets, blue lollipop heads and purple clusters?
7. Which Swiss *Société Anonyme* calls itself 'the world's leading nutrition, health and wellness company' and has named its mission to serve consumers 'Good Food, Good Life'?
8. Established in 1926, which airline is Hong Kong's flag carrier?
9. Stanley Peach is best known for designing which iconic English sporting venue? It was built in 1922 – the year in which Gerald Patterson and Suzanne Lenglen were singles champions.
10. Whose TV roles have included Daniel Ryan, Dr Ben, Derek Noakes, Andy Millman and David Brent?
11. Coined in 1971 by the entrepreneur Ralph Vaerst, which tech-related nickname is given to the South Bay portion of the San Francisco Bay Area in Northern California, occupying roughly the same area as the Santa Clara Valley?
12. Soundtracking a video that showcased a memorable pair of hot pants, which 2000 lead single off the album *Light Years* was Kylie Minogue's first UK no. 1 since 1990?
13. Which cruise ship struck rocks off Giglio in January 2012?
14. What is the only man-made interoceanic waterway in the world?
15. James Gregory (author of the memoir *Goodbye Bafana*), Christo Brand and Jack Swart were three of the best known prison warders of which Nobel laureate, who passed away in 2013?

Answers to General Knowledge: Standard Quiz 12

1. Thousand Island dressing
2. Ireland
3. *Rear Window*
4. Catherine Howard
5. *2001: A Space Odyssey*
6. *Candy Crush Saga*
7. Nestlé
8. Cathay Pacific
9. Wimbledon Centre Court
10. Ricky Gervais (in *Alias, Louie, Derek, Extras, The Office*)
11. 'Silicon Valley'
12. 'Spinning Around' – her first chart-topper since 'Tears on My Pillow'
13. *Costa Concordia*
14. Panama Canal
15. Nelson Mandela

1. *Who You Are* was the 2011 debut album by which English singer and former coach on *The Voice*?

2. Which button on Facebook was originally going to be called 'awesome'?

3. Louvre curator Jacques Saunière is murdered by the albino monk Silas at the start of which novel?

4. The wise and kind centaur Chiron, who taught Achilles among many other heroes in their youth, was placed by Jupiter in heaven among the stars as which zodiacal constellation (it lies between Scorpius and Ophiuchus to the west and Capricornus to the east)?

5. Owned by the Rijksmuseum, this painting appears on the packaging of Dutch Masters cigars. *The Sampling Officials* (1662), aka *Syndics of the Drapers' Guild*, aka *De Staalmeesters* has been described as the 'last great collective portrait' by which painter?

6. What was Charles Alcock proposing in a meeting of 20 July 1871, when he said: 'That it is desirable that a Challenge Cup should be established in connection with the Association, for which all clubs belonging to the Association should be invited to compete'?

7. Which of Rod Stewart's ex-wives starred in the music video for 'Stacy's Mom' by Fountains of Wayne?

8. Starring Robert De Niro and Al Pacino, which 1995 Michael Mann film was a remake of the TV movie *L.A. Takedown*?

9. The Gunpowder Plot of 1605 sought to kill which king?

10. Published in the same year that its editorship was taken on by Graydon Carter, which US magazine's August 1992 issue featured a cover photo of 'Demi's Birthday Suit' – Demi Moore covered in a body painting by Joanne Gair?

11. Which Berkshire racecourse held its first horse race, Her Majesty's Plate, with a purse of 100 guineas on 11 August 1711?

12. Palma de Mallorca is the capital city of which archipelago?

13. Which diarist grew up to have a child with Sharon Bott instead of his teenage paramour and love of his life, Pandora Braithwaite?

14. Nomophobia has become an increasingly common malady during the last decade. It is the fear of which type of technological deprivation?

15. In which chess variant does a piece moved on one board pass 'through the looking glass' onto the second board?

1. Jessie J/Jessica Ellen Cornish
2. Like button
3. *The Da Vinci Code* by Dan Brown
4. Sagittarius
5. Rembrandt
6. The FA Cup – Alcock was the Football Association secretary
7. Rachel Hunter
8. *Heat*
9. James I (and VI of Scotland)
10. *Vanity Fair*
11. Ascot
12. Balearic Islands
13. Adrian Mole
14. Having no mobile phone/not being in mobile phone contact
15. Alice chess

1. Championship Vinyl is a London record store in which 1995 Nick Hornby novel?
2. Which plant's shoots account for 99% of a giant panda's diet?
3. Emmet Brickowski, a builder from Bricksburg, is the hero of which 2014 film?
4. Which recurring cast member on the hospital TV comedy *E/R* then starred as Dr Doug Ross in the hospital TV drama *ER*?
5. Who measures 111 feet 6 inches from her heel to the top of her head, has a 420-inch waistline and weighs around 32,140 stone?
6. In a will dated 1279, a Genoese soldier named Ponzio Bastone left a box of _____ to his family. This bequest was the earliest known reference in Italian to which type of food?
7. Minamoto no Yoritomo was the first person to hold which title as the military dictator of feudal Japan? It was later used for the title of a 1975 novel by James Clavell and the UK's name for the Mitsubishi Pajero SUV.
8. Which celestial body accounts for about 99.86% of the total mass of the solar system?
9. Newly discovered evidence has resulted in the Australian machine-gunner Cedric Popkin being credited with shooting down which fighter ace on 21 April 1918?
10. Which form of physical augmentation, involving a silicone prosthesis was pioneered by the surgeons Thomas Cronin and Frank Gerow at the University of Texas in 1962?
11. Which movie review aggregator website began as a spare-time project by Berkeley student Senh Duong on 12 August 1998? The first film featured was *Your Friends and Neighbors*.
12. Who won a Grammy for his 1986 comedy LP, *A Night at the Met*?
13. Launched in 2007 by *Wallpaper** founder Tyler Brûlé, which unashamedly upmarket lifestyle/global affairs magazine shares its name with a type of eyeglass?
14. Which footwear/clothing brand began in 1970 when Frenchman Daniel Raufast saw a poster for the musical *Hair* and saw that its exciting but barefooted cast of youngsters deserved suitably exciting and youthful things to wear on their feet, like shoes made of nubuck cattle leather?
15. Which mural by Leonardo da Vinci depicts a scene of Jesus with his Twelve Disciples as told in the Gospel of John, 13:21?

Answers to General Knowledge: Standard Quiz 14

1. *High Fidelity*
2. Bamboo
3. *The Lego Movie*
4. George Clooney
5. The Statue of Liberty
6. Pasta – it referred to 'macaronis'
7. Shogun
8. The sun
9. Manfred Freiherr von Richthofen aka 'The Red Baron'
10. Augmentation mammoplasty/breast augmentation – using the Cronin–Gerow implant
11. Rotten Tomatoes
12. Robin Williams
13. *Monocle*
14. Kickers
15. *The Last Supper*

1. Which Croydon-born supermodel performed a pole dance in the video for the White Stripes' 2003 single 'I Just Don't Know What to Do With Myself'?

2. Which London fish market name has become a word for coarsely abusive language?

3. In 1903, which US inventor and advocate of direct current (DC) electrocuted Topsy the Elephant in a horrifying demonstration of the dangers of alternating current?

4. Which French fashion designer and former *Eurotrash* TV presenter introduced the men's skirt in the mid-1980s?

5. Founded in 1845, New York's Temple Emanu-El is the world's largest house of prayer of which type?

6. The former army drill instructor R. Lee Ermey played Gunnery Sergeant Hartman in which Vietnam War film?

7. In a 1983 front page headline, the *Sun* asked 'Do You Really Want This Old Fool to Run Britain?' about which politician?

8. The casino gambling tables of which country are closed to its citizens, who are forbidden from entering the gaming rooms?

9. Which London dry gin was created by James Burroughs in a Chelsea distillery that he purchased in 1862?

10. In 1970, which member of the Beatles made his art gallery debut with the *Bag One* collection of lithographs? His (second) wife's seminal performance work is *Cut Piece* (1964).

11. In 1905, which immigrant from Vetschau, Germany, opened a delicatessen on New York City's Columbus Avenue, where he used his wife's recipe to sell the first ready-made mayonnaise?

12. Which Costa del Sol resort is situated between Malaga and the Gibraltar Strait in the foothills of the Sierra Blanca? This Andalusian city is also the destination of an annual trip by the reality TV stars of *The Only Way is Essex*.

13. Before her career was torpedoed by 'the Gwen Troakes Incident' in 1976, which TV cook wrote the autobiography *Something's Burning* (1960) and the novel *The Lormes of Castle Rising* (1975)?

14. In 1970, which US boxer knocked out Jimmy Ellis in five rounds to become undisputed World Heavyweight Champion; later fighting three classic bouts with Muhammad Ali.

15. Which Eltham-born comedian's book *I Never Left Home* was 1944's bestselling non-fiction book in the US?

1. Kate Moss
2. Billingsgate
3. Thomas Edison
4. Jean-Paul Gaultier
5. Synagogue
6. *Full Metal Jacket*
7. Michael Foot – the then Labour Party leader
8. Monaco
9. Beefeater
10. John Lennon
11. Richard Hellmann
12. Marbella
13. Fanny Cradock (born Phyllis Nan Sortain Pechey)
14. Joe Frazier
15. Bob Hope (born Leslie Townes Hope)

1. Which fast food restaurant chain is known for its Bender in a Bun with Cheese?

2. The Australian actor Keith Michell is best known for his TV and film performances as which king, starting with a 1970 BBC series of six television plays?

3. Which Puccini opera's historical setting, the Forbidden City, has been called 'laughably inaccurate' because it was built hundreds of years after the events of the opera supposedly take place?

4. Which USC graduate, best known for his singles 'I Need a Dollar' and 'The Man' and for writing and performing vocals on Avicii's 'Wake Me Up', was born Egbert Nathaniel Dawkins III in 1979?

5. Which African mountain was first conquered in 1889 by Hans Meyer and Ludwig Purtscheller?

6. Nick Nack was the diminutive sidekick of which triple-nippled Bond villain and hit man-for-hire?

7. In the title of an HBO TV show, who are Hannah Horvath, Marnie Michaels, Jessa Johansson and Shoshanna Shapiro?

8. Launched in 2009 by Travis Kalanick and Garrett Camp, which San Francisco-based mobile app connects passengers with drivers of vehicles for hire and ridesharing services?

9. The Mission, the Tenderloin and 'the Wall Street of the Twenty Teens', SoMa (the docklands south of Market Street) are central areas of which Californian city?

10. The Christian Church celebrates the birth of three people. Christ on 25 December, and who else on 24 June and 8 September?

11. Which German luxury sports car maker has created the $848,000 887-horsepower super-hybrid, the 918 Spyder?

12. In 2003, Dong Hyun Kim founded which high street Japanese food chain in London's embankment?

13. In 1962, which DIY company introduced the world's first cordless outdoor product – the cordless hedge trimmer? It also made the world's first portable electric drill for consumers (1946).

14. Who won the French Open in the year (2009) Rafael Nadal suffered his first ever singles defeat at the tournament (by Robin Söderling)?

15. Which Hampshire port-city served as the launching point of the *Mayflower* and the *Titanic*?

Answers to General Knowledge: Standard Quiz 16

1. Wimpy
2. Henry VIII – the TV series was *The Six Wives of Henry VIII*
3. *Turandot*
4. Aloe Blacc
5. Kilimanjaro
6. Francisco Scaramanga – in *The Man with the Golden Gun*
7. *Girls*
8. Uber, founded as UberCab
9. San Francisco
10. John the Baptist and Virgin Mary
11. Porsche
12. Wasabi
13. Black + Decker
14. Roger Federer
15. Southampton

1. Which British peninsula is said to have given its name to an informal test for whether a tumescent penis can be broadcast on television?

2. 'The surface is fine and powdery . . . I can pick it up loosely with my toe.' Which American said these words in 1969 after saying something far more famous?

3. The Piedmont town of Ivrea holds a festival each spring in which local people throw which citrus fruit at one another?

4. A former husband of painter Georgia O'Keeffe, Alfred Stieglitz is credited with turning what into a recognised art form?

5. In 2013 which carnivorous mammal was discovered in the western hemisphere, the first such discovery since 1978?

6. Led by Vivian Stanshall, which eccentric British band's album *Gorilla* contains tracks called 'Cool Britannia', the origin of that phrase, and 'Death Cab for Cutie', the origin of the band name?

7. A report prepared in 2006 by economist Nicholas Stern warned that what could, if left unchecked, reduce global per capita consumption by up to 20% each year?

8. The paralytic disease konzo is believed to be caused by cyanide poisoning from eating what staple food when improperly prepared?

9. The forename and surname of which current South African bowler is an anagram of 'Steely Dan'?

10. The aria 'Che gelida manina' comes from which Puccini opera featuring Mimi and Rodolfo?

11. Native American adherents of the ghost dance movement were slain at which 1890 battle?

12. Which Skopje-born nun was the first winner of the Templeton Prize, awarded for 'affirming life's spiritual dimension'?

13. Part of an abbreviation seen on high streets the world over, what is Swedish for 'hers'?

14. Which late US entertainer's portrayal of the Japanese character Yunioshi in *Breakfast at Tiffany's* has come to be condemned over the years as racial stereotyping?

15. So called because the crux of the story often lies below the surface, iceberg theory is a term given to the style of which US author of works such as *The Sun Also Rises*?

Answers to General Knowledge: Standard Quiz 17

1. Mull of Kintyre
2. Neil Armstrong (on landing on the moon)
3. Oranges
4. Photography
5. Olinguito
6. Bonzo Dog Doo-dah Band
7. Climate change
8. Cassava or manioc or yuca
9. Dale Steyn
10. *La Bohème*
11. Wounded Knee
12. Blessed Mother Teresa of Calcutta or Agnes Bojaxhiu
13. Hennes (as in Hennes & Mauritz)
14. Mickey Rooney
15. Ernest Hemingway

1. Which snake is the only animal species whose full scientific name is identical to its common name?

2. Which is the only non-South American mountain with a peak which is further from the centre of the earth than Everest?

3. Which country's space agency, the National Aerospace Development Administration, has the unfortunate acronym NADA?

4. What television sporting venue links Hammerhead, Wilson, Gambon, Bacharach and Bentley?

5. England footballer Daniel Sturridge appeared alongside Pele in an advert for which sandwich chain shortly before the 2014 FIFA World Cup?

6. Sounding like it belongs in a bottle, which coefficient is a measure of the inequality of a distribution, between 0 and 1?

7. What name links a domed building in Rome built by Agrippa and a building in Paris that houses the remains of great French citizens such as Victor Hugo and Marie Curie?

8. What was the (in)famous surname of the Italian jazz musician Romano, who married Sophia Loren's sister with whom he had a famous daughter?

9. Which author of 'The Rover' and 'Oroonoko' is the first English-woman to have earned her living from writing?

10. Which two words complete the quote by Tom Stoppard? 'Skill without imagination is craftsmanship . . . imagination without skill gives us _____ _____.'

11. What is the name for the sudden and unexplained loss of fine motor skills needed to play a sport (such as golf) effectively?

12. Whose Symphony No. 1 in G minor is nicknamed *Winter Daydreams*?

13. Replaced by the forint in 1946 after undergoing the most severe hyperinflation in history, the pengő was a currency unit in which European nation?

14. Which film had three of the five nominations for Best Original Song at the Academy Awards ceremony held in 1995, including the eventual winner, 'Can You Feel the Love Tonight'?

15. Niels Finsen, who won the 1903 Nobel Prize in Medicine remains the only Nobel laureate from which self-governing part of the Kingdom of Denmark?

Answers to General Knowledge: Standard Quiz 18

1. Boa constrictor
2. Kilimanjaro
3. North Korea or People's Republic of Korea
4. The *Top Gear* test track (they are the names of corners)
5. Subway
6. Gini coefficient
7. Pantheon or panthéon
8. Mussolini
9. Aphra Behn
10. "Modern art"
11. Yips
12. Piotr Tchaikovsky
13. Hungary
14. *The Lion King*
15. Faroe islands

1. Which father and son horticulturalists give their name to the genus of plants which includes the wandering jew?

2. Which art exhibition was set up in 1863 to exhibit works rejected by the jury of the official Paris Salon, which included Manet's *Déjeuner sur l'herbe*?

3. Which woman has been called 'the first woman to run the government' for the role she played when her husband the serving US President, suffered a stroke in 1919?

4. What punk band with members including Sid Vicious were the subject of the Julien Temple documentary *The Filth and the Fury*?

5. Popular at weddings, by what two-word name is Jeremiah Clarke's 'Prince of Denmark's March' better known?

6. Which saint is said to have been able to see a mass on the wall of her room despite being too ill to attend it, leading to her being made the patron saint of television?

7. In cinema, what links Vladimir Nabokov in 1962, Arthur C. Clarke in 1968, William Makepeace Thackeray in 1975 and Stephen King in 1980?

8. Which world capital city is located at the confluence of the Blue and White Nile?

9. In May 1968, which east London tower block partially collapsed after a resident decided to put the kettle on?

10. Maurice Gatsonides won the 1953 Monte Carlo Rally, a fact which makes which later invention by him, designed to discourage speeding, ironic?

11. Which German author wrote the novels *Steppenwolf* and *The Glass Bead Game*?

12. Which former astronaut and one-time senator for Ohio was the only individual recipient of an email from Bill Clinton during Clinton's time as President?

13. Which hirsute French rugby union player, who retired in 2014, was nicknamed 'the Caveman'?

14. Who wrote the 2nd century mathematical and astronomical treatise *The Almagest*, containing theories on planetary movements accepted until Copernicus?

15. The song 'Tossed Salads and Scrambled Eggs' closed each episode of which US sitcom which ran from 1993 to 2004?

1. John Tradescant
2. Salon des Refusés
3. Edith Wilson (wife of Woodrow Wilson)
4. Sex Pistols
5. 'Trumpet Voluntary'
6. St Clare of Assisi
7. Stanley Kubrick directed film adaptations of their work in those years
8. Khartoum, Sudan
9. Ronan Point
10. Speed camera
11. Hermann Hesse
12. John Glenn Jr.
13. Sébastian Chabal
14. (Claudius) Ptolemy
15. *Frasier*

1. In which English city do the rugby union club the Chiefs play at Sandy Park, while in football the Grecians play at St James Park?

2. Which British coin worth a quarter of a penny ceased to be legal tender in 1960?

3. Known for their scrawny bodies, curly fur and big ears, the Devon and Cornish Rex are breeds of what domesticated animal?

4. Tamora, Queen of the Goths, features in which Shakespeare play, said to be his most violent?

5. According to urbandictionary.com, which Berkshire town gives its name to fans of a particular British heavy metal band?

6. The name of the French village of Domrémy-la-Pucelle commemorates which French heroine who was born there?

7. Which man, more famous for his skills in a different context, hosted the British game show *Every Second Counts* between 1986 and 1993?

8. Which UK tax developed from capital transfer tax, which replaced estate duty in 1975?

9. Its first store opened in 1975; which fashion chain, the flagship brand of the Inditex group, is known for its zero-advertising policy?

10. The singer and poet Victor Jara, shot to death in a right-wing coup in 1973, is a folk hero in which South American country?

11. Which composer was partly responsible for the design of the Festspielhaus in Bayreuth, Germany, at which his operas are performed?

12. What is the English translation of the paradoxical words beneath René Magritte's painting of a pipe, *The Treachery of Images*?

13. The Indian sage Mahavira may be regarded as the founder of which religion associated with the very strict observance of the doctrine of ahimsa, or non-violence?

14. In which classic 1942 film does Captain Renault utter the words 'I'm shocked . . . shocked to find that gambling is going on in there'?

15. The towns of Rennes, Brest and Quimper are found in which French region?

1. Exeter
2. Farthing
3. Cat
4. *Titus Andronicus*
5. Maidenhead (Iron Maiden)
6. Joan of Arc or Jeanne d'Arc
7. Paul Daniels
8. Inheritance tax
9. Zara
10. Chile
11. Richard Wagner
12. 'This is not a pipe'
13. Jainism
14. *Casablanca*
15. Brittany

1. The once-exclusive resort of Varosha, now a ghost town, lies on which Mediterranean island, whose northern part is under Turkish control?

2. 'ATliens', 'Aquemini'and 'Stankonia' are early albums by which innovative American hip-hop duo comprising André 3000 and Big Boi?

3. Which art movement with practitioners including Tristan Tzara, was said to be named after a French term for a hobby horse?

4. The one-act opera *The Village Soothsayer*, was composed by which Swiss man, who wrote works of political philosophy such as *The Social Contract*?

5. Flock, gaggle and skein are collective nouns for which type of bird?

6. In chemistry, what name is given to the group of 15 metallic elements ending with element 103, lawrencium?

7. Running since 2009, which US sitcom centres on Los Angeles resident Jay Pritchett, his Colombian second wife Gloria, and their large, unconventional family?

8. Prime Ministers of which Scandinavian country include Tage Erlander, who served for 23 years, and Fredrik Reinfeld, the current incumbent?

9. In Italian folklore, an old woman called Befana delivers gifts on the eve of which Christian feast day?

10. Which Roman statesman is said always to have ended his speeches with some variation on the words *Carthago delenda est*, meaning 'Carthage must be destroyed'?

11. Which French composer adapted a Mallarmé work into the tone poem 'Prélude à l'après-midi d'un faune'?

12. What is the common birthday (month and day) of British Olympic legends Mo Farah, Chris Hoy and Steve Redgrave?

13. *Bad Boys* and *The Rock* were the first two films directed by which US director of high-budget action films, more recently including the *Transformers* franchise?

14. Which striped mammal is, along with the giraffe, the only living member of the family Giraffidae?

15. Complete this (translated) quote from Jean-Paul Sartre's *No Exit*: 'Hell is _____ _____.'

Answers to General Knowledge: Standard Quiz 21

1. Cyprus
2. Outkast
3. Dada(ism)
4. Jean-Jacques Rousseau
5. Goose
6. Actinides or actinoids
7. *Modern Family*
8. Sweden
9. Epiphany
10. Cato the Elder or Marcus Porcius Cato
11. Claude Debussy
12. 23 March
13. Michael Bay
14. Okapi
15. 'Other people'

1. António Egas Moniz received a (with hindsight) controversial Nobel Prize for developing which neurological procedure involving cutting away connections between the frontal lobes of the brain?

2. The US art critic Mario Amaya received minor wounds when he was shot in June 1968. In which US artist's office was he at the time?

3. The actress Marion Davies is best remembered for her relationship with which very powerful US tycoon (1863–1951)?

4. Banned or censored by several opera companies at the time which German composer made his name with the opera 'Salome' (1905)?

5. Van Dyke, soul patch and goatee are types of what male facial feature?

6. US television drama *Breaking Bad* predominantly is set in which US State?

7. The only land border between territory held by which two western European nations is on the Caribbean island of St Martin?

8. French chef Bernard Loiseau shot himself in 2003 over rumours he was about to lose what prestigious culinary achievement?

9. What name is given to the Vietnamese lunar new year festival, and also to a military operation which begun on that date in 1968?

10. With lyrics written by Paul Anka and most famously sung by Frank Sinatra, which song has led to killings in 'karaoke rage' attacks in the Philippines?

11. What word precedes 'Al-Fitr' and 'Al-Adha' in the names of separate festivals celebrated by Muslims?

12. The splendidly named Laura Chinchilla was President of which Central American state from 2010 to 2014?

13. The Californian and the Andean are the two species of which large New World vulture?

14. The famous line 'Of arms and the man I sing', which inspired the title of one of George Bernard Shaw's plays, begins which epic work by Virgil?

15. Which world city hosted the first home cricket Test match for two nations, in 1955 and 2000 respectively?

1. Prefrontal Lobotomy or Leucotomy
2. Andy Warhol
3. William Randolph Hearst
4. Richard Strauss
5. Beard
6. New Mexico
7. The Netherlands and France
8. Three Michelin stars
9. Tet (as in Tet Offensive)
10. 'My Way'
11. Eid
12. Costa Rica
13. Condor
14. *The Aeneid*
15. Dhaka (for Pakistan and Bangladesh respectively)

1. The art nouveau designer Hector Guimard designed many of the famous entrances to what in Paris?

2. Republican Alf Landon experienced one of the worst electoral college defeat ever in the 1936 US Presidential election when he lost 523–8 to which long-serving Democrat President?

3. The critically acclaimed Fernando Meirelles film *City of God* was set in the *favela* of that name in which South American city?

4. 'In Memory of W.B. Yeats', 'Epitaph on a Tyrant' and 'Funeral Blues' are poems by which Anglo-American poet whose first forename was Wystan?

5. For what reason was the Ukrainian city of Pripyat abandoned in 1986?

6. Which Scotsman won the men's 100 metres at the 1980 Moscow Olympics?

7. For what purpose is the AZERTY layout used in some European countries?

8. Which Italian-American scientist gives his name to element number 100, the class of particles that obey Pauli's exclusion principle, and the paradox that earth has not yet been contacted by advanced life elsewhere in the galaxy?

9. What four-letter word is given to the short tail of a rabbit, hare or deer?

10. Which US musician, whose UK hits include 'The Lonely Bull', 'Spanish Flea' and 'This Guy's in Love with You', founded A&M Records in 1962 with Jerry Moss?

11. Which 'depth charge' cocktail involves pouring a shot of a particular German herbal liqueur into a glass of Red Bull?

12. The son of Septimus Severus, which Roman emperor gives his names to the Roman baths complex at which the Three Tenors gave their first performance in 1990?

13. The science fiction short film *La Jetée*, directed by Chris Marker, influenced which Terry Gilliam movie which starred Brad Pitt?

14. Dmitri Shostakovich's Symphony No. 7 in C major is named after which Russian city, besieged by the Germans during World War II?

15. Parents Jackie and Martin, and sons Adam, played by Simon Bird, and Jonny, played by Tom Rosenthal, make up the Goodman family in which Channel Four sitcom which has run since 2011?

1. Metro stations
2. Franklin D. Roosevelt
3. Rio de Janeiro
4. W.H. Auden
5. Because of radiation from the Chernobyl accident
6. Allan Wells
7. A computer keyboard
8. Enrico Fermi
9. Scut
10. Herb Alpert
11. Jäger bomb or Jäger bull
12. Caracalla or Marcus Aurelius Severus Antoninus Augustus
13. *Twelve Monkeys*
14. Leningrad (accept St Petersburg)
15. *Friday Night Dinner*

1. Which TV 'personality' was created by Rocky Morton and Annabel Jankel and voiced by the Canadian actor Matt Frewer?
2. Eaten with cheeses such as Manchego, with which fruit is the Spanish paste *membrillo* made?
3. From which country did chimichurri sauce originate?
4. Which African desert is thought to be the world's oldest?
5. Which archipelago lying 570 miles east of North Carolina was historically known as 'the Isle of Devils'?
6. Mentioned in the Quran, which trading city may have been destroyed about 1,500 years ago when a giant sinkhole opened up without warning, swallowing the city?
7. An Arctic species of which whale can live to 200 years, making it the planet's longest-living mammal?
8. Who was described by Charles Dickens as 'a spot of blood and grease on the history of England'?
9. The Romans destroyed not only Carthage in 146 BC but also which other city state?
10. The Colosseum in Rome took its name from a colossal statue of which figure located nearby?
11. The word Copt is derived from the Greek word for what?
12. At which Olympic Games did track athletes start the current practice of running anticlockwise?
13. Doyle Brunson's *Super/System* (1978) is a seminal book on which topic?
14. Which actress released *Anywhere I Lay My Head*, a 2008 album of cover versions of Tom Waits songs?
15. *The Score* (2001) was which actor's last film role and the only time he appeared in a film with Robert De Niro?

Answers to General Knowledge: Standard Quiz 24

1. Max Headroom
2. Quince
3. Argentina
4. The Namib
5. Bermuda
6. Ubar – rediscovered in 1992 by a team led by Sir Ranulph Fiennes
7. Bowhead whale
8. Henry VIII
9. Corinth
10. Nero
11. Egyptian – Aigyptos
12. Antwerp – 1920
13. Poker. The chapter on seven-card stud was written by David Reese
14. Scarlett Johansson
15. Marlon Brando

1. Parsifal, the title character of a Wagner opera, is the father of the title character of which other Wagner opera?
2. In 1996, Crowded House played their final gig to 120,000 people outside which famous building?
3. In what country is the tangerine flavoured liqueur Van Der Hum produced?
4. What is the meaning of Egoli, a Zulu name for Johannesburg?
5. Which is the largest island wholly owned (consulates, embassies etc. excepted) by Indonesia?
6. One of the most important palaeontological sites in the world, the Messel Pit is located about 35 km south-east of which German city?
7. Andre Geim and Konstantin Novoselov of the University of Manchester won the 2010 Nobel Prize in Physics for their work on which form of carbon?
8. The bible used by Barack Obama at his swearing in as the 46th President had last been used at which other President's inauguration?
9. A face mask depicting which real-life figure features extensively in the film *V for Vendetta* and is frequently worn by 'Occupy' protesters?
10. Which palace on the island of Lovon, a private residence of the Swedish royal family, has been a UNESCO World Heritage Site since 1993?
11. In which country will you find the 4 km-high Marree Man, a geoglyph thought to have been created recently using bulldozers and GPS technology by persons unknown?
12. Won by Britons Tommy Simpson in March 1967 and Bradley Wiggins in 2012, which week-long cycling classic is known as the Race to the Sun?
13. Retiring in 2011, which quarterback made a record 297 consecutive regular season NFL starts?
14. Which country has the largest population of Portuguese speakers?
15. Which Oscar-winning actress wrote a 1971 cookbook named *In Cucina con Amore*?

Answers to General Knowledge: Standard Quiz 25

1. Lohengrin
2. The Sydney Opera House.
3. South Africa
4. City of Gold
5. Sumatra
6. Frankfurt am Main
7. Graphene
8. Abraham Lincoln
9. Guy Fawkes
10. Drottningholm Palace
11. Australia (Southern Australia)
12. Paris–Nice
13. Brett Favre
14. Brazil
15. Sophia Loren

1. What creatures forced the Kings of Leon to quit a performance at the St Louis Verizon Amphitheatre in 2010?

2. Antonio Stradivari made the Fleming in 1717 to his 'Forma B' pattern, which has been the model for most examples of which instrument made ever since?

3. Veev is billed as the world's first spirit made from which berry?

4. The extremely expensive Serbian Pule cheese is made from the milk of which creature?

5. 'Nkosi Sikele' iAfrika' is the national anthem of which nation?

6. Which planet in our solar system is much the closest to the earth in terms of both mass and size?

7. Bavarian scientist Carl von Linde (1842–1934) was a major early pioneer in which important technology?

8. The Lemelson–MIT prize is known as the 'Oscar for _____' who/what?

9. Which famous figure became the first African-American editor of the prestigious *Harvard Law Review* in 1990?

10. Founded in 1876, in which US city is the eminent Johns Hopkins University?

11. After working with the shoe designer Roger Vivier, who worked briefly as a landscape gardener before setting up his own company in 1991 noted for the use of vivid red soles?

12. Shaffron was medieval armour for the head of which animal?

13. Which game was invented by Leslie Scott and originally named *Takoradi Bricks* after some building blocks handmade by a carpenter in Takoradi, a Ghanaian port?

14. Cyclist Chris Froome has to ingest a pesticide every six months to deal with which long-standing condition contracted during his boyhood?

15. What is the real forename of actor Christopher Walken?

1. Pigeons – many droppings from the rafters
2. Cello
3. Acai
4. Donkey
5. South Africa
6. Venus
7. Refrigeration
8. Inventors. Douglas Engelbart won it in 2007
9. Barack Obama
10. Baltimore
11. Christian Louboutin
12. Horses
13. Jenga
14. Bilharzia/Schistosomiasis
15. Ronald

1. Born Arthur Jacob Arshawsky, which band leader and clarinettist counted Ava Gardner and Lana Turner among his eight wives?

2. Which Sheffield band's *The Dignity of Labour* was an early concept album, a four-part story about Yuri Gagarin's first space flight?

3. Which edible berry (*Vaccinium oxycoccos*) is usually harvested by flooding the plant beds with water and using special harvesters to collect the fruit?

4. Which country's primary stocks and shares index is named the *Straits Times*?

5. Isla de la Juventud is the second largest island of which country?

6. What name is given to a native of Mumbai?

7. Discovered in the Burgess Shale in Canada, the 500-million-year-old filter feeder *Siphusauctum gregarium* gets its English name from the similarity of its shape to which common flower?

8. Which Roman emperor, the last of the so-called Five Good Emperors, died in AD 180 and was succeeded by his son Commodus?

9. Named after an American state, on which warship moored in Tokyo Bay were surrender documents signed by Japan on 2 September 1945?

10. In which Indian city will you find the Hawa Mahal (the Palace of the Winds)?

11. Which Dutch humanist (1466–1536) wrote *In Praise of Folly*?

12. What is the name of the Samoa rugby union squad's pre-match war dance?

13. Why is the nickname of a South Vietnamese soldier, Nguyen Phong, now known all over the world?

14. *Aunts Aren't Gentlemen* (1974) was the last novel (by the original author) to feature which lead characters?

15. Which Bangalore-born Briton directed the so-called Mick Travis trilogy of films : *If . . . .* (1968), *O Lucky Man!* (1973) and *Britannia Hospital* (1982)?

Answers to General Knowledge: Standard Quiz 27

1. Artie Shaw
2. The Human League
3. Cranberry
4. Singapore
5. Cuba
6. Mumbaikar
7. Tulip – the tulip animal
8. Marcus Aurelius
9. USS *Missouri*
10. Jaipur
11. (Desiderius) Erasmus
12. Siva Tau
13. He was the inspiration for the naming of Eldrick 'Tiger' Woods
14. Jeeves and Wooster (P.G. Wodehouse)
15. Lindsay Anderson

1. Queen Latifah was Oscar-nominated for playing Mama Morton in which 2002 musical film?

2. Which Pittsburgh-born self-taught pianist (1923–77), a master of swing playing and improvisation, composed the jazz standard 'Misty'?

3. On which mountain is Agioritiko red wine made?

4. The berry of *Synsepalum dulcificum*, when eaten, causes sour foods subsequently consumed to taste sweet, leading to which apt name?

5. Dettifoss and Gullfoss are major waterfalls in which country?

6. Lying in the delta of the Padma, Brahmaputra and Meghna rivers, which National Park, a UNESCO World Heritage Site approximately 10,000 km² in area, is split between India and Bangladesh?

7. One of the world's most powerful instruments, the VLT or Very Large Telescope is operated at a high desert altitude on Cerro Paranal, a mountain in which southern hemisphere country?

8. In which country will you find the Flaming Cliffs palaeontological site at which numerous very important fossil finds have been made?

9. In what context was the Queen Mother 'Tay Bridge', Princess Margaret 'Chelsea Bridge' and Margaret Thatcher, for a time, 'Iron Bridge'?

10. The primary residence of the Ottoman sultans for approximately 400 years, in which city is the Topkapi Palace?

11. In which city near Los Angeles is the leading private research university Caltech (California Institute of Technology) based?

12. Which former World Heavyweight Champion's thunderous right hand was nicknamed 'the Hammer of Thor' or, more lightheartedly, 'Ingo's bingo'?

13. What is the first name of Ayrton Senna's nephew, who drove for the Williams-Renault team in the 2012 Formula One season?

14. Which 2001 animated film won the very first Academy Award for Best Animated Feature awarded in 2002?

15. Which British author wrote *Madame Doubtfire* (1987), which was filmed as *Mrs Doubtfire* (1993), and has won the Carnegie Medal twice with *Goggle-Eyes* (1989) and *Flour Babies* (1992)?

1. *Chicago*
2. Erroll Garner
3. Mount Athos
4. Miracle fruit
5. Iceland
6. Sundarbans
7. Chile
8. Mongolia
9. Code names used when planning their official funerals
10. Istanbul
11. Pasadena
12. Ingemar Johansson
13. Bruno
14. *Shrek*
15. Anne Fine

1. Which film's climax features an attack on the title quartet by the giant Stay-Puft Marshmallow Man?
2. Which Apollo 11 astronaut, once dubbed 'the loneliest man in the universe', wrote the book *Carrying the Fire*?
3. What is the world's largest and oldest youth charity?
4. In 1863, Hermann Brehmer opened the Heilanstalt für Lungenkranke in Görbersdorf (now Sokołowsko, Poland), the first German sanatorium for the systematic open-air treatment of which infectious disease?
5. *Treasury of Loyal Retainers*, *Yoshitsune and the Thousand Cherry Trees* and *Sugawara and the Secrets of Calligraphy* are the three 'famous plays' in which form of classical Japanese dance-drama?
6. *Tōji* is the job title of a master brewer of which fermented-rice drink of Japanese origin?
7. Thanks to more precise mapping technology, which doubly landlocked Alpine country has had a quarter-acre shaved off its official territory, leaving 62 square miles for its 37,000 residents?
8. Including 'Lazy Sunday' and 'Afterglow', which album by the Small Faces was originally released on vinyl in a giant tobacco tin modelled on a brand produced in Liverpool since 1899?
9. Founded by Ukrainian immigrants in 1882, Rishon LeZion is the fourth largest city in which Middle East country?
10. In German, it's 'spaghetti', in Korean 'kimchi', Castilian Spanish '*patata*' (potato), Bulgarian 'zele' (cabbage), Thai 'Pepsi' and Danish '*appelsin*' (orange), while in India, it is 'paneer'. Which foodstuff is the English equivalent?
11. A powdered form of which element, the most abundant metal in the earth's crust, is extracted via the Wöhler process?
12. Which alias links two-time US Presidential election loser Adlai Stevenson, the Marvel villain Elihas Starr, a *Batman* TV villain played by Vincent Price, and a BBC2 TV show?
13. Which pink-coloured bubblegum was invented by Walter Dierner, an employee of the Frank H. Fleer Company, in 1928?
14. At 6 foot 5 inches, who is the tallest member of the comedy group Monty Python?
15. Which flower genus is named after the ancient Greek word for 'star', referring to the shape of the flower head?

1. *Ghostbusters*
2. Michael Collins – whose fellow Apollo 11 crew members were Neil Armstrong and Buzz Aldrin
3. YMCA (Young Men's Christian Association)
4. Tuberculosis
5. Kabuki
6. Sake
7. Liechtenstein
8. *Ogdens' Nut Gone Flake* (modelled on Ogden's Nut-Brown Flake)
9. Israel
10. Say 'Cheese' – they are 'watch the birdie', smile-for-the-camera words in those languages
11. Aluminium
12. Egghead
13. Double Bubble
14. John Cleese
15. Aster

1. Who was succeeded as MP for Finchley by Hartley Booth?
2. *The Fascist/Il Federale* (1961) was the first film scored by which Italian composer, whose later credits include *The Good, the Bad and the Ugly, Once Upon a Time in America* and *The Untouchables*?
3. According to a 1996 *Inventory Manual* co-written by social psychologist Chistina Maslach, Overwork, Frustration, Resentment and Depression are the four stages of which state of long-term exhaustion and diminished interest in work?
4. Born as Asfaw Wossen Taffari in the walled city of Harar, Amha Selassie (1916–97) was the last reigning empress of which African country?
5. In which film does Michael Caine's title character say to Bryan Mosley (aka *Coronation Street*'s Alf Roberts): 'You're a big man, but you're in bad shape. With me it's a full-time job. Now behave yourself'?
6. In 1998, the government set the first national minimum wage at what hourly rate for those aged 21 and over?
7. What was the Lahore Stadium in Pakistan renamed after the visit of a prominent Libyan in 1974?
8. A biscuit joiner is a tool used for what purpose?
9. DJ Mike Read's musical about which Irish playwright became an infamous West End disaster when it closed after just one performance in 2004?
10. Which spy novelist, whose recent books include *Our Kind of Traitor* and *A Delicate Truth*, is the father of Nick Harkaway, author of the 2008 debut novel *The Gone-Away World*?
11. Telling the story of their rise to fame, which British group played themselves in the 1981 film *Take It or Leave It*? They had their first top 10 hit with 'One Step Beyond' (1979).
12. The American 'Payola' scandal of the late 1950s involved the giving of bribes to who?
13. What is the oldest currency still in use?
14. In America, the inventor Philo T. Farnsworth is known as the 'father of . . .' which entertainment medium?
15. In June 2009, which Scottish breakfast TV personality was made an honorary colonel of the Black Watch cadets?

Answers to General Knowledge: Standard Quiz 30

1. Margaret Thatcher
2. Ennio Morricone
3. Occupational burnout – the *Maslach Burnout Inventory* is the most studied measurement of burnout
4. Ethiopia
5. *Get Carter*
6. £3.60
7. Gaddafi Stadium
8. Joining two pieces of wood together in woodworking
9. Oscar Wilde – title: *Oscar*
10. John le Carré
11. Madness
12. Radio DJs
13. Pound Sterling
14. Television
15. Lorraine Kelly

1. Which 2014 Wimbledon finalist is a Canadian who was named after a princess born in 1990?
2. Which planet was hit by the fragments of comet Shoemaker–Levy 9 in 1994?
3. Which country's flag calls (in translation) for 'order and progress'?
4. In the week of 4 April 1964, the Beatles achieved the unique feat of holding the top five places in the US charts. Which of the five songs (it was no. 2) was not a Lennon and McCartney composition?
5. International trade in which fruit is dominated by the variety called Cavendish?
6. Which 2013 film (released in the UK in 2014), directed by Peter Landesman and dealing with events in the immediate aftermath of the John F. Kennedy assassination, takes its name from that of the hospital at the centre of those events?
7. Tourists in Africa often hope to see the 'big five' game animals. These are lion, elephant, rhino, leopard and . . . what?
8. The so-called 'Surgeon's Photograph' published in the *Daily Mail* was one of the first and most famous photographs of what, supposedly?
9. Which leading member of the UK royal family was the subject of an attempted kidnapping in the Mall in London in 1974?
10. Acts called Bingo Players, Nicky Romero and Martin Garrix all had UK number one hits in 2013. What is their shared nationality?
11. How many stars are there on the flag of the European Union?
12. In the French version of which quiz show were departing contestants told: 'Vous êtes le maillon faible, au revoir!'?
13. Bolero Square in Nottingham is named in honour of which pair's gold-winning performance at the 1984 Winter Olympics?
14. Born Elizabeth Grant, which US singer had her breakthrough hit with 'Video Game', the lead single off her album *Born to Die*? In 2014, she topped the album chart with her second LP, *Ultraviolence*.
15. Which Asian country is the world's largest producer of film?

Answers to General Knowledge: Standard Quiz 31

1. Eugenie Bouchard – named after Princess Eugenie of York
2. Jupiter
3. Brazil
4. 'Twist and Shout'
5. Bananas
6. *Parkland*
7. Cape Buffalo
8. The Loch Ness Monster
9. Princess Anne
10. Dutch
11. 12
12. *The Weakest Link* – translation: 'You are the weakest link, goodbye!'
13. Jane Torvill and Christopher Dean
14. Lana del Rey
15. India

1. Lindenstrasse, the setting of a very popular German soap opera, is supposedly located in which German city?
2. In 2012, which song became the first video to reach 1 billion views on YouTube?
3. The Indian company Godrej & Boyce was the last manufacturer in the world of what items when it ceased production at a Mumbai plant in 2011?
4. What was opened at St James's Gate in Dublin in 1759 on a 9,000-year lease of £45 per annum?
5. Lying in the Indian Ocean and noted for unusual flora and fauna, the archipelago of Socotra belongs to which country?
6. Which city in Indiana was the birthplace of Michael Jackson and was adopted as a forename by the actor who went on to win Best Actor Oscars for roles in *Sergeant York* and *High Noon*?
7. With a length of 345 m and a beam of 53.8 m, Q-Max type ships are the largest LNG (liquefied natural gas) carriers in the world. What does the Q stand for?
8. What was special about a baby named Injaz born in Dubai in 2009 after an 'uncomplicated' gestation period of 378 days?
9. Referred to as 'Flying over the Hump', what other nickname was given to the World War II supply route from Jorhat in Assam to Kunming in China on account of the number of aeroplanes and crew lost on it?
10. Sharing his surname with a major city in Ohio, who is the only US President to have served two non-consecutive terms?
11. Which Fourth Dynasty pharaoh gives his name to the smallest of the three main pyramids at Giza?
12. Republican Linda McMahon has run for the US Senate several times. She is a senior figure in which profitable organisation?
13. What sort of creature was the green-haired Zakumi, the mascot for the 2010 South African World Cup?
14. Which novel was finished with difficulty in 1877, being described by its author as a 'tawdry story of adulterous love'?
15. What is the name of the 2013 'autobiography' of Terry the cairn terrier from *The Wizard of Oz*?

1. Munich
2. 'Gangnam Style'
3. (Mechanical) typewriters
4. The Guinness Brewery
5. Yemen
6. Gary
7. Qatar – Q-Max defines the maximum size of ship able to dock at the LNG terminals in Qatar
8. It is the world's first cloned camel
9. The Aluminium Trail
10. Grover Cleveland
11. Menkaure/Menkaura/Mykerinos/Menkheres
12. WWE – World Wrestling Entertainment, Inc.
13. Leopard
14. *Anna Karenina*
15. *I, Toto* (: *The Autobiography of Terry, the Dog Who Was Toto*)

1. Which real person was played by Kiri Te Kanawa in the TV drama *Downton Abbey* in 2013?
2. The Black Eyed Peas released a 2009 album entitled *The E.N.D.* What do these letters stand for?
3. Japanese researchers have developed a fire alarm for the hearing impaired based on what foodstuff?
4. The French town of Castelnaudary styles itself 'the world capital of . . .' which dish?
5. In which country is the carbon-neutral city of Masdar being built?
6. The westernmost 7,000-metre peak in the world, Noshak is the highest mountain in which country?
7. Which famous archaeological site doubled as Yavin 4, the moon from which Luke Skywalker and the Rebel Alliance set off to destroy the Death Star in the first *Star Wars* film?
8. Which non-profit organisation, sharing its name with a Russian city, plans to produce millions of clones of the biggest trees that ever lived, creating redwood forests in places like Britain to halt and reverse climate change?
9. Which leader's 'dad-dancing' to the song 'American Boy' by girl group Kombinatsiya became a YouTube hit in 2011?
10. By what unorthodox method did the Swedish army invade Denmark in 1657?
11. In which palace would you find the Malachite Room?
12. Translating as 'The Boys', *Bafana Bafana* is the nickname of which country's international football team?
13. Rochambeau and Roshambo are other names for which game?
14. Which author's 2008 memoirs were titled . . . : *Miracles of Life – Shanghai to Shepperton*?
15. Which role in a 1963 film was secured by Hugh Edwards when he wrote to the director Peter Brook saying, 'Dear Sir, I am fat and I wear spectacles'?

1. Dame Nellie Melba
2. *The Energy Never Dies*
3. Wasabi (horseradish)
4. Cassoulet
5. UAE – Abu Dhabi specifically
6. Afghanistan
7. Tikal
8. Archangel
9. President Dmitri Medvedev (Russia)
10. They marched across the frozen Baltic
11. The Winter Palace, St Petersburg
12. South Africa
13. Rock, Paper, Scissors/Paper-Scissors-Stone/ick-ack-ock
14. J.G. Ballard – author of *Empire of the Sun* and *Crash*
15. Piggy in *The Lord of the Flies*

1. In the TV drama *K-Ville*, which city is K-Ville?

2. Which series started with a 2004 pilot 'Everybody Lies' and ended 176 episodes later with a final installment, 'Everybody Dies', in 2012?

3. What is the main ingredient of the Sicilian dish *caponata di melanzane*?

4. Gina Rinehart is an extremely wealthy Australian business-woman. She is the daughter of which iron ore magnate who discovered the world's largest deposits of iron ore in the Pilbara Range of Western Australia in 1952?

5. Thought to house the largest single concentration of mammals in the world, the Bracken Cave, home to 40 million Mexican free-tail bats, is near which major US city?

6. The word Burkinabe refers to something or someone from which country?

7. In June 2009, who released a rap track 'Rocket Experience' commemorating the 40th anniversary of the first lunar landing?

8. Filmed in 1894 in wobbly black and white and lasting only 18 seconds, *The Execution of Mary Queen of Scots* may be the first historical film. Who made it?

9. Which US operation in the Vietnam War was code-named Frequent Wind?

10. Name either of the two grandchildren of William the Conqueror who fought each other in a war sometimes known as the Anarchy?

11. Where would a Sikh boy wear a *patka*?

12. In which sport is the Vardon Trophy awarded annually in the US?

13. Which star of *Seinfeld* went on to star in *The New Adventures of Old Christine* and *Veep*?

14. Under what pseudonym does a Coventry-born former Granada TV executive named Jim Grant write the bestselling Jack Reacher novels?

15. Who played Dr Cate Banfield in *ER*, Tina Turner in *What's Love Got to Do with It* (1993) and voiced Michelle Obama's character when she appeared in *The Simpsons*?

1. New Orleans, i.e. Katrinaville
2. *House*
3. Aubergine (eggplant)
4. Lang Hancock
5. San Antonio
6. Burkina Faso
7. Buzz Aldrin
8. Thomas Edison – using the Edison kinetoscope
9. The evacuation of Americans from Saigon in 1975
10. Stephen or Matilda
11. On his head – it is a cut-down Sikh turban
12. Golf – awarded for the lowest scoring average over a minimum of 60 rounds
13. Julia Louis-Dreyfus
14. Lee Child
15. Angela Bassett

1. In 2008 John McCain was told to stop using the song 'My Hero' for campaign purposes by which lead singer?

2. Pre-eminent in the world of music, which puzzle and mystery game fanatic was named by Anthony Shaffer as a partial inspiration for the central protagonist Andrew Wyke in his 1970 play *Sleuth*?

3. In medieval times, while dogs and young children were also harnessed for this job, what could a good goose keep spinning for up to 12 hours?

4. At just 260 square kms in area, which is the smallest of the United Arab Emirates?

5. What is the *Frecce Tricolori*?

6. Which creature, the largest living species of lizard, takes its common name from one of the few Indonesian islands on which it is found in the wild?

7. Which Apollo 13 astronaut was elected a Republican congressman for a Colorado district in 1982 but died before he could take his oath of office?

8. Why were there sausage bans in Germany in World War I?

9. In 1862, Nathaniel Gordon became the only American to be executed for what?

10. What book of 1611 is the subject of both David Hare's play *Written on the Heart* and Melvyn Bragg's book *Book of Books*?

11. What was Rodin's first major work (1876), which caused a furore when exhibited, being so lifelike that he was (wrongly) accused of casting from a live model?

12. Billed as the world's toughest one-day cycle race, which 269 km race runs from Bumthang to Thimphu tackling 3,780 metres of ascent and 3,950 metres in descent?

13. At which sport at the 2012 Olympics did Sun Yang (China), Ranomi Kromowidjojo (Netherlands) and Katie Ledecky (US) all win multiple gold medals?

14. The opening scene of which 1931 film, where he buys a flower from a blind flower seller, took two years and 342 takes until Charlie Chaplin was satisfied?

15. *American Tabloid*, *The Cold Six Thousand* and *Blood's a Rover* comprise which author's Underworld USA trilogy of novels?

1. Dave Grohl of the Foo Fighters
2. Stephen Sondheim
3. A joint of meat being roasted on a spit. The goose was contained in a treadmill!
4. Ajman
5. The Italian Air Force display team
6. Komodo dragon
7. Jack Swigert
8. The intestines were needed for Zeppelin manufacture. It took the intestines of more than 250,000 cows to make the gas holding cells for a single Zeppelin
9. Slave-trading
10. The King James Bible
11. *The Age of Bronze*
12. Tour of the Dragon
13. Swimming
14. *City Lights*
15. James Ellroy

1. Cabo da Roca, the European mainland's most westerly point, is in which country?
2. The controversial drug Lariam (mefloquine hydrochloride) is used to fight which disease?
3. Named after its original chief designer George Davies, the clothing range George was created in 1990 for which supermarket chain?
4. In 1911, who were paid for the first time ever, with an annual salary of £400 per year?
5. The story of army officer Anna Leonowens being appointed a governess to 82 children was turned into which musical?
6. Which *Father Ted* star wrote the 1998 novel *The Talk of the Town*?
7. Five drops of grenadine is the oft-forgotten ingredient in which champagne and orange juice cocktail?
8. Jokingly attributed to him by a mischievous Liverpool team-mate, which Welsh footballer never actually said that 'living in Italy is like being in a foreign country'?
9. Featured prominently in *The Thomas Crown Affair* remake, *San Giorgio Maggiore at Dusk* was painted by which French Impressionist?
10. In a 1999 hoax discovery, the 'Archaeoraptor' fossil looked like the true missing link between dinosaurs and which creatures?
11. Which US saxophone player's crimes against humanity include the albums *Duotones*, *Miracles*, *Breathless*, *Paradise*, *Moments* and *Rhythm & Romance*?
12. Which luxury British sports car maker dropped the 'Cygnet' model after an embarrassing failure to sell more than 150 of these city cars?
13. Keith Waterhouse took the title of his 1989 play *Jeffrey Bernard is Unwell* from the apology that was printed whenever the title character failed to file his 'Low Life' column left a blank page in which political magazine?
14. The sole tyre supplier for the NASCAR series, which Tire & Rubber Company and blimp fleet operator was founded in 1898 by Frank Seiberling in Akron, Ohio?
15. Using sieving to determine and average out size, what term does the invariable Udden–Wentworth scale use to classify a grain if it is 0.0625 mm to 2 mm in size? Anything bigger is gravel, anything smaller is silt.

Answers to General Knowledge: Standard Quiz 36

1. Portugal
2. Malaria
3. Asda
4. British Members of Parliament
5. *The King and I*
6. Ardal O'Hanlon
7. Buck's Fizz
8. Ian Rush
9. Claude Monet
10. Birds
11. Kenny G or Kenny Gorelick
12. Aston Martin
13. *The Spectator*
14. Goodyear
15. Sand

1. What was started in 1824 when the House of Commons agreed to buy the 38-painting collection of banker John Julius Angerstein for £57,000?

2. Madrid's Museo Taurino is dedicated to which spectacle?

3. Founded by Alan Schaaf in 2009, which online image hosting service uses a giraffe mascot that was created as an April Fool's Day joke, but was 'too cute to give up'?

4. Which Socialist President of France kept his illegitimate daughter Mazarine Pingeot secret for 20 years?

5. Nitta Sayuri is the Japanese title character and first-person narrator of which 1997 Arthur Golden novel?

6. Who won his third major and first Open Championship at the Royal Liverpool Golf Club in 2014?

7. Using T-Discs, which 'Hot Beverage System' is a single-serve coffee machine that was first introduced in France in 2004? The original machines were made by Saeco.

8. Mark Shand, the author of the travel classic *Travels on My Elephant*, died in April 2014 after a fall outside the Rose Bar of the Gramercy Park Hotel. He was the brother of which duchess?

9. Soviet documents prove that which man was born Yuri Irsenovich Kim during his father's exile to Soviet Khabarovsk in 1941, and not on Mount Baekdu, as his home nation claims?

10. Which annual world championship has been held in the village of Willaston, near Nantwich in Cheshire, since 1980 when local man Tom Shufflebotham won on 5 July? The competition's 18 rules include the banning of water (as a stimulant drug) and each competitor using a 3 × 3 m area.

11. Launched in 1929, Bib-Label Lithiated Lemon-Lime Soda originally had seven secret ingredients. What is its current name?

12. Daniel Vangarde co-wrote the Ottawan hit 'D.I.S.C.O.'. Vangarde's son Thomas Bangalter forms half of which music duo?

13. The noblewoman Vannozza dei Cattanei gave birth to which infamous Italian woman at Subiaco on 18 April 1480?

14. The Uganda Cowries (1895), the Hawaiian Missionaries (1851) and the Moldavian Bull's Heads (1858) are famous examples of which collectible items?

15. The title of which 2012 novel by Iain Banks is the two-word term for the absence of sound when a radio broadcast is in progress?

1. National Gallery
2. Bullfighting
3. Imgur – referring to the Imguraffe
4. François Mitterrand
5. *Memoirs of a Geisha*
6. Rory McIlroy
7. Tassimo
8. Duchess of Cornwall, Camilla
9. Kim Jong-Il, the late North Korean President
10. Worm charming
11. 7 Up
12. Daft Punk
13. Lucrezia Borgia
14. Postage stamps
15. *Dead Air*

1. *Nam chim* means 'dipping sauce' in which language?
2. The Naughty Boy no. 1 'La La La' featured vocals by which singer, whose album *In the Lonely Hour* topped charts around the world in 2014?
3. According to the US historian Eric H. Cline, which Middle Eastern city has been destroyed at least twice, placed under siege 23 times, been attacked another 52 times, and been captured and recaptured 44 times?
4. Christopher Boone, a 15-year-old with Asperger's, is the hero of which 2003 novel by Mark Haddon?
5. Egypt became a Roman province after the 30 BC suicide of which ruler from the Greek-speaking Macedonian Ptolemaic dynasty?
6. Which former US Secretary of State is the author of *Dear Socks, Dear Buddy*, *It Takes a Village* and *Hard Choices*?
7. In around 2500 BC, Heliopolis became known as the centre for which Egyptian sun god's cult?
8. In a footballing context, what links Ronald Reagan, Lionel Richie and James Bond?
9. Which type of crocus is known as the 'Red Gold of La Mancha'?
10. Named after Dr Michael Somogyi, who first wrote about it, the Somogyi effect refers to a swing to a high level from an extremely low level of which substance in the blood? The swing is caused by the release of stress hormones to counter the low levels of the said substance.
11. Which of New York City's five boroughs is the only mainland borough?
12. In 2004, the metals tycoon Viktor Vekselberg paid $90 million to the Forbes family for a collection of which Fabergé items?
13. How is Amy Dunne described in the title of a novel by Gillian Flynn?
14. The 'muggle' form of what has been described, on the website iqaworldcup.com, as 'a co-ed contact sport with a unique mix of elements from rugby, basketball, and dodgeball'?
15. Which movie hero's instantly recognisable get-up is a near-exact replica of Charlton Heston's costume (fedora, leather jacket, white shirt etc.) in the 1954 adventure film *Secret of the Incas*?

1. Thai
2. Sam Smith
3. Jerusalem, according to Cline's book *Jerusalem Besieged*
4. *The Curious Incident of the Dog in the Night-Time*
5. Cleopatra (VII)
6. Hillary Clinton
7. Ra
8. Top footballers were named after them: Cristiano Ronaldo, Lionel Messi, James Rodríguez
9. Saffron/*Crocus sativus*
10. Glucose (sugar)
11. The Bronx
12. Imperial Easter eggs
13. *Gone Girl*
14. Quidditch
15. Indiana Jones

1. Complete the movie line Lawrence Walsh (Joe Mantell) says to Jake Gittes (Jack Nicholson): 'Forget it. Jake, it's . . .' what?

2. Which English scientist was Einstein describing when he said 'in one person, he combined the experimenter, the theorist, the mechanic and, not least, the artist in exposition'?

3. Who was the first ever Muslim MP in the UK?

4. Which civil rights activist said of a 1955 bus journey in Montgomery, Alabama: 'All I was doing was trying to get home from work'?

5. Cataglottism is the scientific term for which type of kissing?

6. In 1966, Más a Tierra Island in Chile's Juan Fernández Islands was renamed after which Daniel Defoe character?

7. Which frequent visitor to Seattle's Cafe Nervosa was previously married to Lilith Sternin?

8. Discovered in 1828 by the Norwegian mineralogist Morton Thrane Esmark, element atomic number 90 was named by the Swedish chemist Jöns Jacob Berzelius after which Norse god?

9. Which three-dimensional solid object gives its name to a mini MPV (multi-purpose vehicle) that Nissan first produced in 1998?

10. Which 2004 film features the quotes: 'On Wednesdays, we wear pink!', 'Gretchen, stop trying to make "fetch" happen! It's not going to happen!', 'She's the queen bee, the star, those other two are just her little workers' and 'One time she punched me in the face . . . it was awesome'?

11. In 2010, *Modern Rome: Campo Vaccino* fetched £29.7 million and broke the auction record for a painting by which English artist?

12. Patented in 1979, which fruit is a cross between a blackberry and a red raspberry and is named after a major river in Scotland?

13. Jean Pierre Blanchard and John Jeffries made the first crossing of the English Channel using which mode of transport?

14. The largest noctuid found in the continental US, the black witch (*Ascalapha odorata*) aka duppy bat and Papillon-devil is considered a harbinger of death in Mexican and Caribbean folklore. What type of insect is it?

15. Prince George, the Duke and Duchess of Cambridge's son, was baptised like many royal babies before him with water from which Middle Eastern river?

1. '. . . Chinatown' – in the film *Chinatown*
2. Isaac Newton
3. Mohammad Sarwar – the former MP for Glasgow Govan became Governor of Punjab in 2013
4. Rosa Parks
5. French kissing or kissing using the tongue
6. Robinson Crusoe
7. Frasier Crane
8. Thor – as in thorium
9. Cube
10. *Mean Girls*
11. J.M.W. Turner
12. Tayberry
13. Hot-air balloon
14. Moth
15. River Jordan

1. Ronnie Ross, who taught a young David Bowie to play saxophone, performed the sax solo that plays over the fade-out of which song by Lou Reed, the B-side to his 1972 single 'Perfect Day'?

2. What links the popes St Pontian, Benedict IX and his successor Sylvester III (both in 1045), St Celestine V and Benedict XVI?

3. What links Gerd Müller, Jorge Burruchaga, Andreas Brehme, Andrés Iniesta and Mario Götze?

4. What are La Recoleta, Brookwood, Rookwood, Zentralfriedhof, San Michele, Vyšehrad, Assistens, Cathays and Highgate?

5. Given musical accompaniment by Sir Hubert Parry, what is the better known title of William Blake's poem 'And did those feet in ancient time', taken from the preface to his epic poem *Milton*?

6. Miles Davis and an 'orchestra under the direction of Gil Evans' released their version of which 1935 George Gershwin opera on Columbia Records in 1958?

7. Inner Circle's song 'Bad Boys' is the famous theme song of which 1989–2013 Fox TV show?

8. Which Eric Linklater film, made over a period of 12 years, charts the growing up of Mason Jr (Ellar Coltrane)?

9. During the winter of 1918–19, the Berlin doctor Kurt Huldschinsky demonstrated how UV light-emitting mercury-quartz lamps could treat children who had which medical condition, a defective mineralisation of the bones?

10. 'Semper fidelis' (always faithful) is the motto of which US fighting force?

11. In a 2014 film title, who are Peter Quill, aka Star-Lord, Gamora, Rocket Raccoon, Drax the Destroyer and Groot?

12. What four-letter word for air pollution found in large urban areas was coined in 1905 by Dr Henry Antoine Des Voeux of the Coal Smoke Abatement Society?

13. Despite riding an unprecedented wave of popularity, which US President declined to run again for the presidency in 1908, instead anointing his Secretary of War, William Taft, as his successor?

14. Which diarist wrote about her crush on Peter Schiff, aka 'Petel', and later, her affection for Peter van Daan?

15. Founded in 2011 by Jonathan Wegener and Benny Wong, which smartphone app collects old photos and posts from Facebook, Instagram, Twitter and Dropbox photos and replays past?

1. 'Walk on the Wild Side'
2. They resigned – the first three apocryphal, the last two canonical resignations
3. They all scored the winning goal in a World Cup final – 1974, 1986, 1990, 2010, 2014
4. Cemeteries (Buenos Aires, Surrey, Sydney, Vienna, Venice, Prague, Copenhagen, Cardiff, London)
5. 'Jerusalem'
6. *Porgy and Bess*
7. *Cops* – Fox's longest-running TV show was cancelled and moved to Spiked
8. *Boyhood*
9. Rickets
10. American Marine Corps
11. *Guardians of the Galaxy*
12. Smog
13. Theodore Roosevelt
14. Anne Frank
15. Timehop

1. 'Take it to the hole', 'bump the cutter', 'I got back' and 'nothin' but net' are phrases in which sport?
2. Which Nobel Prize has been won by Sweden's Selma Lagerlöf, Verner von Heidenstam, Pär Lagerkvist, Eyvind Johnson and Tomas Tranströmer?
3. Which French political scandal is the subject of the 2013 novel *An Officer and a Spy* by Robert Harris?
4. Four hundred and four years after his death, the remains of which painter were buried near the Tuscan coastal town of Porto Ercole in a memorial park that opened in July 2014?
5. Which Beatles song did East German Communist leader Walter Ulbricht claim to be symbolic of the decadent culture of the West: 'The monotony of the yeah, yeah, yeah, and whatever it is called'?
6. The 2013 film of The Proclaimers' musical *Sunshine on Leith* ends with a flash mob performance in Edinburgh's Princes Street Gardens of which song?
7. The World Games/Paralympic sport of powerlifting consists of three attempts at maximal weight on three canonical exercises: the squat, the deadlift and which lift – an exercise of the upper body performed by a person on their back?
8. In 2014, which double Oscar-winner married the photographer and actress Alexandra Hedison?
9. Which Shakespeare comedy play centres on the young Athenian lovers Lysander, Helena, Demetrius and Hermia?
10. According to the writer who created him, whose full name is Oscar Zoroaster Phadrig Isaac Norman Henkel Emmannuel Ambroise Diggs?
11. *Dawlat al-'Imārāt al-'Arabiyyah al-Muttaḥidah* is the Arabic name of which country?
12. The residents of Arles wrote a petition to evict which artist, whom they nicknamed the 'Fou Roux' (mad redhead), from the Yellow House?
13. The Shamus Awards are given to writers in which genre of fiction?
14. Steve Carell, Stephen Colbert, John Oliver and Ed Helms are 'graduates' of which topical Comedy Central show?
15. Mass panic caused the Khodynka Tragedy of 1896 in which a stampede killed 1,389 people. It took place at the coronation of which Russian Tsar?

1. Basketball
2. Literature
3. The (Alfred) Dreyfus Affair
4. Caravaggio/Michelangelo Merisi
5. 'She Loves You'
6. 'I'm Gonna Be (500 Miles)'
7. Bench press
8. Jodie Foster
9. *A Midsummer Night's Dream*
10. The Wizard of Oz – created by L. Frank Baum
11. United Arab Emirates
12. Vincent Van Gogh
13. Crime
14. *The Daily Show with Jon Stewart* – they are former 'correspondents'
15. Nicholas II

1. The martial art Krav Maga is particularly associated with the military of which country?
2. Which work by Sylvia Plath, her only novel, begins 'It was a queer, sultry summer, the summer they executed the Rosenbergs . . .'?
3. Which artist features on three of the ten biggest selling singles of the 2010s in the UK?
4. Which conspiracy thriller, which is broadcast on Channel 4, concerns a group of people battling against a shadowy force called 'the Network'?
5. The army officer Grigory Potemkin was the lover and a key influence on which Russian empress who ruled from 1762 to 1796?
6. Thesis, antithesis and synthesis are the three stages of a philosophical dialectic named after which German philosopher?
7. In grams, what is the recommended UK daily allowance of salt for an adult?
8. Which bodily organs would be affected by one of the range of diseases known as glomerulonephritis?
9. It can also be found in the Shar Pei, but a blue/black tongue is most characteristic of which dog breed?
10. Causing controversy in the UK in the mid-1970s, the artwork *Equivalent VIII* by Carl Andre was made of what items normally used in construction?
11. Adapted into a stage musical and the film *Sommersby*, which 16th-century French peasant was said to have successfully impersonated for three years by an impostor?
12. Which composer's works include the tone poem 'The Carnival of the Animals' and the opera *Samson and Delilah*?
13. The new Wembley Stadium has 107, whereas the old Wembley Stadium appropriately had thirty-nine, of what?
14. With which book, whose title refers to a York cultural institution, did Kate Atkinson win the Whitbread Book of the Year Prize in 1995?
15. In US politics, which figure is known by the acronym FLOTUS?

1. Israel
2. *The Bell Jar*
3. Pharrell Williams ('Happy', 'Blurred Lines' and 'Get Lucky')
4. *Utopia*
5. Catherine II or Catherine the Great
6. Georg Hegel
7. Six
8. The kidneys
9. Chow chow
10. (Fire) bricks
11. Martin Guerre
12. Camille Saint-Saëns
13. Steps up to the Royal Box
14. Behind the Scenes at the Museum
15. First Lady of the United States

1. In which war was the last shot fired on 22 June 1865?
2. *SAW* – the Ride, the Swarm (the UK's first winged roller coaster), Nemesis Inferno and Stealth are 'Extreme Thrill' rides at which Surrey theme park?
3. Fuleco the Armadillo was the mascot of which 2014 sporting event?
4. In which film does Joel (Jim Carrey) enlist the services of Lacuna Inc. to erase the memories of his former lover Clementine, who has already erased her memories of him?
5. 'This Messiah Needs Watching', 'Eagle Tax' and 'What Are They Doing in Heaven Today?' are songs on Mogwai's soundtrack for which French TV drama?
6. The Equestrian Statue of Marcus Aurelius from AD 173 in the Campidoglio, Rome, survived destruction during the late Roman Empire after being mistaken for which Christianising emperor, who died in 337?
7. Anaconda, Guillotine, Peruvian Necktie and Rear-Naked are types of which martial arts submission hold?
8. Using a rotating mirror and a stationary mirror about 20 miles away, the Fizeau–Foucault apparatus (1850) was designed by the French physicists Hippolyte Fizeau and Léon Foucault for measuring the speed of what?
9. The Bouclier de Brennus is given to the French club champions, winners of the Top 14 league, in which sport?
10. King Gustav Vasa's sword of state and King Erik XIV's crown are treasures in the state regalia of which country?
11. Dentin, cementum, dental pulp and which other major tissue – the body's hardest substance – forms a tooth?
12. Who are brothers and sister Dick, Julian and Anne, cousin Georgina ('George') and Timmy the dog?
13. In 1921, who became the first woman to win the Pulitzer Prize for literature, for a novel published the previous year, *The Age of Innocence*?
14. Dick Grayson, Jason Todd and Tim Drake have all taken on the role of which comic book sidekick?
15. Which song, a percussive cover of A.P. Carter's 1931 tune 'When I'm Gone', was popularised by the actress Anna Kendrick in the film *Pitch Perfect*?

1. American Civil War
2. Thorpe Park
3. FIFA World Cup
4. *Eternal Sunshine of the Spotless Mind*
5. *Les Revenants/The Returned*
6. Constantine the Great/Constantine I
7. Choke
8. Light
9. Rugby union
10. Sweden
11. Tooth enamel
12. The Famous Five
13. Edith Wharton
14. Robin
15. 'Cups'

1. What is the nickname of *Dirty Dancing* heroine Frances Houseman?
2. Which World Heavyweight boxing champion began his career as a 12-year-old under the tutelage of Louisville policeman Joe Martin?
3. Known as 'America's pastor', which evangelist made his book debut with *Calling Youth to Christ* (1947)? His later works include *Till Armageddon*.
4. Which spoof movie featured the characters Lone Starr, Dark Helmet, Pizza the Hutt and Yogurt?
5. Which notorious London football club gives its name to a 'brick', a nasty club made by twisting and turning a newspaper until it is compacted into a rock-hard nightstick?
6. Which Rolling Stones song opens with the lyrics: 'Please allow me to introduce myself / I'm a man of wealth and taste'?
7. Costa da Caparica, Europe's largest beach, is in what country?
8. In *The Flintstones*, what is the name of Betty and Barney Rubble's adopted son?
9. Which Russian-born *Foundation* series novelist married the children's science fiction author J.O. Jeppson in 1973?
10. In her 2002 book *Portrait of a Killer*, the crime writer Patricia Cornwell presented the theory that the Camden Town Group painter Walter Sickert was which infamous man?
11. Assassinated near Stanger (now KwaDukuza) by Dingane and Mhlangana in 1828, which Zulu king was played by Henry Cele in a 1986 South African TV series?
12. The 61 EL, aka the 'Hog', Heritage Classic and FXST Softail are classic motorcycles produced by which company?
13. In 1962, Hans Gugelot and Gerd Alfred Müller designed the Sixtant electric shaver for which German company?
14. Yambuku, a small village in northern Democratic Republic of Congo, was the site of the first known outbreak of the Zaire strain of which haemorrhagic fever virus? Making its first appearance on 26 August 1976, it killed 280 of 318 identified cases.
15. Styled the 'father of the Canadian crown' thanks to his being the first royal family member to live in North America for more than a short visit (1791–1800), Prince Edward, Duke of Kent and Strathearn, was the father of which monarch?

Answers to General Knowledge: Standard Quiz 44

1. 'Baby'
2. Muhammad Ali, who was a 12-year-old Cassius Marcellus Clay, Jr.
3. Billy Graham/William Franklin Graham, Jr.
4. *Spaceballs*
5. Millwall
6. 'Sympathy for the Devil'
7. Portugal
8. Bamm-Bamm
9. Isaac Asimov
10. Jack the Ripper
11. Shaka – the TV drama was *Shaka Zulu*
12. Harley-Davidson
13. Braun
14. Ebola – Yambuku is on the Ebola River
15. Queen Victoria

1. Judge (Joseph) Dredd made his first ever appearance in the second issue of which British comic in 1977?
2. Black, speed, doom, thrash and power are subgenres of which form of rock music?
3. Which former Indian Prime Minister was assassinated by alleged Tamil Tiger member Thenmozhi Rajaratnam in 1991?
4. 'Hello, my name is Inigo Montoya. You killed my father. Prepare to die' is a much-repeated quote, spoken by Mandy Patinkin in which film, based on a William Goldman novel?
5. What is the nickname of New Zealand's rugby league team?
6. Zowie Bowie directed the films *Moon* and *Source Code*. He is better known by which name?
7. Which fictional structure was given an estimated $850 quadrillion construction cost when the White House turned down a petition to build it in January 2014?
8. *Songs of Enchantment* and *Infinite Riches* are sequels to which Booker Prize-winning novel by Ben Okri?
9. Formerly known as Thalang, which popular holiday destination is Thailand's largest island?
10. Galimard, Molinard and Fraginard are all perfumeries based in which historic Provençal town, a key setting in Patrick Suskind's novel *Perfume*?
11. *Persil* is the French word for which herb?
12. Which brand of bourbon whiskey, produced in Clermont, Kentucky, was introduced in 1795 by the first of seven generations of the same family?
13. In 2006, the Conservative politician Stephen Harper defeated Paul Martin to become Prime Minister of which country?
14. The jejunum, ileum and duodenum form the small . . . what?
15. So impressed was she, Beryl Bainbridge was prompted to ask Colin Dexter why which novel – the one that saw him kill off Inspector Morse – never made the Booker shortlist?

Answers to General Knowledge: Standard Quiz 45

1. *2000 AD*
2. Heavy metal/metal
3. Rajiv Gandhi
4. *The Princess Bride*
5. The Kiwis
6. Duncan Jones
7. *Star Wars'* Death Star
8. *The Famished Road*
9. Phuket
10. Grasse
11. Parsley
12. Jim Beam
13. Canada
14. Intestine
15. *The Remorseful Day*

1. In which 1934 novel by James M. Cain does trouble begin when drifter Frank Chambers embarks on a steamy affair with diner owner Nick Papadakis's wife Cora?

2. In 1928, cousins Edward M. Knabusch and Edwin J. Shoemaker designed which reclining chair – the world's first – as 'nature's way of relaxing'?

3. The art critic Louis Vauxcelles coined which term when discussing Georges Braque's *House at L'Estaque* being fashioned with certain shapes in 1908?

4. Who released the 1970s albums *The Wild, the Innocent and the E-Street Shuffle*, *Born to Run* and *Darkness on the Edge of Town*?

5. Which vestigial third molars did human ancestors use to help grind down plant tissue?

6. Sent off to join the Royal Navy at 13 years old, which future king saw service at the Battle of Cape St Vincent in 1780?

7. The Symphony No. 9 in C major, known as the 'Great', was which Austrian composer's final completed symphony?

8. NASA's Goddard Space Flight Center, opened in 1959, was its first such facility, and is still in operation. In which eastern seaboard US state is it situated?

9. Which footballing great, who died in July 2014, was nicknamed 'la Saeta Rubia' (the Blond Arrow)?

10. Which US company in 2014 topped *Fortune* magazine's annual list of the world's 500 largest corporations (by revenue)?

11. Since the upgrading of Ceres from the status of asteroid to that of dwarf planet, in 2006, which has been the largest asteroid, by size, in our solar system?

12. A statue of a woman named Alice Nutter, shown wearing chains, was unveiled in 2012 in Roughlee, Lancashire, her home village, near the 400th anniversary of her death. She was a victim of which notorious event?

13. What, in architectural terminology, is an oculus?

14. Invented in 1936 by Oklahoma City supermarket owner Sylvan Goldman, the 'folding basket carrier' is much better known by which name?

15. The first of which messages was sent on 3 December 1992 from Neil Papworth of Sema Group using a PC to Richard Jarvis of Vodafone using an Orbitel 901 handset?

1. *The Postman Always Rings Twice*
2. La-Z-Boy
3. Cubism
4. Bruce Springsteen
5. Wisdom teeth
6. William IV – the 'Sailor King'
7. Franz Schubert
8. Maryland
9. Alfredo di Stéfano
10. Wal-Mart Stores
11. Pallas
12. The Pendle Witch Trials
13. A circular window
14. Shopping cart/shopping trolley
15. SMS message (Short Message Service)/text message

1. Which former Soviet leader founded the environmental organisation Green Cross International in 1993?

2. Which mountain range derives its name from the Sanskrit for 'abode of snow'?

3. Founded in 1961 by Mitoshi Uyehara, the US magazine *Black Belt* covers which subject?

4. In 2010, which retired Brazilian footballer was named the Honorary President of the New York Cosmos?

5. Known as the 'father of modern linguistics', which US political commentator co-wrote the 1988 book *Manufacturing Consent: The Political Economy of the Mass Media*?

6. Who defeated Zina Garrison in the 1990 Wimbledon final to win her 18th and last grand slam singles title?

7. In 1993, which food-related title did motivational speakers Jack Canfield and Mark Victor Hansen give to the first in a series of highly successful books consisting of inspirational true stories?

8. What is hypodontia?

9. In 1868, there were two almost simultaneous uprisings against Spanish colonial rule known rather poetically as 'The Cry (El Grito) of Yara' and 'The Cry of Lares'. Name either colonial territory involved (not far apart geographically).

10. A common stuffing for Spanish green olives, which red chilli pepper is named after the Portuguese word for 'bell pepper'?

11. Which Central American country, whose capital is Tegucigalpa, has the world's highest murder rate?

12. Which 'pudding' is supposed to have been invented due to a misunderstanding between Mrs Graves, Mistress of the Inn at the White Horse Inn (now the Rutland Arms Hotel), and her kitchen assistant in the 1860s?

13. Which Tracey Emin artwork, bought at auction for £2.54 million, has been described by its new owner Count Christian Duerckheim as 'a metaphor for life, where troubles begin and logics die'?

14. Native to Central America, which fruit is also known as the pitaya and in its yellow form resembles a mini-pineapple crossed with a banana? It is named after a mythical beast.

15. Which 1977 sports film is about the wild antics of the Charlestown Chiefs ice hockey team?

1. Mikhail Gorbachev
2. Himalayas
3. Martial arts and combat sports
4. Pelé
5. Noam Chomsky
6. Martina Navratilova
7. *Chicken Soup for the Soul*
8. The development of fewer than the usual number of teeth
9. Cuba or Puerto Rico respectively
10. Pimento
11. Honduras
12. Bakewell pudding
13. *My Bed*
14. Dragon fruit
15. *Slap Shot*

1. Which mythical creature is traditionally given the body and head of a horse, the hind legs of a stag, the tail of a lion and a single horn in the middle of the forehead?

2. According to popular belief, the Vazimba were the first inhabitants of which island country in the Indian Ocean?

3. Haruspices were Roman priests who made predictions based upon the study of what?

4. The chemist Carl Djerassi, also a novelist and playwright, is perhaps best known for his contribution in the 1950s to which medical breakthrough?

5. The artists Franz Marc, Henri Gaudier-Brzeska, Isaac Rosenberg, August Macke and Raymond Duchamp-Villon all died during which conflict?

6. Designed in the Dutch Classicist style by Jacob van Campen, which royal picture gallery overlooking the Hofvijver Lake is flanked by The Hague's parliamentary buildings and was built in 1644 for a governor of Brazil?

7. Appearing on the album cover with her cat Telemachus in what was then her living room in Laurel Canyon, which songwriter has sold 24 million copies of her LP *Tapestry*?

8. The musician Giovanni Bottesini was known to some as the 'Paganini' of which bowed string instrument?

9. It has an olive green or dark green pelage with yellow and black bands and a white belly, as well as an elongated muzzle with a red stripe down the middle and blue ridges on the sides. What is the most colourful primate?

10. Which country formed the elite counterterrorism unit GSG-9 (Grenzschutzgruppe 9 or Border Protection Group 9)in 1973?

11. Established in 1899, the Permanent Court of Arbitration (PCA) is based in which city?

12. The first modern general purpose version of which ubiquitous item was introduced in the USA by Diners Club in 1950?

13. Which boozily named tax protest in Western Pennsylvania was suppressed by US President George Washington in 1791?

14. Louie Miller, Suky Tawdry, Jenny Diver and Miss Lotte Lenya are implied victims of which song's title character?

15. In which novel by Ray Bradbury does Guy Montag horrify his wife's friends by reading the poem 'Dover Beach' aloud?

Answers to General Knowledge: Standard Quiz 48

1. Unicorn
2. Madagascar
3. Animal entrails
4. The oral contraceptive pill
5. World War I
6. The Mauritshuis
7. Carole King
8. Double bass
9. Mandrill
10. West Germany
11. The Hague
12. Credit card
13. Whiskey Rebellion
14. 'Mack the Knife' composed by Kurt Weill, lyrics by Bertolt Brecht
15. *Fahrenheit 451*

1. Professor Yaffle, in the children's TV series *Bagpuss*, was based on which Nobel laureate (1950 – Literature), someone Oliver Postgate had encountered as a child?

2. A nine-foot-high bronze statue of which comedian was unveiled in his home town of Caerphilly by Sir Anthony Hopkins, a big fan?

3. A red variant of this relish is produced with the addition of beetroot. Found in Jewish cuisine, chrain is made from which grated vegetable?

4. The Bury (flattish with almonds), the Devizes (star-shaped with fruit) and the Shrewsbury (complex with 11 marzipan balls – for the apostles minus Judas) are all variations of what?

5. Which city, the second largest in Sicily, lies to the south of Mount Etna?

6. The *Case Histories* series of crime novels by Kate Atkinson and the Inspector Rebus series by Ian Rankin are generally set in which British city?

7. Which island, at 228,900 square miles in area the fourth largest in the world, separated from India around 88 million years ago?

8. *Geococcyx californianus* is a type of cuckoo. Under what name is it more commonly known, featuring in numerous Warner Brothers cartoons as an obsession of Wile E. Coyote?

9. A swelling of the thyroid gland usually caused by an iodine deficiency, how is the medical condition also known as Derbyshire neck more commonly known?

10. Which criminals, the so-called Resurrection Men, are thought to have supplied Dr Robert Knox with at least 17 bodies for anatomical dissection?

11. Einstein died and Bill Gates was born in which year?

12. In 622, Muhammad and his followers fled Makkah to Yathrib, a town to the north. By what name is Yathrib known today?

13. Which Aberdeen-born trainer of four Derby winners and of the super sprinter Frankel died in June 2013 aged 70?

14. The US state of Idaho has declared 1 October to be _____ _____ Day after which native son, a star of *Breaking Bad*?

15. Which Blackpool-born actress, who played Jasmine Thomas in *Emmerdale*, became the *Doctor Who* assistant Clara Oswald?

Answers to General Knowledge: Standard Quiz 49

1. Bertrand Russell
2. Tommy Cooper
3. Horseradish
4. Simnel cake
5. Catania
6. Edinburgh
7. Madagascar
8. The Roadrunner
9. Goitre
10. Burke and Hare (both William)
11. 1955
12. Medinah
13. Sir Henry Cecil
14. Aaron Paul (Day)
15. Jenna-Louise Coleman

1. Known as the 'Gate to Mecca', the Saudi Arabian city of Jeddah is situated on the eastern shore of which sea?

2. The Campaign for Real Ale suggests that a duck main course should be matched with which Belgian beer, made by fermenting limbic with sour morello cherries?

3. Felipe V, formerly Philip, Duke of Anjou, was the first member of the House of Bourbon to rule as king of which country?

4. Which white abolitionist's attempt to lead a slave revolt in the South by raiding Harper's Ferry in 1859 helped spark the American Civil War?

5. Who was the only female competitor not required to submit to a sex test at the 1976 Montreal Olympics?

6. The first British banknote to feature a living non-royal person was issued in 2005 by the Royal Bank of Scotland. Which US golfer appeared on this £5 note?

7. Featured in Martin Scorsese's *Hugo*, which 1902 work by Georges Méliès was the first movie to be designated as a UNESCO World Heritage film?

8. Vlad III, Prince of Wallachia, aka Vlad Ţepeş, is now commonly referred to by the name of which title character in an 1897 novel?

9. Which major river gives its name to a delta that is Europe's most extensive wetland and the world's largest reed bed – heaven for birdwatchers as millions of birds winter there?

10. Which album by Green Day spawned a musical adaptation that features the songs 'Jesus of Suburbia', 'Good Riddance (Time of Your Life)' and 'Boulevard of Broken Dreams'?

11. Which star of *Avatar* and the rebooted *Star Trek* married the Italian artist Marco Perego in 2013?

12. Which Ancient Wonder of the World was a statue of the Greek Titan–god of the sun Helios?

13. Whose 'beauty is beyond compare / With flaming locks of auburn hair / With ivory skin and eyes of emerald green'?

14. Sharing its name with a Cuban musical form, which Australian surf and street clothing brand was launched in 1984 by Dare Jennings and Andrew Rich in the Sydney suburb of Alexandria?

15. Named after the Hebrew word for 'cessation', what is the Jewish day of rest and seventh day of the week?

1. Red Sea
2. Kriek
3. Spain
4. John Brown
5. Princess Anne
6. Jack Nicklaus
7. *A Trip to the Moon/Le Voyage dans la lune*
8. Dracula – referring to the novel by Bram Stoker
9. Danube – as in the Danube Delta
10. *American Idiot*
11. Zoe Saldana
12. The Colossus of Rhodes
13. Jolene – in the song by Dolly Parton
14. Mambo
15. Shabbat

Pop Music

1. What is the Japanese-related stage name of German rapper Anis Mohamed Youssef Ferchichi (b.1978)?

2. '212' (featuring Lazy Jay, whose song 'Float My Boat' it sampled) was the 2011 debut single by which US rapper?

3. Which former NWA member released the solo albums *AmeriKKKa's Most Wanted*, *Death Certificate* and *The Predator*?

4. Which 1987 debut album features the tracks 'The Magic Number', 'Eye Know', 'Potholes in My Lawn' and 'Me Myself and I'?

5. Which 1987 song by Eric B. & Rakim, from their namesake album, was given a hugely popular remix by dance duo Coldcut that Eric B. dismissed as 'girly disco music'?

6. Willard Carroll Smith Jr and Jeffrey Allen Townes won their first Grammy for Best Rap Performance in 1989 for 'Just Parents Don't Understand'. What was their stage name?

7. In 1993, which Latino hip hop group had hits with 'Insane in the Brain' and 'I Ain't Goin' Out Like That'?

8. Born Horst Christian Simco, Riff Raff is a Texas-based rapper who released his debut album *Neon Icon* in June 2014. He claims that James Franco stole his outlandish look for the role of Spider in which cult film?

9. Who had a Billboard Hot 100 no. 1 in 2014 with 'Timber'?

10. Which trio was founded in 1981 by Joseph Simmons, Darryl McDaniels and Jason Mizell?

11. A former Fulham and Spurs player, which US footballer released the rap single 'Don't Tread' in time for the 2006 World Cup, and has since released the 2014 album *The Redux*?

12. Formed in 1989, which superstar French rap group includes the classical-Egyptian-culture-inspired members Akhenaton, DJ Khéops, Imhotep and Kephren?

13. 'Witness (1 Hope)' has featured in the films *Children of Men* and *Kidulthood*, and the TV shows *Charlie Brooker's Screenwipe*, *Skins* and *The Wire*. It is from the 2001 album *Run Come Save Me* by which London rapper?

14. Who has had chart hits with 'I Luv U', 'Fix Up Look Sharp', 'Stand Up Tall', 'Dance Wiv Me' and 'Bonkers'?

15. As well as being the main character in the video for 'Good Morning', the mascot Dropout Bear is the cover star of three studio albums by which hip hop artist?

1. Bushido
2. Azealia Banks
3. Ice Cube (O'Shea Jackson)
4. *3 Feet High and Rising* by De La Soul
5. 'Paid in Full'
6. DJ Jazzy Jeff & the Fresh Prince (you know, Will Smith)
7. Cypress Hill
8. *Spring Breakers*
9. Pitbull featuring Kesha
10. Run-D.M.C. (aka Run, D.M.C. and Jam Master Jay)
11. Clint Dempsey
12. IAM – other members: Shurik'n and Freeman
13. Roots Manuva (Rodney Hylton Smith)
14. Dizzee Rascal (Dylan Mills)
15. Kanye West

1. Which US jazz pianist released the best-selling recording *The Koln Concert* in 1975?

2. With the forenames Theodore Walter, which jazz tenor saxophonist released *Saxophone Colossus* in 1956?

3. Which much-covered traditional American song appeared on Bob Dylan's eponymous debut album in 1962 and on Rod Stewart's debut album in 1970, but is probably best known for featuring in the film *O Brother, Where Art Thou?* (2000)?

4. Despite suffering severe hand injuries in a fire when aged 18, which Belgian-born Romani guitarist became a jazz guitar virtuoso?

5. Which man from Montreal switched from trumpet to piano at the age of five because of tuberculosis, going on to become a globally acclaimed jazz pianist?

6. By what nickname was Earl Hines, the innovative jazz pianist and band leader from Philadelphia, known?

7. Which forceful Chicago bluesman who made noted recordings of 'Smokestack Lightnin', 'Killing Floor' and 'Little Red Rooster' was born Chester Arthur Burnett?

8. Who, in 1987, became the first female solo artist inducted into the Rock and Roll Hall of Fame?

9. Which 1970s soul singer of songs such as 'Let's Stay Together' and 'Tired of Being Alone' was ordained a pastor in 1976 and has served in Memphis ever since?

10. Noted for the personalised guitars he plays, which blues musician followed his first solo album, *Dog House Music*, with *I Started out with Nothin and I Still Got Most of It Left*?

11. Which giant of blues, soul and jazz released *Modern Sounds in Country and Western Music* in 1962?

12. New Orleans-born Malcolm John 'Mac' Rebennack, Jr. appeared in the film *The Last Waltz* performing under what name?

13. A recording of which Texan bluesman's song 'Dark Was the Night, Cold Was the Ground' was included on the Golden Record mounted on both of the *Voyager* probes?

14. The Grammy Award-winning blues musician Henry Saint Clair Fredericks shares his stage name with which noted building?

15. Which Mississippi-born bluesman (1917–2001) dueted with Carlos Santana on 'The Healer' but is best known for songs like 'Boogie Chillen' (1948) and 'Boom Boom' (1962)?

Answers to Jazz, Soul and Blues: Pop Music Quiz 2

1. Keith Jarrett
2. Sonny Rollins
3. 'Man of Constant Sorrow'
4. Django Reinhardt
5. Oscar Peterson
6. Fatha
7. Howlin' Wolf
8. Aretha Franklin
9. Al Green
10. Seasick Steve (Wold)
11. Ray Charles
12. Dr John
13. Blind Willie Johnson
14. Taj Mahal
15. John Lee Hooker

1. Which band whose hits include 'Love Shack' named themselves after a hairstyle which took its name from a Boeing aeroplane nicknamed the Stratofortress?

2. One had hits including 'Tour de France' while the other had hits including 'Some Like It Hot'. Name these two bands whose names are translations of one another.

3. The 1990 hit 'I'm Free' was the biggest hit for which band named after a character in *The Clangers*?

4. Which band originally named themselves after basketball star 'Mookie' Blaylock? They eventually changed it but named their album *Ten* after his jersey number instead.

5. Oasis are said to have named themselves after a leisure centre in which Wiltshire town?

6. The Killers named themselves after a fictional rock band in the video to 'Crystal' by which British band?

7. Which US rock band takes its name from Marlon Brando's gang in the film *The Wild Ones*?

8. A surname used by Paul McCartney when booking hotel rooms was taken by Jeffrey Hyman, John Cummings, Douglas Colvin and Thomas Erdelyi as the name of which punk band?

9. The name of a Danish board game testing memory skills was taken by which US rock band led by Bob Mould?

10. Which enigmatic Canadian band of the 1970s named themselves after the alien in *The Day The Earth Stood Still*?

11. The 1980s band whose name was a squiggle, claimed to be pronounced 'Freur', included Karl Hyde and Rick Smith, who went on to form which electronic dance act?

12. Which Liverpool electronic band took its name from a track on Roxy Music's eponymous debut album?

13. Which US rock band takes their name from a phrase in the Book of Genesis referring to Cain?

14. Which British indie band of the early 2000s took their name, with a slight spelling change, from an addition to the Elementary Education Act 1870?

15. Which band is named after a question David Brent posed in *The Office* about his alcohol consumption?

Answers to Band Names: Pop Music Quiz 3

1. B-52s
2. Kraftwerk and the Power Station
3. Soup Dragons
4. Pearl Jam
5. Swindon
6. New Order
7. Black Rebel Motorcycle Club
8. The Ramones
9. Hüsker Dü
10. Klaatu
11. Underworld
12. Ladytron
13. Avenged Sevenfold
14. The Cooper Temple Clause (after the Cowper-Temple clause on funding for denominational schools)
15. Does It Offend You, Yeah?

1. *Viva Hate* (1988) was the first solo album by which former lead singer of the Smiths?
2. Captain Sensible had a UK number one hit in 1982 with a cover of which song from the soundtrack of *South Pacific*?
3. The opening lines of which major UK hit of 1994 are 'I feel it in my fingers / I feel it in my toes'?
4. What was the surname of brothers Neil and Tim, members of Split Enz and later Crowded House?
5. Which person who used her city of birth as her stage surname founded Shakespears Sister with Siobhan Fahey and had solo hits including 'I Believe'?
6. Bob Holness's daughter Ros was in which band, whose major hit was 'I Eat Cannibals Part 1'?
7. Mark Hollis was lead singer of which British band, whose album *Spirit of Eden* is nowadays regarded as a classic?
8. The Proclaimers featured Scottish brothers Craig and Charlie Reid, but which band featured Scottish brothers Jim and William Reid?
9. 'Police Officer' was a 1984 hit for which reggae singer, who ironically and sadly died during a police raid on his house in 2011?
10. Born Kevin Donovan, which US house DJ released seminal electro-influenced hip hop tracks like 'Planet Rock'?
11. *Exile on Coldharbour Lane* which contains 'Woke Up This Morning', the theme of *The Sopranos*, was the first album by which British band?
12. Which German Europop group had a worldwide hit in 1996 with 'Coco Jamboo'?
13. Which Scottish footballer appeared twice in the same episode of *Top of the Pops* in 1982, firstly with his nation's World Cup squad, and then with his club teammates at Tottenham Hotspur?
14. Dream Academy's 'Life in a Northern Town' was dedicated to which English folk singer?
15. They won an online 'Comedy God' poll in 2010 after a campaign inspired by Stewart Lee; which Japanese female art-pop group got into John Peel's Festive 50 in 1984 with 'Blue Canary'?

Answers to 1980s and 1990s: Pop Music Quiz 4

1. Morrissey
2. 'Happy Talk'
3. 'Love Is All Around' by Wet Wet Wet
4. Finn
5. Marcella Detroit
6. Toto Coelo (known as Total Coelo in the US)
7. Talk Talk
8. The Jesus and Mary Chain
9. Smiley Culture
10. Afrika Bambaataa
11. Alabama 3 (known as A3 in the US)
12. Mr President
13. Steve Archibald
14. Nick Drake
15. Frank Chickens

1. *Saturday Night Live*'s 'More Cowbell' sketch starred Will Ferrell as the Blue Oyster Cult's cowbell player being encouraged by which actor playing record producer Bruce Dickinson?

2. Burton Cummings and Randy Bachman belonged to which Canadian band, whose hits include 'American Woman' (1970)?

3. Founded by Chris Karrer in 1969, which Krautrock pioneers released the LPs *Phallus Dei* and *Yeti*? Like Karrer's previous band, it was spawned by a namesake Munich art commune.

4. Which group, featuring the songwriting talents of singer Jean-Louis Aubert, had become perhaps France's biggest rock band by the time of its 1986 split? Their hits include 'Ça c'est vraiment toi', 'Cendrillon' and 'New York avec toi.'

5. Which 1975 song by the band Arrows was made famous thanks to a 1982 cover by Joan Jett and the Blackhearts?

6. Which band pioneered art punk with its 1977 debut *Pink Flag*?

7. Which Japanese idol-heavy metal fusion trio's name came to creator Kobametal as a 'divine message'? Their 2014 self-titled debut LP includes the songs 'Head Bangya!!' and 'Gimme Chocolate!!'.

8. Which Russian rock band was formed in Leningrad in 1972 by lead singer Boris Grebenshchikov, the only original remaining member over its 40-year history? Its LPs include *Sinii Albom* ('The Blue Album'; 1981), *Tabu* (1982) and *Radio Africa* (1983).

9. Which 'father of Chinese rock' is famed for the 1986 song 'Nothing to My Name', a Tiananmen Square protest anthem, and his 1991 cover of the revolutionary song 'Nanniwan'?

10. Iron Maiden topped the singles charts with which 1991 song?

11. 'Imagine Neu! covering 'Dancing in the Dark' – the *Guardian*'s description of the 2014 album *Lost in the Dream* by which US indie rock band, whose frontman is Adam Granduciel?

12. Which Macedonian singer, the 'Elvis Presley of the Balkans', was given an official state funeral after he died aged 26 in a car crash on the Zagreb-Lipovac A3 highway in 2007?

13. *Mistaken for Strangers* is a documentary directed by Tom Berninger about his brother's band. Fronted by Matt Berninger, which group released the albums *Boxer*, *Alligator* and *High Violet*?

14. Which Tool frontman is known as MJK?

15. The science-fiction rock opera *Lifehouse* was which band's intended follow-up to *Tommy*?

1. Christopher Walken
2. The Guess Who
3. Amon Düül II – the commune also gave rise to Amon Düül, Karrer's former band
4. Téléphone
5. 'I Love Rock 'n' Roll'
6. Wire
7. Babymetal – it is a play on 'heavy metal'
8. Aquarium
9. Cui Jian
10. *Bring Your Daughter . . . To The Slaughter*
11. The War on Drugs
12. Todor 'Toše' Proeski
13. The National
14. Maynard James Keenan
15. The Who

Sport

1. Elected to the IOC in 1999, who is the only man to have won Olympic gold in the 100 m and 200 m men's freestyle in consecutive Olympics?

2. In 2012, who became the first men's singles player to retain the Olympic badminton title?

3. Whose 2010 autobiography is entitled *9.58*?

4. With six wins, who has won the most NBA MVP awards?

5. Americans Kerri Lee Walsh Jennings and Misty May-Treanor won Olympic gold in which event in 2004, 2008 and 2012?

6. Born in Colombia, Orlando Duque is a major star in which sport, winning the first ever gold medal at the 2013 World Aquatics Championships in Barcelona?

7. By 2014, which female squash player had won the British Open five times and the World Open a record seven times?

8. Prior to Kim Clijsters in 2009, who was the last woman to win a grand-slam tennis singles title after giving birth?

9. Which man trained three consecutive Cheltenham Gold Cup winners in 1953, 1954 and 1955 and won four Cheltenham Gold Cups in the six years from 1948?

10. Which American identical twins dominated men's doubles tennis in the early 21st century?

11. In 2012, which All Black open-side flanker became the first rugby union player to achieve 100 international wins?

12. Which all-time great won three consecutive Olympic Greco-Roman Super Heavyweight gold medals in 1988, 1992 and 1996?

13. Among the key career records that Tiger Woods is chasing are Jack Nicklaus's 18 major wins and which golfer's 82 PGA titles?

14. Philippe Quintais has won which sport's world championship 12 times?

15. Which French cross-country mountain biker, widely regarded as an all-time great, won gold medals at the Athens and Beijing Olympics?

1. Alexander Popov (Russia)
2. Lin Dan (China)
3. Usain Bolt
4. Kareem Abdul-Jabbar (born Ferdinand Lewis Alcindor Jr. formerly Lew Alcindor) (US)
5. Beach volleyball (W)
6. High diving
7. Nicol David (Malaysia)
8. Evonne Goolagong Cawley – Wimbledon as a 29-year-old in 1980
9. Vincent O'Brien
10. Bob and Mike Bryan
11. Richie McCaw
12. Alexander Karelin
13. Sam Snead – as of April 2014, Woods has won 79
14. Petanque
15. Julien Absalon

1. Against which team did Pelé score his first World Cup goal, in 1958?

2. Who in 1978 became probably the only unattached World Cup winner of all time, although he was signed by Birmingham City soon after the tournament?

3. Who did former England manager Sven-Göran Eriksson manage at the 2010 World Cup?

4. Who in 1934 became the first player to play in the final of two World Cups?

5. He won three consecutive South American Footballer of the Year titles; who was the only player to appear at both the 1966 and 1982 World Cups?

6. Who were the first team eliminated from a World Cup finals without losing a game?

7. Which national side holds the record of 559 minutes of World Cup finals games without conceding a goal?

8. Who scored the first golden goal in World Cup finals history, against Paraguay in 1998?

9. Which goalkeeper in 2010 became the oldest player to make his debut in a World Cup finals match, aged 39 years and 322 days?

10. Which team has played a record nine World Cup finals matches without victory?

11. At the 2014 World Cup, James Rodríguez scored in his first five World Cup appearances, the first person to do this since who at the 1970 and 1978 tournaments?

12. Which side, knocked out in the first round, beat El Salvador by a record scoreline of 10–1 in 1982?

13. Bora Milutinovíc is one of two coaches who have managed five national teams at the World Cup finals. Who is the other, who has also won the tournament when coaching the nation of his birth?

14. In the 1974 World Cup, Dino Zoff's two-year run without conceding a goal for Italy was ended by a goal scorer from which country?

15. Both the semi-finals in 1930 finished with what scoreline?

Answers to The FIFA World Cup: Sport Quiz 2

1. Wales
2. Alberto Tarantini
3. Côte d'Ivoire or Ivory Coast
4. Luis Monti (for Argentina in 1930 and Italy in 1934!)
5. Elias Figueroa
6. Scotland (in 1974)
7. Switzerland (extending across seven matches from 1994 to 2010)
8. Laurent Blanc
9. David James
10. Honduras
11. Teófilo Cubillas
12. Hungary
13. Carlos Alberto Parreira
14. Haiti
15. 6–1

1. During the Ancient Olympics, all of Greece underwent a complete cessation of hostilities. What was this truce called?

2. Uniquely which Austrian Olympic Committee president won a silver medal in the Team Sabre event at Stockholm 1912?

3. In 2004, who became the oldest woman athlete to win both the 800 m and 1,500 m?

4. Christa Luding-Rothenburger of East Germany is the only athlete to win medals at Winter and Summer Olympics in the same year. In 1988, she won a silver and gold in which sports?

5. In 1988, who became the first competitor to represent Great Britain in Olympic ski-jumping?

6. Which five-time Olympic champion played himself in the films *Cannibal Attack* (1954), *Jungle Moon Men* (1955) and *Devil Goddess* (1955)?

7. Which Canadian was the first sprinter not from the US to win two golds at one Olympics?

8. Defeating Dong Jiong of China in 1996, which Dane remains the only non-Asian player – male or female – to win badminton singles gold since its Olympic introduction in 1992?

9. What was unique about the gold- and silver-winning rowing teams in the coxless pairs at the 1980 Moscow Olympics?

10. At the 1924 Paris Olympics, which US athlete broke the long jump world record of 7.76 m? Unfortunately, he was competing in the pentathlon and came third, while the actual long jump champion won with a jump that was 32 cm shorter.

11. Shot in the face during a March 1996 carjacking, which athlete became the first black South African to win Olympic gold when he won the marathon at the Atlanta Games?

12. Which Danish cyclist died as a result of a drug overdose during the men's road race at Rome in 1960?

13. Which sport in the Winter Olympics originated in a discipline called Military Patrol, under which name it was first contested?

14. Amy Williams (2010) and Lizzy Yarnold (2014) both won gold for Great Britain in which event?

15. Helping Japan win men's team gold at the 1976 Montreal Games, which gymnast famously performed on a broken right knee after breaking his leg on the floor exercise?

1. Ekecheiria
2. Otto Herschmann – he remains the only sitting National Olympic Committee president to win a medal at an Olympic Games
3. Kelly Holmes
4. Cycling (silver) and speed skating (gold)
5. Eddie 'The Eagle' Edwards
6. Johnny Weissmuller – Tarzan won his golds in swimming
7. Percy Williams, who won the 100 m and 200 m in 1928
8. Poul-Erik Høyer Larsen
9. Both crews were twin brothers – Bernd and Jörg Landvoigt (East Germany), Nikolai and Yuri Pimenov (USSR)
10. Bob LeGendre – DeHart Hubbard won the long jump becoming the first black athlete to win an Olympic gold at an individual event
11. Josia Thugwane
12. Knud Jenson – his death resulted in the International Cycling Federation becoming the first international body to introduce drug tests
13. Biathlon
14. Skeleton bob
15. Shun Fujimoto

1. Which rider, nicknamed 'the Badger', remains the last French winner, in 1985?

2. The 2013 Tour began in which *région* of France, until then the only *région* in France's European territories which the Tour had never visited?

3. Regular Tour spectator Dieter 'Didi' Senft is known for dressing as what?

4. Which Luxembourg rider became in 2010 the most recent of the four cyclists to win the Young Rider and General Classification jerseys in the same year?

5. From 1904 to 1967, the Tour finished at which Parisian sporting venue?

6. What French term describes those climbs more difficult than category one?

7. Which French cyclist won the 1956 Tour de France but achieved little else of note in his cycling career?

8. Which Belgian won a joint-record eight stages in his debut Tour in 1976, ultimately finishing in eighth place, and winning the green jersey?

9. For which team did Lance Armstrong ride for his seven subsequently annulled Tour victories (they were called Discovery Channel for the last)?

10. Which Spaniard interrupted Eddy Merckx's otherwise consecutive run of Tour wins when he won the 1973 Tour in the great Belgian's absence?

11. Which rider became the first rider to die on the Tour in 1910, unusually doing so from a jellyfish sting while swimming rather than while on his bicycle?

12. Which Dutchman won the 1980 Tour on his 10th attempt? He finished every one of his 16 Tours and never finished below 30th.

13. Which small town just to the north of the Pyrenees has hosted over 60 stage starts or finishes, putting it third behind Paris and Bordeaux?

14. Which Belgian *soigneur* to the Festina team was stopped in his car in 1998 with large quantities of doping products, starting a major Tour scandal?

15. Which Scotsman placed fourth in the 1984 Tour de France, also winning the King of the Mountains competition?

Answers to Tour de France: Sport Quiz 4

1. Bernard Hinault
2. Corsica
3. The devil
4. Andy Schleck
5. Parc des Princes
6. *Hors catégorie* (above categorisation)
7. Roger Walkowiak
8. Freddy Maertens
9. US Postal Service
10. Luis Ocaña
11. Adolphe Hélière
12. Joop Zoetemelk
13. Pau
14. Willy Voet
15. Robert Millar

1. Which East German sprinter won Olympic gold in the 200 m and 4 × 100 m races at the 1976 and 1980 Olympics?
2. Winner of the 5,000 m Olympic title in Sydney, who became Romania's Minister of Youth and Sports in March 2014?
3. Which German, who joined the Portland Thorns in January 2014, was named FIFA Women's World Player of the Year in the same month? She is the first goalkeeper to win it.
4. Olympic champion in the slalom and alpine combined (both 1992), which Austrian was the first female alpine skier to win in all five World Cup events?
5. Winner of the 1963 BBC Sports Personality of the Year, which 1962 European champion athlete in the 100 m has a stadium in Cudworth, Barnsley, named in her honour?
6. The 1994 Lou Marsh Trophy winner, who is the only Canadian to have won an Olympic medal in the biathlon? She won the 7.5 km sprint and the 15 km individual at Lillehammer.
7. On 7 February 2005, which sailor broke the world record for the fastest solo circumnavigation of the globe?
8. Which Australian tennis player was only 17 when she won the first of seven straight singles titles at 1960's Australian Open?
9. The only European-born player in the WNBA Top 15 Players of All Time poll, which Portuguese guard for the Sacramento Monarchs is the all-time WNBA leader in assists (2,560)?
10. The Germans Sylke Otto (2002 and 2006), Tatjana Hüfner (2010) and Natalie Geisenberger (2014) all won which Olympic title?
11. Competing for the USSR, then the Unified Team and finally Russia, who is the only woman to have become an Olympic champion in two winter sports: cross-country skiing and biathlon?
12. Which Australian, from 1910 to 1918, was regarded as the world's greatest female swimmer of all distances? She won the inaugural Olympic women's 100 m freestyle event in 1912.
13. The 1993 world champion in ladies' singles, Oksana Baiul is the first and so far only figure skater to win gold at the Winter Olympics (in 1994) representing which country?
14. Which gymnast won Olympic gold at the 1980 Olympics in the Floor Exercise and the Beam?
15. Which country's national field hockey team are nicknamed *Las Leonas* ('The Lionesses')?

1. Bärbel Wöckel
2. Gabriela Szabo
3. Nadine Angerer
4. Petra Kronberger
5. Dorothy Hyman
6. Myriam Bédard
7. Ellen MacArthur
8. Margaret Court, née Smith
9. Ticha Penicheiro
10. Luge
11. Anfisa Reztsova, née Romanova
12. Fanny Durack
13. Ukraine
14. Nadia Comâneci
15. Argentina

Miscellaneous I

1. A cereologist studies which phenomenon?
2. In an 1989 movie, Harry was what type of mysterious North American human-like creature?
3. Who was the German youth who appeared in 1828 claiming to have been brought up in a darkened cell, and died from a stabbing in 1833?
4. What name was given to the mysterious creature, able to bound over walls and rooftops, who terrorised the UK in the 19th century?
5. Never identified, what was the assumed name of the man who hijacked an airliner over the north-western US in 1971, parachuting out of the plane with $200,000 of ransom money?
6. Which Russian student gives his surname to the mountain pass in the Urals where in February 1959 he and eight others died for reasons still unknown?
7. A popular mystery claims that 'angels' protected British troops at which 1914 World War I battle?
8. Which Nova Scotia island is home to a so-called 'Money Pit', the scene of many attempts to recover reputed buried treasure?
9. Also called a 'blob', what name is given to any unidentified organic mass which washes up on the shore of a body of water?
10. Which Malian tribe has been credited with advanced astronomical knowledge of mysterious origin, particularly regarding the star Sirius B?
11. They ceased to be used in the 19th century and have resisted all attempts at decipherment; what name is given to the carved glyphs once used on Easter Island?
12. Which 20-year-old Australian pilot disappeared in 1978 while flying a Cessna light aircraft, having reported being followed by a strange craft?
13. What Persian phrase was written on paper in the pocket of a mystery man found dead on a South Australia beach in 1948, and gives its name to that baffling case?
14. What name is given to the massive undersea rock formation located off the Japanese coast whose flat parallel faces and sharp edges have led to suggestions that it is man-made?
15. Which hilltop village in southern France is the centre of conspiracy theories centred on the cleric Bérenger Saunière?

1. Crop circles
2. Bigfoot or Sasquatch
3. Kaspar Hauser
4. Spring-heeled Jack
5. D.B. Cooper or Dan Cooper
6. Igor Dyatlov
7. Mons
8. Oak Island
9. Globster
10. Dogon
11. Rongorongo
12. Frederick Valentich
13. Tamam shud (often misspelt as Taman shud)
14. Yonaguni monument or Yonaguni-jima Kaitei Chikei
15. Rennes-le-Château

1. Which Nobel Economics laureate (1994) is the subject of a 2001 film which won the Best Picture Oscar ?

2. Which lawyer and human rights campaigner, Iran's first female judge, was awarded the 2003 Nobel Peace Prize?

3. Which Nobel Prize was awarded to Norman Borlaug in 1970 for his role in the 'Green Revolution', developing strains of cereals that transformed food production worldwide?

4. Which future Nobel winner (1935) lectured on radioactivity whilst detained at Ruhleben internment camp during World War I?

5. Winning the Physics Prize in 1907, which Russian-born US scientist is best known for conducting a landmark 1887 experiment with E.W. Morley?

6. Which winner of the 1913 Nobel Prize in Physics had, in 1908, become the first man to liquify helium?

7. Which Australian, who shared the 2005 Nobel Prize in Medicine, self-experimented to demonstrate the role played by the bacterium *Heliobacter pylori* in gastritis and peptic ulcers?

8. What is the surname of the father and son who shared the Nobel Prize in Physics in 1915 'for their services in the analysis of crystal structure by means of X-rays'?

9. Which double Nobel laureate is the only female scientist to be seen in the celebrated group photograph from the great Fifth Solvay conference of 1927 on 'Electrons and Photons'?

10. Which theoretical physicist shared the 1979 Nobel Prize in Physics, becoming the first Pakistani to receive a Nobel Prize and also the first Muslim to win a Nobel Prize in science?

11. What connects the Nobel winners Erik Axel Karlfeldt (Literature, 1931), Dag Hammarskjöld (Peace, 1961), William Vickrey (Economics, 1996) and Ralph M. Steinman (Medicine, 2011)?

12. Thomas Mann was awarded the 1929 Nobel Prize in Literature with which of his novels of 1901 being cited as '. . . one of the classic works of contemporary literature'?

13. Were you to sort the Nobel Literature laureates by surname in alphabetical order, which winner, from 1935, would come last?

14. Who, in 1938, became the first US woman to win the Nobel Prize in Literature?

15. Which English Nobel Prize winner acted in the theatre and occasionally on film and TV, under the stage name David Baron?

1. John Forbes Nash Jr. – *A Beautiful Mind*
2. Shirin Ebadi
3. Nobel Peace Prize
4. James Chadwick – he won for the discovery of the neutron
5. Albert Michelson
6. Heike Kamerlingh Onnes
7. Barry Marshall
8. Bragg – Sir William Henry Bragg and William Lawrence Bragg
9. Marie Curie
10. (Mohammad) Abdus Salam
11. They did not live to receive their awards in person
12. *Buddenbrooks*
13. William Butler Yeats
14. Pearl S. Buck
15. Harold Pinter

1. Which German astronomer wrote about a fantasy voyage to the moon in the Latin-language work *Somnium* (The Dream)?

2. Deriving its title from the Greek for 'sad', which 1956 sci-fi poem by Swedish Nobel laureate Harry Martinson relates in 103 cantos the tragedy of a spaceship that gets ejected from the solar system?

3. Which prolific Russian pop culture writer (b.1962) is the author of the novels *Omon Ra*, *Generation 'Π'*, *The Sacred Book of the Werewolf* and *S.N.U.F.F.*?

4. In the title of a TV show, who were the student Quinn Mallory, Wade Wells, Professor Arturo and soul singer Rembrandt Brown?

5. Widely assumed to be an inspiration for Superman, *Gladiator* is a 1930 novel by which US author?

6. Which 2000 cyberpunk action RPG has the player assume the identity of the 'nano-aug' UNATCO agent J.C. Denton?

7. Called the most important French sci-fi writer since Verne, who wrote the 1969 time travel novel *Le temps n'a pas d'odeur*?

8. Based on a Bulgakov play, which 1973 Soviet comedy film has the engineer Shurik Timofeev send back building superintendent Ivan Bunsha (Yuri Yakovlev) and burglar George to the time of Ivan the Terrible, while the Tsar is sent to modern-day Russia?

9. Which Czech sci-fi trailblazer is said to have inspired *Solaris*, *Star Trek* and *Alien* with the stark design and psychological style of his 1963 film, the socio-realist space odyssey *Ikarie XB-1*?

10. Commissioned by one of the Great Houses, General Martouk's B'rel-class raiding and scouting vessel, the IKS *Rotarran*, is a notable example of which type of ship?

11. Which much-acclaimed episode of the new *Dr Who* featured Carey Mulligan in the guest role of Sally Sparrow?

12. In *Blake's 7*, Roj Blake (Gareth Thomas), captain of the *Liberator*, waged war on which quasi-fascist stellar government?

13. *The Windup Girl* is which US writer's 2009 debut novel?

14. Based on a story by Richard A. Lupoff, 1990's Oscar-nominated short *12:01 PM* had a *Groundhog Day* premise, but repeated an hour instead of a day. It stars which *Robocop* actor as Myron Castleman, a man locked in a time-loop?

15. Which 2012 Swedish sci-fi TV drama is set in an alternate version of modern-day Sweden where humanoid robot workers/servants – dubbed 'hubots' – are commonplace?

1. Johannes Kepler
2. *Aniara*
3. Victor Pelevin
4. *Sliders*
5. Philip Wylie
6. Deus Ex
7. Gérard Klein, who also uses the pseudonym Gilles d'Argyre
8. *Ivan Vasilievich Changes Profession/Ivan Vasilievich: Back to the Future*
9. Jindřich Polák
10. Klingon Bird-of-Prey
11. 'Blink'
12. The Terran Federation or the Federation
13. Paolo Bacigalupi
14. Kurtwood Smith– who played Clarence Boddicker in *Robocop*
15. *Real Humans/Äkta människor*

1. Its early R-1340 Wasp engine powered the aircraft of Wiley Post and Amelia Earhart. Which Connecticut-based company is one of the 'big three' manufacturers of aero engines along with General Electric and Rolls-Royce?

2. Every 7 October since the 1950s, which airline has celebrated its founding in 1919 by presenting special, very collectible, gin bottles to its World Business Class customers?

3. What two-word name is given to the Boeing WC-135, used by the United States Air Force to 'sniff' out atmospheric evidence of nuclear detonations?

4. The company that made MiG fighter aircraft took its name from the surnames of two co-founders. Give either surname.

5. Manufactured by Airbus, and making its first flight in 2005, what is the designation of the world's largest passenger airliner?

6. Prohibited from making aircraft after World War II, which aircraft company made the six-foot-long microcar named the Kabinenroller?

7. What surname is shared by brothers Burt, an American aerospace engineer, and Dick, who co-piloted the Burt-designed *Voyager*, which was, in 1986, the first aircraft to fly around the world without stopping or refuelling?

8. Which Lockheed reconnaissance aircraft, now retired, has held the speed record for air-breathing manned aircraft (Mach 3.3 – 2,193.2 mph) since 1976?

9. Which figure from Greek mythology gave its name to the engines used to power the Harrier jump jet?

10. The primary Japanese naval fighter in World War II, by what name was the Mitsubishi A6M better known to the Allies?

11. An airship used by the US Navy for scouting, which 'flying aircraft carrier' crashed into the ocean off Monterey Bay, California, in 1935?

12. Francis Rogallo, the inventor of the Rogallo wing, was dubbed the 'father of _____' what?

13. What do the letters XWB stand for in plane names such as the Airbus A350XWB?

14. The Orteig Prize ($25,000) led to which historic feat of 1927?

15. Name either of the British aviators who made the first non-stop transatlantic flight in June 1919, flying a modified World War I Vickers Vimy bomber from Newfoundland to Ireland.

Answers to Aviation: Miscellaneous I Quiz 4

1. Pratt & Whitney
2. KLM. Each miniature depicts a real Dutch house
3. Constant Phoenix
4. (Artem) Mikoyan and (Mikhail) Gurevich
5. A380
6. Messerschmidt
7. Rutan
8. SR-71 'Blackbird' (aka Habu)
9. Pegasus
10. Zero
11. USS *Macon*
12. Hang-gliding
13. eXtra-Wide-Body
14. Lindbergh's solo flight across the Atlantic
15. John Alcock or Arthur Brown

1. Which World Chess Champion's namesake 'gun', sees a queen backing up two rooks on the same file?
2. In 2005, the first World Championship in Chessdarts was won by a future Women's World Chess Champion and the 2004 BDO World Darts Champion. Name either.
3. During the Candidates tournament in Zürich in 1953, which future World Chess Champion (1957–58) used his fine baritone voice to sing extracts from opera on Swiss radio?
4. In 2003 a biography subtitled *It's Only Me* was published about which late English chess grandmaster?
5. Name either of the grandmasters whitewashed 6–0 in successive matches by Bobby Fischer in 1971 in the Candidates Tournament to find a challenger to the World Champion Boris Spassky?
6. Whose reign as World Champion was first interrupted by Vasily Smyslov and then later by Mikhail Tal, making him the only man to hold the world title for three non-consecutive periods?
7. Which leading proponent of hypermodern chess wrote the influential book *Mein System* (*My System*) in 1925?
8. The men's team from which country with a population of just over 3 million won the European Team Championship in 1999, the World Team Championship in 2011 and the Chess Olympiad in 2006, 2008 and 2012?
9. Containing a hidden chess player, it was a sensation for decades. By what name was the Automaton Chess-player constructed by Wolfgang von Kempelen in the late 18th century better known?
10. In May 2014, who achieved a record Elo rating of 2,882?
11. What move is represented in chess notation by 0–0–0?
12. The English opening (1. c4) derives its name from its use by which English (unofficial) world champion, who played it during his 1843 match with Saint-Amant?
13. Taking its name from the English and Austrian players who analysed it in 1886, which chess opening is characterised by the opening moves 1. e4 c6?
14. Which Dresden-born millionaire grandmaster (1928–2013), heir to the Karl May publishing house refereed the Fischer–Spassky match in Reykjavik in 1972?
15. In 2010, who, at the age of 16, became the youngest ever Women's World Chess Champion?

1. Alekhine – Alekhine's gun
2. Alexandra Kosteniuk or Andy Fordham
3. Vasily Smyslov
4. Tony Miles (an anagram of his name)
5. Mark Taimanov (USSR) or Bent Larsen (Denmark)
6. Mikhail Botvinnik
7. Aaron Nimzowitsch
8. Armenia
9. The Turk
10. Magnus Carlsen
11. Queenside castling or long castling
12. Howard Staunton
13. Caro–Kann Defence
14. Lothar Schmid
15. Hou Yifan (China)

Social Sciences and Religion

1. The German philosopher Adam Weishaupt (1748–1830) was the founder of which secret society?

2. Who wrote the 1881 treatise *The Art of Being Right*?

3. Which 'father of Russian Marxism' was instrumental in the 1898 creation of the Russian Social Democratic Workers' Party, and believed that Russia must pass through industrialisation and capitalism before reaching socialism? Siding with the Mensheviks against Lenin, he died in Finnish exile in 1918.

4. Which 17th-century English philosopher's social contract includes ideas surrounding the 'state of nature', 'government with the consent of the governed' and the natural rights of life, liberty and estate?

5. Which Cynic was called 'a Socrates gone mad' by Plato?

6. Which two-word term was coined in 1973 by the Norwegian philosopher and mountaineer Arne Naess to describe the concept that we must recognise we are part of nature, and not separate from it, if we are to avoid environmental catastrophe?

7. Which philosopher, born in Aosta, Italy, in 1033, was made Archbishop of Canterbury in 1093, despite his protestations?

8. What are *Dukkha, Samudaya, Nirodha* and *Magga*?

9. Which Denver-born philosopher is perhaps best known for his 'Chinese room' argument against 'strong' artificial intelligence?

10. As a young man, Jean-Paul Sartre became interested in philosophy after reading 'Time and Free Will', an essay by which French winner of the 1927 Nobel Prize in Literature?

11. First making her name in the 1970s with the books *Deviant Logic* and *Philosophy of Logics*, which English philosopher introduced the epistemological theory of foundherentism in the 1993 work *Evidence and Inquiry*?

12. What did Aristotle call 'the highest good, being a realisation and perfect practice of virtue'?

13. 'Striking his fist with mighty force against a large stone, till he rebounded from it – "I refute it thus"' – whose famous response to Bishop Berkeley's thesis that matter does not exist?

14. Carrying a copy wherever he went, Mahatma Gandhi referred to which 700-verse scripture as his 'moral dictionary'?

15. Which 1918 paper by Bertrand Russell holds that language can be analysed into fundamental atoms of meaning?

Answers to Philosophy: Social Sciences and Religion Quiz 1

1. The Order of the Illuminati
2. Artur Schopenhauer – it is subtitled *38 Ways to Win An Argument*
3. Georgi Plekhanov
4. John Locke
5. Diogenes
6. 'Deep ecology'
7. St. Anselm of Canterbury
8. The Four Noble Truths of Buddhism – e.g. *Dukkha* refers to the truth of suffering
9. John Searle
10. Henri Bergson
11. Susan Haack
12. Happiness
13. Dr Samuel Johnson
14. The Bhagavad gita – contained within the classical Sanskrit epic poem, the Mahabharata
15. 'The Philosophy of Logical Atomism'

1. In which 2005 video game does the player control Kratos, a Spartan tasked by Athena with killing Ares, the title deity?

2. Consecrated to an eponymous Semitic god, the Temple of Bel formed the centre of religious life in which ancient Aramaic city in central Syria, once called the 'Bride of the Desert'?

3. The Ésagila – 'house of the raised dead' – was a temple dedicated to which protector god of Babylon?

4. One of the world's longest epics, *La Galigo/Sureq Galigo* is a creation myth of the Bugis people from which Indonesian island?

5. Which legendary founder of Mycenae invented the quoit?

6. Now named after a Roman god, which planet, as long as 3,000 years ago, was named Nergal by Babylonian astronomer-astrologers after their god of death and pestilence?

7. Which deity, whose name means 'Throne', was the first daughter of Geb, god of the earth, and Nut, the sky goddess?

8. Who was the Roman goddess of fruitful abundance?

9. Crafted by Brokk and Sindri, which weapon is supposed to be given to Magni after Thor's death?

10. Salvador Dalí signed a licensing agreement with Jean-Pierre Grivory of COFCI (now Cofinluxe) in 1982, thus creating the Salvador Dalí perfume brand. Dalí designed the company's bottles. They represented the nose and lips of a figure from one of his paintings. Name the goddess.

11. The father god and creator, Achamán was the supreme god of the Guanches on which island?

12. The Trojan Horse was built in three days under the leadership of which cowardly Greek soldier and son of Panopeus?

13. The Mexica/Aztec were said to be guided by which god of will and the sun, whose name means 'Hummingbird from the South'?

14. Dumuzid the Shepherd's consort, Inanna, the Sumerian goddess of love, fertility, and warfare, was the goddess of the E-Anna temple at which city, her main centre, situated on the ancient dry former channel of the Euphrates River in Iraq?

15. Which Norse goddess presides over the realm of the dead with her blood-drenched dog Garmr, making sure that the souls of the dishonoured and those undeserving of Valhalla stay there?

Answers to Mythology: Social Sciences and Religion Quiz 2

1. *God of War*
2. Palmyra
3. Marduk
4. Sulawesi, formerly known as Celebes
5. Perseus
6. Mars
7. Isis – she married her brother Osiris and conceived Horus with him
8. Pomona
9. Thor's hammer Mjölnir
10. Aphrodite – from his painting *Apparition of the Face of Aphrodite of Knidos*
11. Tenerife – his name means 'the skies'
12. Epeios
13. Huitzilopochtli – may also mean 'left-handed hummingbird'
14. Uruk
15. Hel – ruler of Helheim

1. A church in Axum claims to house the Ark of the Covenant containing the tablets with the Ten Commandments, but it is kept under guard and not even Indiana Jones can get at it. In which African country is the holy city of Axum?
2. Said to be the tunic worn by the Virgin Mary at Christ's birth, the *Sancta Camisa* is a relic in which French cathedral?
3. The National Emblem of India is an adaptation of the Lion Capital of Ashoka, the sculpture that was originally placed atop the Aśoka pillar at which Buddhist site in Uttar Pradesh?
4. Which religious organisation is known for its 'Lassies' wearing a bonnet with a red band and large ribbon bow?
5. Completed on 30 August 1604, the original copy of which holy scripture – whose name means 'the beginning scripture' – still exists today and is kept at the Indian town of Kartarpur?
6. Which religion has 'Mansions' that followers identify with, including the Nyahbinghi, and the Bobo Ashanti?
7. Which South American country, unusally, has a population that is less than 50% practicing Roman catholic?
8. Which daughter of Imran and Hannah is the only woman mentioned by name in the Quran?
9. The *San Zeno Altarpiece* is a triptych by Andrea Mantegna located in a namesake basilica, in which northern Italian city?
10. Home to the 16th-century Basilica of Our Lady of Copacabana, Bolivia's patron saint, Copacabana is the main Bolivian town on the shore of which lake?
11. According to Deuteronomy, who was shown the Promised Land from the top of Mount Nebo and told: 'I have caused thee to see it with thine eyes, but thou shalt not go over thither'?
12. Which five-letter name, Tibetan for 'new year', is given to Tibetan New Year? It is preceded by the celebration Nyi Shu Gu and the traditional eating of the noodle soup *Guthuk*.
13. Which colour was traditionally used to indicate a saint's day or other Christian festival in the calendar?
14. Founded by Father Michael J. McGivney in 1882, what is the world's largest Catholic fraternal service organisation?
15. Which Hindu god of beginnings and patron of intellectuals, has the large Indian bandicoot rat for his vehicle (*vahana*) in this world, symbolising his status as the remover of obstacles?

1. Ethiopia
2. Chartres Cathedral
3. Sarnath deer park
4. Salvation Army
5. Adi Granth – the compilation of Sikh scriptures finished by the fifth Sikh guru, Guru Arjan Dev Ji, and installed at Harmandir Sahib Ji on 1 September
6. Rastafarianism
7. Uruguay – CIA Factbook claims 47.1%; Uruguay has been called the 'most secular place in Latin America'
8. Mary or Maryam
9. Verona – as in the Basilica di San Zeno
10. Lake Titicaca
11. Moses
12. Losar
13. Red – it is the source of the phrase 'red letter day'
14. The Knights of Columbus
15. Ganesha

International Business:
Social Sciences and Religion Quiz 4

1. Now headquartered in Houston, which company, the world's largest oilfield services company, was founded in 1926 by namesake French brothers Conrad and Marcel?

2. Hutchinson Whampoa, Jardine Matheson and Shaw Brothers Studio are companies headquartered in which city?

3. Wrapped in wax paper and made by Haribo since 1986, what is the palindromic name of the most popular fruity chew in Germany?

4. Which company (NYSE code LVB) has manufacturing facilities in New York and Hamburg with its flagship model being the D-274?

5. In 2009, after a run of 74 years, Eastman Kodak stopped producing which product immortalised in a 1973 Paul Simon hit?

6. What sort of disposable product is made by the firm Travel John?

7. Separating from Samsung in the 1990s, in which city is Shinsegae's flagship outlet, the world's largest department store, which surpassed Macy's department store in New York City in 2009?

8. Founded in 1873, which major metals and mining corporation takes its name from a river in south-western Spain, which has run red since mining began there about 5,000 years ago?

9. In the past Bloehm + Voss has built aircraft, submarines and warships including the *Bismarck* and *Admiral Hipper*. In recent times it has built numerous superyachts including *Eclipse* and *Dubai*. In which city is it based?

10. Which Danish business conglomerate has been the largest container ship operator in the world since 1996?

11. Noted for tyre manufacture, which company's name derives from a translation of the name of the founder, Shojiro Ishibashi?

12. Founded by Ivor Tiefenbrun in Glasgow in 1973, which company has produced high-end audio equipment including the Sondek LP12 turntable and the Isobarik speaker?

13. Headquartered in Linz, Plasser & Theurer is an Austrian manufacturer, the world's largest in its segment, of equipment used for the construction and maintenance of what?

14. What did the acronym ARM stand for when the semiconductor and software design company was founded in 1990?

15. Founded in 2003, Rovio Entertainment Limited is best known for creating which very popular video game in 2009?

Answers to International Business:
Social Sciences and Religion Quiz 4

1. Schlumberger
2. Hong Kong
3. MAOAM
4. Steinway & Sons. At 8'11¾ the D-274 is a 274 cm long grand piano. LVB stands for Ludwig van Beethoven
5. Kodchrome
6. Disposable/portable urinals
7. Busan (Centum City), South Korea
8. Rio Tinto (Group)
9. Hamburg
10. Maersk (A.P. Moller – Maersk Group)
11. Bridgestone – (Ishi = Stone, Bashi = Bridge)
12. Linn
13. Rail track – they make distinctive yellow track maintenance and track-laying machines
14. Advanced RISC Machines
15. *Angry Birds*

1. *Indian Currency and Finance* was the first major work by which giant of economics?
2. The idea that consumers rein in their spending if government spending increases, because they anticipate future tax rises, is given what name?
3. Which two words come next in the quote by Milton Friedman: 'Inflation is always and everywhere a . . .'?
4. What is the name of those commodities, often staple foods for the poor, for which demand paradoxically rises if the price rises?
5. Referring to a combination of high inflation and high unemployment, the word 'stagflation' is said to have been first used by which future Chancellor of the Exchequer?
6. In 2013, students at which British university founded the Post-Crash Economics Society, calling for a rethink of the way economics is taught?
7. Which phrase originating from Juvenal was applied by Nassim Nicholas Taleb to refer to hard-to-predict but critical events?
8. Which curve in economics shows combinations of goods between which a consumer has no preference?
9. In the textbook *Principles of Economics*, which economist was the first to publicise the classic supply-and-demand graph used in microeconomics?
10. *23 Things They Don't Tell You About Capitalism* is a work by which Korean economist based at Cambridge University?
11. François Quesnay was one of the leaders of which 18th century French school of economics who stressed the primacy of agriculture in generating wealth?
12. The economist George Akerlof showed how the existence of defective items or 'lemons' in a market can cause prices generally to drop, by studying which market?
13. The former President of Harvard Larry Summers is the nephew of two Nobel Prize-winning economists. Who are they?
14. In his 2013 work *Capital in the Twenty-First Century*, economist Thomas Piketty argues that economic inequality is caused by what being higher than the rate of economic growth over the long term?
15. Of the eight rounds of talks held under the General Agreement on Tariffs and Trade, only one was in the United Kingdom. In which resort town was it held?

Answers to Economics: Social Sciences and Religion Quiz 5

1. John Maynard Keynes
2. Ricardian equivalence (after David Ricardo)
3. 'Monetary phenomenon'
4. Giffen goods
5. Iain Macleod
6. University of Manchester
7. Black swans
8. Indifference curve
9. Alfred Marshall
10. Ha-Joon Chang
11. Physiocrats or physiocracy
12. Used cars
13. Paul Samuelson and Kenneth Arrow
14. The rate of return on capital ('r')
15. Torquay

Literature

1. Who links Jerusalem, Pyongyang, Shenzhen and Burma?

2. The first online comic, published on CompuServe in 1985, was Eric Millikin's *Witches and Stitches*, an unauthorised parody of which book series and movie musical?

3. Which Daniel Clowes graphic novel centres on 'supremely ironic' teens, Enid Coleslaw and Rebecca Doppelmeyer?

4. Who is the British creator of the comic strip serials *Gemma Bovery* (2000) and *Tamara Drewe* (2005–6)?

5. Which graphic novel by Joe Sacco tells the story of 'July 1, 1916: The First Day of the Battle of the Somme'?

6. Who created the series *Rork*, (its spin-off) *Capricorne* and *Arg*?

7. Played by Lewis Wilson, which crime fighter first appeared on the big screen in a 1943 film serial battling the villainous scientist Dr Daka in a piece of anti-Japanese propaganda?

8. Which comic book crime fighter drives a camouflaged sport coupé called the Redbird?

9. Which ex-My Chemical Romance frontman created *The Umbrella Academy* (2008), a comic about a dysfunctional family of super-heroes with names like The Rumor?

10. Goku is the hero of which 1984–95 manga series by Akira Toriyama? Its 42 volumes have sold over 230 m copies.

11. Which film noir-style comic by Spanish authors Juan Diaz Canales and Juanjo Guarnido is set in 1950s America with characters that, like the title feline private eye, are all anthropo-morphic animals? Celeb cameos include Senator Joseph McCarthy as the cockerel Senator Gallo.

12. 'The mother of manga', Riyoko Ikeda, began her most famous series in 1972. Focusing on Brigadier Oscar François de Jarjayes (a girl raised as a man), which 1,700-plus-page manga was set at King Louis XIV's court and began a trend for historical manga?

13. Who usurped Biffo the Bear from the front cover in the 14 September 1974 issue of the *Beano*?

14. Written by Brian K. Vaughan, which epic space opera centres on a husband and wife from long-warring races, the winged Alana from the planet Landfall and the horned Marko from Landfall's moon Wreath, and their newborn daughter Hazel?

15. Credited as the first underground comic, *The Adventures of Jesus* was published in 1962 by which Texan cartoonist?

1. Guy Delisle – the Quebec-born author of comic book travelogues about those locations including *Burma Chronicles*
2. *The Wizard of Oz*
3. *Ghost World*
4. Posy Simmonds
5. *The Great War*
6. Andreas – the German-born Belgain comics artist Andreas Martens
7. Batman
8. Robin
9. Gerard Way
10. *Dragon Ball*
11. *Blacksad* – the title character is black cat John Blacksad, his sometime sidekick, the least weasel Weekly
12. *The Rose of Versailles/Lady Oscar*
13. Dennis the Menace
14. *Saga*
15. Frank Stack under the name Foolbert Sturgeon

1. Which Ivorian novelist, who died in 2003, wrote about how power corrupted Africa's leaders in *Waiting for the Wild Beasts to Vote*? *The Suns of Independence* was his 1970 debut.

2. In *The Captive*, Proust's Bergotte dies looking at a little patch of yellow wall in which Vermeer painting?

3. Who first brought the horrific reality of South Africa's apartheid system to international attention with his novel *Mine Boy* (1946)?

4. Italy's best-selling post-war book is *Va' dove ti porta il cuore* (1994), a long letter from a dying woman in Trieste, telling her granddaughter in America to *Follow Your Heart*. Who wrote it?

5. The 1985 novel *Ardent Patience* by Chilean author Antonio Skármeta was the inspiration for which 1994 movie?

6. Completed in 1257 what was the first book of poetry by Saadi? Its Persian title means 'the fruit orchard'.

7. João Guimarães Rosa is best known for which 1956 novel, regarded by some as the Brazilian *Ulysses*? It is the story of Riobaldo, a *jagunço* (bandit) who undergoes an existential quest.

8. Which Pakistani author wrote *A God in Every Stone* (2014)?

9. A Bolshevik fighter in the Civil War, Pavel Korchagin is the protagonist of which 1936 novel by Nikolai Ostrovsky, whose Soviet sales of 36.4 m bettered *War and Peace*?

10. Charter 77's youngest signatory, which Czech author wrote the novels *City Sister Silver/Sestra* and *Gargling with Tar*?

11. In which debut novel by Milan Kundera does writing the postcard message – 'Optimism is the opium of the people! A healthy atmosphere stinks of stupidity! Long live Trotsky!' – have grave consequences for Ludvik Jahn?

12. Introducing the titular orphan, *Memed, My Hawk* (1955) has been called the greatest Turkish novel of the 20th century. The first book in a tetralogy, it was whose debut novel?

13. His four novels include *A Burnt Child* and 1949's *Wedding Worries*. Which prolific Swedish author, who also wrote short stories, plays and travelogues like *German Autumn* and gave his name to a literary prize, committed suicide in 1954 aged 30?

14. 'A Madman's Diary' (1918) is the first story in *Call to Arms*, a short story collection by which Chinese writer?

15. Which Nigerian novelist wrote *My Life in the Bush of Ghosts* and *The Palm-Wine Drinkard*?

Answers to Foreign Literature: Literature Quiz 2

1. Ahmadou Kourouma
2. *View of Delft*
3. Peter Abrahams
4. Susanna Tamaro
5. *Il Postino* – the novel now bears the title *El Cartero de Neruda* (Neruda's Postman)
6. *Bustan*
7. *Grande Sertão: Veredas/The Devil to Pay in the Backlands*
8. Kamila Shamsie
9. *How the Steel was Tempered*
10. Jáchym Topol
11. The Joke/*Pert*
12. Yaşar Kemal (born Kemal Sadık Gökçeli in 1923)
13. Stig Dagerman
14. Lu Xun, the pen name of Zhou Shuren
15. Amos Tutuola

1. What is the nickname of Marco Buratti, the Skoda-driving unlicensed investigator that writer Massimo Carlotto based on himself and writes about in such novels as *The Master of Knots*?
2. France's leading political crime writer, who penned *Murder in Memoriam*, *A Very Profitable War* and *Nazis in the Metro*?
3. Which Polish crime writer is best known for his series of five Chandleresque novels set in pre-war Breslau (now Wroclaw) with the policeman Inspector Eberhard Mock as the protagonist?
4. Which US crime writer, best known for his Cork O'Connor series of Minnesota-set books, won the 2013 Best Novel Edgar Award for his stand-alone novel *Ordinary Grace*?
5. Which private eye looks 'rather pleasantly like a blond satan'?
6. The Inspector Montalbano novels are set in which fictional town modelled on author Andrea Camilleri's hometown Porto Empedocle, which changed its name to reflect the association in 2003?
7. *A Dark-Adapted Eye* (1986) was the first psychological thriller written by Ruth Rendell using which pen-name?
8. Cecil Day-Lewis writing as Nicholas Blake, supposedly based the detective Nigel Strangeways on which fellow poet?
9. Which Havana-born Spanniard's novel *The Athenian Murders* features the Poirot-like 'decipherer of enigmas', Heracles Pontor?
10. A morphine and opium addict, which 'Swiss Simenon' died in 1938 due to a stroke he suffered on the eve of his wedding? Germany's most prestigious crime-writing prize is named after this Sergeant Studer mysteries author.
11. Shortlisted for the Gold Dagger in 2003 for *Almost Blue* (part of the Inspector Grazia Negro series), which Parma-born former Progetto K punk band singer previously wrote the Fascist-era Inspector Da Luca novels, starting with *Carte Blanche* (1990)?
12. Centring on writer Erica Falk and detective Patrik Hedström, Camilla Läckberg's crime novels – such as *The Ice Princess* – are set in which small Swedish west coast town where she grew up?
13. Author of the Johanna Vik/Inspector Stobo series, Anne Holt held which offce in the Norwegian government during 1996–97?
14. Who solved his first case in *The Mysterious Affair at Styles* (1920)?
15. Which US author's Inspector Ebenezer Gryce debuted in *The Leavenworth Case* (1878), making her the first major woman writer of detective fiction?

1. 'The Alligator'
2. Didier Daeninckx
3. Marek Krajewski
4. William Kent Krueger
5. Sam Spade in *The Maltese Falcon* by Dashiell Hammett
6. Vigàta – Porto Empedocle changed its official denomination to Porto Empedocle Vigata
7. Barbara Vine
8. W.H. Auden
9. José Carlos Somoza
10. Friedrich Glauser
11. Carlo Lucarelli
12. Fjällbacka
13. Minister of Justice
14. Hercule Poirot
15. Anna Katherine Green

1. Nicholas Garrigan, a physician who works for Ugandan dictator Idi Amin, is the central character of which 1998 novel by Giles Foden?

2. What name is given to Evelyn Waugh's trilogy of World War II novels, centred around the protagonist Guy Crouchback?

3. Sixteen-year-old Frank is the protagonist of *The Wasp Factory*, the debut novel by which British writer who died in 2013?

4. With *The Girl at the Lion d'Or* and *Charlotte Gray*, which novel makes up Sebastian Faulks' 'French Trilogy'?

5. Which 1990 Booker Prize winner concerns the relationship between two fictional Victorian poets, Randolph Henry Ash and Christabel LaMotte?

6. In which country is Malcolm Lowry's 1947 novel *Under the Volcano* set?

7. Which science fiction/fantasy author explored the history of the UK capital in his 1988 novel *Mother London*?

8. *Nineteen Seventy-Four*, *Nineteen Seventy-Seven*, *Nineteen Eighty* and *Nineteen Eighty-Three* make up which quartet of novels by David Peace?

9. The city of Unthank is a surreal representation of Glasgow in which work by Alasdair Gray, comprising four books intended to be read out of order?

10. Which British writer wrote the novels *The Infernal Desire Machines of Doctor Hoffma*n and *Nights at the Circus*?

11. In which classic 1980 novel is gay writer Kenneth Toomey, 81, asked to work on the memoirs of fictional pope Gregory XVII?

12. Later adapted into a television mini-series, which very long novel set in the Indian Raj was written by M.M. Kaye and first published in 1978?

13. Which 2005 novel by Zadie Smith is loosely based on E.M. Forster's *Howard's End*?

14. Which Chinese-British novelist has been Booker shortlisted for *Sour Sweet, An Insular Possession* and *The Redundancy of Courage*?

15. An archetypal everyman, who narrates Anthony Powell's novel sequence *A Dance to the Music of Time*?

1. *The Last King of Scotland*
2. *Sword of Honour*
3. Iain Banks
4. *Birdsong*
5. *Possession* (by A.S. Byatt)
6. Mexico
7. Michael Moorcock
8. The *Red Riding* quartet
9. *Lanark*
10. Angela Carter
11. *Earthly Powers* (by Anthony Burgess)
12. *The Far Pavilions*
13. *On Beauty*
14. Timothy Mo
15. Nicholas Jenkins

1. *True* (2000) was the autobiography of which *Eastenders* star?
2. *Good Vibrations: My Autobiography* (1990) is by which percussionist, now a dame?
3. Who is the subject of the 2006 biography *First Man*?
4. Biographer Robert Caro is best known for an enormous and ongoing (38 years' labour so far) multi-volume biography of which US President?
5. Which artist's 2005 autobiography *Strangeland* chronicled her troubled upbringing in Margate?
6. Frequently sent to the Vatican to advocate a beatification, what seven-letter name is given to documents which are effectively a spiritual biography of a person?
7. *No Ordinary Joe* is the autobiography of which British World Champion boxer?
8. Which sportsman wrote the 2002 autobiography *1966 and All That*?
9. Which 19th-century autobiography by Solomon Northup was made into a film which won the Oscar for Best Picture?
10. After Charlotte Brontë's death in 1855, her father Patrick asked which other author to write her biography? Intended to counter several lies then in circulation, it, in turn, proved controversial.
11. *Notes on a Cowardly Lion* was a biography of his father written by John, the son of which actor?
12. *Tall, Dark and Gruesome* (1998) and *Lord of Misrule* (2004) are autobiographies by which film actor?
13. *Neither Shaken Nor Stirred* (1994) by Andrew Yule is a biography of which actor?
14. *The Invisible Woman* (1991) by Claire Tomalin is an acclaimed book about Nelly Ternan and her long affair with which author?
15. Which English author, biographer, critic and broadcaster is remembered in an annual award for the best biography, autobiography or diary in theatre or show business?

Answers to Biography and Autobiography:
Literature Quiz 5

1. Martin Kemp
2. (Dame) Evelyn Glennie
3. Neil Armstrong
4. Lyndon B. Johnson
5. Tracey Emin
6. *Positio* (*Positio super Virtutibus*)
7. Joe Calzaghe
8. Geoff Hurst
9. *Twelve Years a Slave* (film was *12 Years a Slave*)
10. Mrs (Elizabeth) Gaskell
11. Bert Lahr – *The Wizard of Oz*
12. Christopher Lee
13. Sean Connery
14. Charles Dickens
15. Sheridan Morley

Geography

1. Which capital city's name means literally 'City of a thousand warriors'?
2. To the dismay of rival metropolises, which city was confirmed as a new capital in 1858 by Queen Victoria, supposedly inspired by several romantic watercolours?
3. The city of Havana was founded in 1514 by a man who shared both forename and surname with which very famous painter of *Portrait of Pope Innocent X* (1650)?
4. Jorge Chavez International Airport serves which South American capital city?
5. In which capital city did a reported 132,247 spectators, the largest boxing attendance in history, watch Julio Cesar Chavez defeat Greg Haugen to retain his WBC light welterweight title in 1993?
6. The birthplace of sumo yokozunas Hakuho and Asashoryu, which of the world's capital cities lies furthest from the ocean?
7. Seized in 1968, the USS *Pueblo* is moored in which capital city?
8. The majority of Hulhulé Island is occupied by an international airport serving which capital city?
9. Founded in 1498 by Christopher Columbus's brother Bartolome, which capital city has the largest population of any Caribbean city?
10. Near which capital city is Yana Dag (literally 'Burning Mountain'), where natural gas leaks from the ground and burns?
11. The 49 metre-high bronze African Renaissance Monument is located just outside which capital city, the westernmost in mainland Africa?
12. Which capital city was founded in 1886 by Emperor Menelik on land chosen by his Empress Taytu for its pleasant climate in the foothills of the Entoto Mountains?
13. Considered the most populous city in West Asia, which capital is overlooked by the Elburz Mountains and Mt Damavand?
14. Founded in the 18th century, which capital's name arose when the Niare clan named the town Crocodile River in the Bambara langauge because of the numerous crocodiles they saw in the Niger?
15. Lying on the Buriganga River, which fast-growing capital city was the birthplace of structural engineer and architect Fazlur Rahman Khan, a pioneer in very tall skyscrapers?

Answers to Capital Cities: Geography Quiz 1

1. Antananarivo (Madagascar)
2. Ottawa
3. Diego Velazquez
4. Lima (Peru)
5. Mexico City (Mexico)
6. Ulaanbaatar (Mongolia)
7. Pyongyang (North Korea)
8. Malé (Maldives)
9. Santo Domingo (Dominican Republic)
10. Baku (Azerbaijan)
11. Dakar (Senegal)
12. Addis Ababa (Ethiopia)
13. Tehran (Iran)
14. Bamako (Mali)
15. Dhaka (Bangladesh)

1. Named after a British Prime Minister, which stratovolcano is the only recently active volcano on the Antarctic mainland?

2. Which Italian volcano gives its name to those eruptions where spasmodic and discrete explosive bursts eject pyroclastic materials a relatively short distance into the air?

3. Which word, derived from Javanese, describes a type of mudflow arising from volcanic activity and composed of a slurry of pyroclastic material, rocky debris and water?

4. Beerenberg (Bear Mountain) is an active volcano on Jan Mayen Island. To which country does this island belong?

5. What is mined on Chimborazo in Ecuador by locals, the so-called *Hieleros*?

6. Located in the north-western Pacific Ocean and claimed to be 'the biggest single shield volcano ever discovered on earth', the four-letter name of which submarine massif is derived from the initials of a US university?

7. The 1815 eruption of which volcano on the island of Sumbawa was the largest in recorded history, its dust and ash causing 1816 to be known as 'the year without a summer'?

8. In 1991 French vulcanologists Maurice and Katia Kraft lost their lives to an incandescent ash flow when filming on which Japanese volcano?

9. The formation of which Mexican volcano was witnessed from its first appearance in a cornfield in 1943 until it fell dormant in 1952?

10. The Avenue of Volcanoes, culminating in Cotopaxi, the world's highest active volcano at 5,897 metres, is in which country?

11. Which mountain on Papua New Guinea is, at 4,367 metres, the highest volcano in Australasia?

12. The tallest mountain on North Island, New Zealand, which 2,797-metre stratovolcano produced a mudflow in 1953 that destroyed a railway bridge and train, killing 151 people?

13. In which country is Ol Doinyo Lengai, a 2,890-metre stratovolcano that produces the coolest, most fluid lava in the world?

14. Merapi is one of the so-called 'decade volcanoes' selected for study because of their history of large, destructive eruptions and proximity to populated areas. On which island is it located?

15. In the novel *Journey to the Centre of the Earth* (1864), the group enter the earth by descending into which Icelandic volcano?

Answers to Volcanoes: Geography Quiz 2

1. Mount Melbourne (Mount Erebus is on Ross Island)
2. Stromboli
3. Lahar
4. Norway
5. Glacial ice – from Spanish *hielo* for ice
6. Tamu Massif – from Texas A&M University
7. Tambora
8. Mount Unzen
9. Paricutin
10. Ecuador
11. Mount Giluwe
12. Ruapehu
13. Tanzania
14. Java
15. Snaefellsjokull/Snaefell

1. Which main river of the Isle of Wight shares its name with an Asian city?
2. Whip Ma Whop Ma Gate is a memorably named street in which northern English city?
3. Known for over 1,500 years as a place of pilgrimage, and also known for its natural history, which island is located just off the tip of the Lleyn Peninsula in Wales?
4. New Zealand and California are suburbs of which English Midlands city?
5. After Great Britain and the island of Ireland, which Scottish island is the third largest of the British Isles?
6. Which town in Greater Manchester is served by Mumps station, which was on the national railway network until 2009 and has since been converted to serve Manchester's Metrolink light railway?
7. Alfred Wainwright's Coast to Coast Walk runs from Robin Hood Bay on the North Sea to which Cumbrian headland on the Irish Sea?
8. Which Cornish village is home to a large open slate quarry which was in the past the deepest man-made pit in the world?
9. What name is given to the extensive area of karst limestone pavements in County Clare in the Republic of Ireland, one of the largest such areas in Europe?
10. Yorkshire's 'Three Peaks' consist of Pen-y-Ghent, Ingleborough and which other mountain, the highest point in the ceremonial county of North Yorkshire?
11. Stott Hall farm is perhaps one of the most frequently seen farms in the UK. Where is it located?
12. Which town in Dumfries and Galloway has since 1998 styled itself as Scotland's National Book Town in honour of its second-hand bookshops?
13. Which small seaside village near Clacton-on-Sea was in 2011 branded Britain's most deprived community due partly to its large number of crumbling prefabricated bungalows?
14. The Caledonian Canal and the A82 road northeast of Fort William both travel along which geological fault in Scotland?
15. Almost totally enclosed by the Ards peninsula, which sea lough in Northern Ireland is the largest inlet in the British Isles?

1. Medina
2. York
3. Bardsey Island
4. Derby
5. Lewis and Harris
6. Oldham
7. St Bees Head
8. Delabole
9. The Burren
10. Whernside
11. Between the carriageways of the M62
12. Wigtown
13. Jaywick-on-Sea
14. The Great Glen or Glen Mor or Glen Albyn
15. Strangford Lough

1. Rebuilt by Andalusian refugees following the Reconquista, Morocco's most complete medina is found in which of the country's two major ports on the Mediterranean Sea?

2. Known as the 'Ukrainian Pompeii', its ruins are overlooked by St Vladimir's Cathedral. Which ancient city was founded in the 6th century BC by settlers from Heraclea Pontica on the shore of the Black Sea near Sevastopol?

3. In which African country is the Chongoni Rock-Art Area?

4. 'Levuka Historical Port Town' was the first colonial capital of which Pacific country, ceded to the British in 1874?

5. One of the greatest illustrations of Renaissance culture at its most refined, the Villa d'Este is in which ancient town?

6. The Koutammakou landscape is home to the Batammariba people, whose mud tower-houses (*takienta*) have become a symbol of which country?

7. Built by the Portuguese in 1593–96, Fort Jesus was designed to protect the Old Port of which Kenyan city?

8. Lying on the Mediterranean coast about 41 miles west of Libya's capital, which site was the westernmost of the 'three cities' of ancient Tripolitana; the others being Oea and Leptis Magna?

9. The walled coastal town of Al Zubarah flourished as a pearling and trading centre before it was destroyed in 1811. Founded by merchants from Kuwait, it is in which country?

10. Which island, site of a Benedictine abbey, lies between Gnadensee and the Untersee in Lake Constance?

11. Ibiza is a World Heritage Site partly due to the presence of dense prairies of which oceanic seagrass, an important endemic species found only in the Mediterranean basin?

12. The Sian Ka'an Biosphere Reserve is on which peninsula?

13. Which commune in France's Bourgogne region is home to the 12th-century monastic church that is believed to be the resting place of the relics of St Mary Magdalene?

14. Capital of the Roman province Arabia Petraea, which 'Ancient City' in Syria has a majestic 2nd-century AD Roman theatre and a cathedral, completed in 513 by Archbishop Julianus?

15. Situated on the English Channel in Haute-Normandie, severe bomb damage from World War II led to a major 1945–64 reconstruction effort conceived by Auguste Perret. Which city on the Seine?

1. Tétouan, formerly Titawin
2. Chersonesus/Chersonesos Taurica/Korsun/Khersones – the site is called the 'Ancient City of Tauric Chersonese and its Chora'
3. Malawi
4. Fiji
5. Tivoli
6. Togo
7. Mombasa
8. Sabratha
9. Qatar
10. Monastic Island of Reichenau
11. Posidonia/*Posidonia oceanic*/Neptune Grass/Mediterranean tape-weed
12. Yucatán Peninsula, Mexico
13. Vézelay (in the Yonne department)
14. Bosra
15. Le Havre

1. Two African countries have land borders with only one other. One is Lesotho; which is the other, which also borders ocean?

2. What is the English meaning of 'Mosi-oa-Tunya', the local name for the Victoria Falls?

3. Which island in the Comoros, along with a few small surrounding islets, became an overseas département of France in 2011, having voted against joining the rest of the chain as a sovereign state in 1975?

4. One of the seven natural wonders of Africa as chosen in 2013, which river forms a large inland delta in Botswana which is home to a wide variety of wildlife?

5. Lake Volta is entirely located within which African country?

6. Which man who succeeded Bismarck as Chancellor of Germany gives his name to the panhandle of Namibia running east to the Zambesi?

7. Which town in northern Ethiopia is a World Heritage Site known principally for its 11 churches hewn from rock?

8. Which African capital city is known for its array of modernist architecture, and was once linked by an aerial tramway to the city of Massawa, 75 kilometres away?

9. Which lake on the borders of the Democratic Republic of Congo and Rwanda contains huge amounts of methane and carbon dioxide, which poses a risk of huge loss of life if it 'overturns' and escapes the lake?

10. Oldoinyo Lesatima is the highest point in which mountain range in Kenya, which shares its name with a Welsh town?

11. Malabo, the capital of Equatorial Guinea, is located on which island, which used to be called Fernando Po?

12. Agadir is in Morocco, but in which country is the town of Agadez?

13. Which salt lake in Djibouti is the lowest point on land in Africa?

14. What name, which means 'the place where one cannot walk barefoot' in the local language, is given to the karst landscapes of north-western Madagascar?

15. Which city is the capital of the self-declared Republic of Somaliland?

1. The Gambia (bordered only by Senegal)
2. The Smoke That Thunders
3. Mayotte
4. Okavango
5. Ghana
6. Leo Graf von Caprivi (it is the Caprivi Strip)
7. Lalibela
8. Asmara or Asmera
9. Lake Kivu
10. Aberdare Mountains
11. Bioko Island
12. Niger
13. Lake Assal
14. Tsingy
15. Hargeisa or Hargeysa

Other Music

1. Thanks to it soundtracking TV ads for Heinz from 1997, the song 'Inkanyezi Nezazi' is forever associated with baked beans. Which South African group recorded it?

2. In Javanese mythology, which type of musical ensemble was created in the 3rd century by the god-king Sang Hyang Guru?

3. The title means 'swaying'. Which Spanish-language song, recorded in 1987, was a global hit for the French *rumba catalana* band the Gipsy Kings?

4. What is a Schwyzerörgeli?

5. Traditionally, they were made of eagle feathers and tortoise/sea-turtle shell, as well as cow horn (the latter of which are still sold). Modern picks are also made of cellulose plastic. Which Arabic name is given to the plectrum used to play the oud?

6. Which 1963 hit for Kyu Sakamoto was the first US no. 1 to be sung entirely in Japanese and made Sakamoto the first Asian singer to have a no. 1 on the Billboard Hot 100?

7. *Renaissance de la Harpe Celtique* is a 1972 album by which Breton master of the Celtic harp?

8. Which younger sister (b.1933) of the Indian playback singer Lata Mangeshkar was memorialised in a 1998 no. 1 single?

9. Cameroonian saxophonist Manu Dibango's signature tune has been called 'Africa's first truly global hit'. Which 1972 song is partly named after a Duala dialect word for 'twisting dance'?

10. Guinea's Mory Kanté became the first African musician to score a million-selling single with which 1987 Afro-pop classic?

11. Both formed in 1988, the bands B'z and Mr Children are the biggest selling acts of all time in which country?

12. Which title links a 1977 song (and album) by Fela Kuti and Africa 70 and a 1994 hit single for the Cranberries?

13. Rachid Taha's 2004 album *Tékitoi* features a raucous, raï-infused cover of which song by the Clash?

14. The song 'Kothbiro' by the Kenyan musician Ayub Ogada features in which 2005 John le Carré movie adaptation?

15. Known for such albums as 1989's *Soy Gitano* (I am Gypsy), what was the stage name of José Monge Cruz, the late Spanish musician who has been called the 20th century's greatest male flamenco singer?

1. Ladysmith Black Mambazo
2. Gamelan
3. 'Bamboléo'
4. It is a diatonic button accordion from Switzerland
5. Risha/Turkish: Mizrab
6. 'Sukiyaki'/'Ue o Muite Aruk' 'I Look Up as I Walk'
7. Alan Stivell
8. Asha Bhosle – Cornershop topped the singles chart with the Norman Cook remix of 'Brimful of Asha'
9. 'Soul Makossa'
10. 'Yé ké yé ké'
11. Japan – they have sold more than 81 million and 58 milion records respectively
12. 'Zombie'
13. 'Rock the Casbah'
14. *The Constant Gardener*
15. Camarón de la Isla (1950–92)

1. Which Frenchman said: 'In opera, anything that is too stupid to be spoken is sung'?

2. Which Italian composer had his greatest triumphs in Paris with the operas *Les Danaïdes* (1784) and *Tarare* (1787)?

3. Which 1853 Verdi opera features the Gypsies' 'Anvil Chorus'?

4. In a 1983 opera by Olivier Messiaen, which titular saint is represented by themes based on the Blackcap's song?

5. *Alfredo il Grande* (1823), based upon the story of our own Alfred the Great, was an opening night failure, lasting for just the one performance. It was the first venture into British history for which later much more successful composer?

6. Nominated in the 2014 International Opera Awards' 'World Premiere' category, which opera in jazz by Terence Blanchard is about the life of welterweight boxer Emile Griffith?

7. The only French composer to write an original Savoy opera, he conducted the world premiere of Debussy's *Pelleas and Melisande*. Whose 30 operatic works include *Veronique* (1898) and *Monsieur Beaucaire*, based on the Booth Tarkington novel?

8. Whose name is missing from this *Corriere della Sera* bulletin: '_____ _____ the gentle maker of melodies of sorrow and grace, died at 11:30 on 29 November in Brussels. The Maestro died without being able to speak, but he was fully conscious'?

9. Which US composer had his first operatic success with *El Capitan* (1896), an operetta about Don Errico Medigua, Viceroy of Peru?

10. Which play inspired operas by Richard Strauss (1906) and Antoine Mariotte (1908), an orchestral suite by Florent Schmitt (1907) and a 1978 ballet with music by Peter Maxwell Davies?

11. What links *Rosalinda* (1744) by Veracini, *Hermione* (1872) by Bruch, *Cordelia* (1881) by Gobatti, and *At the Boar's Head* (1925) by Holst?

12. In 1891, which French composer announced the premiere of his new opera, *Tristan's Bastard*, a hoax poking fun at Wagner?

13. Which singer's 1904 recording of the tenor aria 'Vesta la giubba' from Leoncavallo's *Pagliacci* was the first sound recording to sell a million copies?

14. At the start of the 20th century, Edward Morris of Covent Garden invented a coin-operated holder for which device?

15. Which German composed the 1917 opera *Palestrina*?

Answers to Opera: Other Music Quiz 2

1. Voltaire
2. Antonio Salieri
3. *Il Trovatore*
4. St Francis of Assisi – opera title: *Saint François d'Assise*
5. Gaetano Donizetti (not exactly historically accurate, it featured a queen called Amalia and Danes called Atkins and Rivers)
6. *Champion*
7. Andre Messager
8. Giacomo Puccini
9. John Philip Sousa
10. *Salomé* (1896) by Oscar Wilde
11. They are all operas based on plays by Shakespeare – *As You Like It*, *A Winter's Tale*, *King Lear*, *King Henry IV Parts 1* and *2*
12. Erik Satie
13. Enrico Caruso
14. Opera glasses/Galilean binoculars – Morris founded the London Opera Glass Company in 1913
15. Hans Pfitzner

1. Monty Norman composed which very famous film theme?
2. Which film director has scored nearly all of his films, most famously *Assault on Precinct 13* and *Halloween*?
3. Film composer Hans Zimmer appeared in the video to which UK number one single in the 1970s, the first to be played on MTV?
4. Who composed the scores to the two highest-grossing films of all-time, *Avatar* and *Titanic*?
5. What nationality is Lalo Schifrin, perhaps best known for composing the theme from *Mission Impossible*?
6. Composer James Newton Howard has scored all the films by which director since *The Sixth Sense* in 1999?
7. What is the surname of the US family of eminent film composers which includes Alfred, his brothers Emil and Lionel, Alfred's children David, Thomas and Maria and others?
8. Which one-time member of the Art of Noise has scored British films including *Bright Young Things*, *The Crying Game* and *The Full Monty*?
9. Bernard Herrmann died almost immediately after finishing the score for which 1976 Martin Scorsese film?
10. Which Italian composer composed the music for the first two *Godfather* films, winning an Academy Award for the second?
11. At the Academy Award ceremony held in 1974, who won the awards for Best Original Score, Best Adaptation Score, and Best Song, the only composer to win three Academy Awards in one year?
12. Malcolm Arnold won an an Ivor Novello Award in 1958 for his score to which film based on the story of nurse Gladys Aylward?
13. Associated with Disney, which composer won successive Academy Awards in the early 1990s for scoring *Beauty and the Beast* and *Aladdin*?
14. Which French composer wrote the music for films such as *The King's Speech* and *Argo*?
15. Which composer was nominated for an Academy Award 15 times without winning, eventually becoming the first composer to win an Honorary award, no doubt to make it up to him?

1. The 'James Bond Theme'
2. John Carpenter
3. 'Video Killed the Radio Star'
4. James Horner
5. Argentinian
6. M. Night Shyamalan
7. Newman (singer Randy is also related)
8. Anne Dudley
9. *Taxi Driver*
10. Giovanni 'Nino' Rota
11. Marvin Hamlisch
12. *The Inn of the Sixth Happiness*
13. Alan Menken
14. Alexandre Desplat
15. Alex North

1. What does the wife of Barak the Dyer lose and then regain in a Richard Strauss opera premiered in 1919?

2. The three movements of Sally Beamish's Violin Concerto are inspired by which famous war novel of 1929?

3. Both of Franz Schubert's song cycles *Die schöne Müllerin* and *Winterreise* are based on verse collections by which German poet?

4. Hans Werner Henze's cello concerto *Ode to the West Wind* (1953) was inspired by which English incident of 1819 which resulted in 15 fatalities?

5. *Variations on a Rococo Theme*, Op. 33, by Tchaikovsky is written for performance by an orchestra and a soloist playing which instrument?

6. Whose 13th Symphony of 1962 was subtitled *Babi Yar*?

7. *Missa Papae Marcelli*, or *Pope Marcellus Mass*, is probably the best known mass by which composer (1525–94)?

8. Kirkpatrick, Longo, Pestelli and Czerny all produced catalogues of the works of which Italian composer?

9. Premiered in Cadiz in the 1780s, which work of seven parts was viewed by Haydn as his greatest achievement?

10. Which composer's *Tudor Trilogy* of operas consists of *Roberto Deveraux*, *Maria Stuarda* and *Anna Bolena*?

11. In 1914, for what reason was Ralph Vaughan Williams apprehended by a boy while writing *The Lark Ascending*?

12. Dedicated to his patron, the Archduke Rudolf, by what single-word name is Beethoven's formidable 45-minute-long Piano Sonata, No. 29 more commonly known?

13. Which Belgian violinist, composer and conductor (1858–1931) wrote *Six Sonatas for Solo Violin*, Op. 27, with each dedicated to a different famous violinist and written in their particular styles?

14. Written in 1935–36 to the 'memory of an angel', whose Violin Concerto was a requiem for Manon, the 18-year-old daughter of Alma Mahler and Walter Gropius?

15. In what sort of non-musical business owned by their friend, artist Richard Serra, did composers Steve Reich and Philip Glass work together in New York City in the 1960s?

1. Her shadow – *Die Frau ohne Schatten* (*The Woman without a Shadow*)
2. *All Quiet on the Western Front*
3. Wilhelm Müller
4. The Peterloo Massacre
5. Cello
6. Dmitri Shostakovich
7. (Giovanni Pierluigi da) Palestrina
8. Domenico Scarletti
9. *The Seven Last Words of our Saviour on the Cross*
10. Gaetano Donizetti
11. Suspected espionage. He was writing in a notebook while looking out to sea – it was World War I and the boy assumed he was a spy
12. *Hammerklavier*
13. Eugène Ysaÿe
14. Alban Berg
15. A furniture removal business – Low-Rate Movers

1. It is made from a large calabash gourd cut in half and covered with cow skin to make a resonator with a long hardwood neck. *The Mandé Variations* (2008) sees virtuoso Toumani Diabaté play which west African 21-string lute-bridge harp?

2. Carlos Nunez is particularly noted for playing the Galician gaita. This is a member of which family of musical instruments?

3. A French musician of Ivorian origin, Manu Katche is a song-writer and a virtuoso on which instrument appearing on albums by Peter Gabriel and Sting?

4. The first album released by Virgin Records carried the name of which instrument?

5. The blind American Piedmont blues musician Sonny Terry was noted for playing which instrument?

6. Which Budapest-born cellist (d.2013) designed a modified name-sake bridge to improve the acoustics of stringed instruments?

7. A builder of various keyboard instruments, which German (with his brother Andreas) is probably best remembered for the organs at the Hofkirche in Dresden and at Freiberg Cathedral?

8. Originally from Peru, which six-sided, box-shaped percussion instrument is played by slapping the front or rear faces (generally thin plywood) with the hands, fingers or various implements?

9. Which instrument is played by the Norwegians Hakan Hardenberger and Tine Thing Helseth and the Briton Alison Balsam?

10. Which Toronto-born pianist built a global reputation as a performer of the works of J.S. Bach only to retire completely from concert performances at the age of 31 to devote his time to studio recording and scholarship?

11. A pannist plays which instrument?

12. Introduced to compete with designs from the National String Instrument Corporation, which resonator guitar was originally made in 1928 by the Dopyera brothers?

13. Noted for tutoring many other rock guitarists, which guitar virtuoso has released his own albums including *Surfing with the Alien* (1987), *The Extremist* (1992) and *Super Colossal* (2006)?

14. Named after Henryk Wieniawski, a competition for players of which instrument is held every five years at Poznan?

15. The bandoneon is a type of concertina particularly linked with the music accompanying which dance style?

Answers to Musical Instruments and Virtuosi:
Other Music Quiz 5

1. Kora
2. Bagpipe
3. Drums
4. Tubular bells
5. Harmonica (aka French harp, blues harp and mouth organ)
6. János Starker
7. Gottfried Silbermann
8. Cajón
9. Trumpet
10. Glenn Gould
11. Steelpan or steel drum
12. Dobro (from DOpyera BROthers)
13. Joe Satriani
14. Violin
15. Tango

Miscellaneous II

1. In 1838, who made the first ever photograph to include a human being with a picture of a figure – a man having his shoes shined – on the boulevard du Temple in Paris?

2. Len Deighton's novel *Bomber* was the first to be written how?

3. Which country was the first to recognise the United States of America as an independent nation?

4. Produced by an eponymous distillery, Penderyn is the first commercially available spirit of which type to be made in Wales since the 16th century?

5. Who won the boxing fight that ended the first *Rocky* film?

6. What was the address of the first ever website to be published, by Tim Berners-Lee, on 6 August 1991?

7. Which former First Lady of France is heiress to the fortune created by the tyre company CEAT?

8. In 1980, what became the first arcade game to be licensed for a home gaming console, the Atari 2600?

9. The world's richest black man, which Nigerian businessman became, in June 2013, the first entrepreneur from Africa to claim a $20 bn fortune, thanks largely to an unprecedented jump in the stock value of his namesake cement company?

10. Founded by Jan Wenner, which music and culture magazine's first cover star, in an issue dated 9 November 1967, was John Lennon, in a still from the film *How I Won the War*?

11. Edwin Hubble is often wrongly credited with being the first person to state it. Which Belgian astronomer and Catholic priest first proposed the theory of the expansion of the universe?

12. In 1875, the mayor of Dover said: 'I make bold to say that I don't believe that in the future history of the world any such feat will be performed by anybody else.' Which feat was he talking about?

13. Josephine Cochran invented the first useful example of which household appliance?

14. At the age of just nine, Picasso completed his first painting. What was this bullfighting-themed work called?

15. Having his first success with Gaspard Burgos, whom he helped to make his first confession, the 16th-century Spanish monk Pedro Ponce de León is believed to have been the first person to develop a method for teaching people with which disability?

1. Louis Daguerre
2. On a word processor – *Bomber*, published 1970 was written on the IBM MT/ST
3. The United Provinces of the Netherlands
4. Whisky
5. Apollo Creed (played by Carl Weathers)
6. info.cern.ch
7. Carla Bruni-Sarkozy
8. *Space Invaders*
9. Aliko Dangote
10. *Rolling Stone*
11. Georges Lemaître
12. Captain Matthew Webb being the first person to swim across the English Channel
13. Dishwasher
14. *Le Picador* (a man riding a horse in a bullfight)
15. Deafness

1. Where is the world's largest bulwarked dry ditch system?

2. Which 'ultimate department store for oligarchs' has a steel-and-glass domed roof designed by Vladimir Shukhov and containing more than 20,000 panes of glass?

3. Which company lays claim to the world's largest hand-basket with its seven-storey HQ in Newark, Ohio, taking the form of its biggest-selling model, the maple wood 'Medium Market Basket'?

4. Which concert venue at 881 Seventh Avenue in Midtown Manhattan is named after the philanthropist who built it in 1891?

5. Built by Savoy (1728–1850) according to architect Ignazio Bertola's design, which fortress guards the access to Turin via the Chisone valley and, with a surface area of 1,300,000 m², is the largest Alpine fortification in Europe?

6. Designed by Enrique Luis Varela, the Modelo Brewery was built in Cotorro, Havana, in 1948 for which company?

7. The *Sacri Monti* ('Sacred Mountains') are nine groups of chapels and other architectural features in which two Italian regions?

8. Built mostly between 1667 and 1670, Claude Perrault's Colonnade is the easternmost facade of which Paris building?

9. Europe's largest building in terms of usable space, the Jean-Luc Lagardère Plant is the assembly hall for which double-deck, wide-body four-engine jet airliner?

10. The tallest building in Africa, the 223 m-tall Carlton Centre skyscraper is found at 150 Commissioner Street in which city?

11. Architect Frank Williams collaborated with M.M. Posokhin on this example of 'structural expressionism'. Which 339 m-tall Moscow office tower overtook the Shard to become the tallest building in Europe?

12. Demolished in 1968, the Imperial Hotel, Tokyo, was designed in 1923 by which US architect?

13. Covering 20 acres, it has a 115 ft deep end and holds 66 million gallons of water. This man-made saltwater lagoon is the world's largest swimming pool and is located at the San Alfonso del Mar resort at Algarrobo in which country?

14. In which city, Bosnia's second largest, was the 16th-century Ferhat Pasha Mosque blown up by Serbian forces in May 1993?

15. The Battenberg Mausoleum is the final resting place of Prince Alexander I (1857–93), the first head of state of which country?

1. Elvas, a fortified 17th century border town in Portugal
2. GUM in Red Square, Moscow – *Glavnyi Universalnyi Magazin* means 'main universal store'
3. Longaberger
4. Carnegie Hall – named after Andrew Carnegie and designed by William Burnet Tuthill
5. Fenestrelle Fort, named after the Piedmont *comune* that it overlooks
6. Compañia Ron Bacardi S.A.
7. Piedmont and Lombardy
8. Palais du Louvre
9. Airbus A380 – world's largest passenger airliner
10. Johannesburg
11. Mercury City Tower
12. Frank Lloyd Wright
13. Chile
14. Banja Luka
15. Bulgaria – he was the first prince (*knyaz*) of modern Bulgaria from 1879 to 1886

1. In Scrabble, which name – that of another game – is given to any word that earns a 50-point bonus when all seven tiles on your rack are used?

2. Invented by Sid Sackson and first published by 3M in 1962, the aim of the game *Acquire* is to develop which businesses?

3. Which roulette-like gambling game has long been played in China and has a name meaning 'repeated divisions'?

4. Using miniature battlefields and models, which Games Workshop 'tabletop battlegame of the far future' is about the Imperium of Man and Marines' fight against such alien races as the Necrons, Dark Eldar and Orks? It celebrated its 25th birthday in 2012.

5. Which 'Game for Your Whole Brain' was created by former Microsoft employees Whit Alexander and Richard Tait in 1998?

6. In 1971, Ohioan barber Merle Robbins came up with the idea of which card game?

7. Which board game features five Soldiers on each side (red or black), Advisors, Elephants who cannot cross the River, Horses, Cannons, Chariots and, most importantly, Generals?

8. What is the most common opening move by White in chess?

9. In Texas Hold 'Em poker, which pair of cards are nicknamed 'pocket rockets'?

10. Which game has a player give a word or line to be matched in rhyme by other players? Its name comes from a word for cabbage.

11. In 2012, it became the first Polish game to be nominated for a Spiel des Jahres award. In which board game by Adam Kałuża are players challenged to climb an eponymous mountain?

12. The American Willie Hoppe won 51 world titles (1906–52) in three forms of which cue sport?

13. In 2008, which brewer built Table Football XXL – the largest table football game in the world?

14. A linguist, soldier, musician, journalist and political activist, which British chess master (1842–88) lost to Wilhelm Steinitz in the 1886 World Chess Championship, the first world title game?

15. Subtitled 'The Cold War, 1945–89', which card-driven strategy war-game for two players became the highest-ranked game on BoardGameGeek in December 2010, surpassing 'Puerto Rico'?

Answers to Board Games and Other Games:
Miscellaneous II Quiz 3

1. Bingo
2. Hotel chains/Hotels
3. Fan-Tan/Fantan
4. Warhammer 40,000/Warhammer 40K
5. Cranium
6. Uno
7. Xiangqi/Chinese chess
8. White, e4 or King Pawn's Game or White King's pawn advances two spaces to e4
9. Two aces
10. Crambo/*crambe* is a latin word for cabbage; crambo has also been called the ABC of Aristotle and capping the rhyme
11. K2
12. Carom billiards/carambole billiards/Carambole – in three-cushion, balkline and cushion caroms
13. Amstel
14. Johannes Hermann Zukertort
15. Twilight Struggle – the title comes from John F. Kennedy's inaugural address: 'Now the trumpet summons us again . . . a call to bear the burden of a long twilight struggle'

1. Named after the Japanese for 'iron fist', which 1994 fighting game featured such locations as Angkor Wat, the Acropolis, Monument Valley and the UK's own Windermere?

2. Released in 2000, what is the best-selling game console of all time, with over 155 million units sold?

3. Created in 1994 by the French graphic artist Michel Ancel, Rayman is the official mascot of which video game publisher?

4. Which 1986 Nintendo platform game has players control Simon Belmont, who must defeat the vampire Dracula?

5. Graphics consisted of black squares and it had four directions. Which game was programmed in 1997 by design engineer Taneli Armanto and installed on the Nokia 6110 handset?

6. Which award-winning iPad game, created by Denis Mikan, has one simple goal: draw and shape a line that collects all coloured circles, avoiding black holes on its route?

7. Based on Andrzej Sapkowski's dark fantasy novels, which sleeper hit series, developed by CD Projekt RED, centres on the sardonic monster-slayer Geralt of Rivia?

8. Which US opera singer voices GLaDOS in the *Portal* video game series and the Jaeger AI in the film *Pacific Rim*?

9. A 2007 documentary subtitled *A Fistful of Quarters* saw gaming legend Billy Mitchell have major problems with newcomer Steve Wiebe breaking his world high score on which 1981 arcade classic?

10. A software program developed to show off the power of the Digital Equipment Corporation PDP-1 minicomputer, which 1962 game heralded the birth of electronic games?

11. Which 2011 game's voice cast featured acting legends Max von Sydow as Esbern and Christopher Plummer as Arngeir?

12. Which US actress created and wrote the comedy web series *The Guild* (2007–), a show that revolves around the lives of a gamers' online guild called the Knights of Good?

13. Players control Joel escorting the young Ellie as they roam a post-apocalyptic USA ravaged by a mutant *Cordyceps* fungus in which acclaimed 2013 video game?

14. Which 1986 arcade game was the first to show blood or gore?

15. Released in 1979, which Milton Bradley-made device was the first handheld console with interchangeable cartridges?

1. *Tekken*
2. Sony PlayStation 2
3. Ubisoft – Rayman is the main character of a namesake series that started in 1995
4. *Castlevania*
5. *Snake*
6. *Blek*
7. *The Witcher*
8. Ellen McLain
9. *Donkey Kong* – the documentary is titled *The King of Kong*
10. *Spacewar!*
11. *Elder Scrolls V: Skyrim*
12. Felicia Day
13. *The Last of Us*
14. *Chiller* – an Exidy light gun game the 'sickest arcade game of all time' was banned in the UK for being gratuitously violent with no redeeming features
15. Microvision

1. Which *Enter the Dragon* star played the title role in *Black Belt Jones* (1974)?

2. Which renowned wushu coach (b.1937) has produced more wushu champions than any coach in China teaching the likes of Hao Zhihua, Kenny Perez (his first US student) and Jet Li?

3. Once taught at the Toyama Military Academy in Tokyo, jūkendō is the Japanese martial art of fighting with which weapon?

4. Which fight choreographer directed *Iron Monkey* (1993)?

5. Which of China's 'Four Dan Actresses' played a t'ai chi-practising dumpling maker who becomes a substitute goalie in the 2001 film *Shaolin Soccer*? In 2013, her directorial debut *So Young* set a box office record in China with takings of over $115 m.

6. Who links Donnie Yen, Tony Leung and Anthony Wong?

7. Who died during the filming of *Game of Death* in 1973, in which he fought with basketball star Kareem Abdul-Jabbar as Mantis – 5th Floor Guardian?

8. Which 1989 Capcom beat 'em up featured Cody, Guy and Metro City mayor Mike Haggar as the playable characters?

9. ROSS, from 'Russian Native System of Self-Defence', is a martial art invented by which Russian Cossack general (b.1955), who gives it a longer name?

10. Emphasising weapons-based fighting with sticks and knives, *eskrima*, *arnis* and *kali* are umbrella terms for the traditional martial arts of which Asian country?

11. The chosen weapon of Elektra (of *Daredevil* fame) and Ninja Turtle Michelangelo, which traditional martial arts weapon consists of one long pointed metal baton and two smaller curved prongs to its side?

12. With over 400 victories in jiu-jitsu, vale tudo, and other combat sports, Rickson _____, son of Brazilian jiu-jitsu founder Hélio, is the champion of which family?

13. Known for his resemblance to Bruce Lee, which Hong Kong actor and lead singer of the band Poet played the martial arts legend in the 50-episode TV series *The Legend of Bruce Lee* (2008)?

14. The *Boxer of Quirinal*, is an ancient bronze Greek sculpture of a sitting boxer wearing which kind of leather hand-wrap?

15. An ancestor of tae kwon do, it is believed to have once been called subak. What is the traditional Korean martial art?

1. Jim Kelly
2. Wu Bin
3. Bayonets
4. Yuen Woo-ping, whose martial arts work is seen in *The Matrix*, and both *Kill Bill* filmes
5. Zhao Wei/Vicki Zhao
6. Ip Man/Yip Man (1893–1972) – they played the martial arts grandmaster/Bruce Lee's teacher in *Ip Man*, *The Grandmaster*, and *Ip Man: The Final Flight*, respectively
7. Bruce Lee
8. *Final Fight*
9. Alexander Retuinskih, as in Retuinskih's System ROSS
10. Philippines
11. Sai
12. Gracie family
13. Danny Chan/Chan Kwok-kwan
14. Cestus
15. Taekkyeon or Taekkyon

TV

1. In *Episodes,* a hit Britcom is reworked by Hollywood into which programme starring Matt LeBlanc as a hockey coach?

2. Which US space opera television series created by writer and producer J. Michael Straczynski was set on a namesake space station between the years 2257 and 2281?

3. Actress Tatiana Maslany plays several identical clones (all born in 1984) in which Canadian sci-fi series?

4. The family patriarch in *American Dad* shares both names with which winner of the Wimbledon men's singles title in 1972?

5. Set in Chicago, *The Beast* centred on an FBI veteran, Charles Barker. This was the last role of which actor, best known for his film work, before his untimely death at the age of 57?

6. In the 2014 TV series *Fargo*, who plays the ruthless killer Lorne?

7. In *Prison Break*, Michael Schofield springs his brother from jail. How does he smuggle in the escape plan details?

8. Name the TV killer, played by Michael C. Hall, who works for a Miami Police department.

9. With his catchphrase 'Happy, happy, happy', Phil Robertson is the family patriarch in which successful US reality TV show?

10. Which 1990s Baltimore-based TV police drama featured actors including Yaphet Kotto, Kyle Secor, Andre Braugher and Melissa Yeo?

11. Which TV crime drama starring Woody Harrelson and Matthew McConaughey is based on *The King of Yellow*, a collection of macabre short stories by R.W. Chambers?

12. Sig Hansen (*Northwestern*), Jonathan Hillstrand (*Time Bandit*), and Keith Colburn (*Wizard*) are among the regular faces appearing in which Alaska-set reality series?

13. How is the Oswald State Correctional Facility known in the title of a very bleak 1990s HBO prison drama?

14. Created by David E. Kelley, which Boston-set comedy-drama television series starred Calista Flockhart in the title role as a young lawyer working in the fictional law firm Cage and Fish?

15. In which US drama do Matthew Rhys and Keri Russell star as all-American couple Philip and Elizabeth Jennings living in Washington DC who are, in fact, Soviet KGB agents?

1. *Pucks!*
2. *Babylon 5*
3. *Orphan Black*
4. Stan Smith
5. Patrick Swayzee
6. Billy Bob Thornton
7. The plans are hidden in an intricate tattoo which covers his entire torso
8. Dexter (Morgan)
9. *Duck Dynasty*
10. *Homicide: Life on the Streets*
11. *True Detective*
12. *Deadliest Catch* – they are crab boat captains
13. *Oz*
14. *Ally McBeal*
15. *The Americans*

1. First shown in 1975, which children's cartoon was narrated by John Le Mesurier and featured a boy who lives in a town with Aunt Flo, PC Copper, Frank the Postman and Farmer Barleymow?

2. In *Jamie and the Magic Torch*, the title device was shone on the floor to open up a hole into which fun dimension?

3. In *The Simpsons*, who sang the immortal line 'I hate every chimp I see from chimpan-A to chimpanzee' in a musical version of *Planet of the Apes*? You may remember him from such self-help videos as *Smoke Yourself Thin* and *Get Confident, Stupid*.

4. Who wields the legendary Sword of Omens?

5. Which Russian animator's masterpiece is the classic short *Hedgehog in the Fog* (1975)?

6. The 1979–80 TV anime series *Mobile Suit Gundam* was created and directed by which animator?

7. Attaining popularity in Japan equivalent to *Garfield* in the US, which robotic cat was created in 1970 by the manga duo Fujiko Fujio (Hiroshi Fujimoto and Motoo Abiko) and is known for his adventures with schoolboy pal Nobita Nobi?

8. Known as the 'Walt Disney of Brazil', which cartoonist (b.1934) based the strip *Monica's Gang* on his daughter and her friends? It was adapted into a TV show that premiered in 1976.

9. Created in 1993, it was about a conflict between two tribes: the brightly coloured airborne Joyces (Verigreens) and the dark, furnace-burning Yuks (Kruds). Which French production was the first completely computer-animated TV series?

10. Created by Justin Roilland and Dan Harmon, which 2013–14 Adult Swim cartoon is about the crazed sci-fi shenanigans of an alcoholic, amoral scientific genius and his 14-year-old grandson?

11. Which character in *Futurama* is named after a 1949 symphonic masterwork by Olivier Messiaen?

12. Which F/X animated series's season five saw its characters become cocaine dealers instead of international spies?

13. 'Yahoos and Triangles' by the Refreshments was the opening theme to which 1997–2010 animated sitcom?

14. In *Family Guy*, who is the Griffin family's youngest member?

15. 'Frog Baseball', a 1992 short film by Mike Judge that first aired on Liquid Television was the pilot of which series?

1. *Bod*
2. Cuckoo Land
3. Troy McClure – voiced by Phil Hartman
4. Lion-O – the leader and 'Lord of the Thundercats'
5. Yuriy Norshteyn
6. Yoshiyuki Tomino
7. Doraemon
8. Mauricio de Souza
9. *Insektors*
10. *Rick and Morty*
11. Leela or Turanga Leela, named after the ten-movement *Turangalîla-Symphonie*
12. *Archer*
13. *King of the Hill*
14. Stewie – the villainous one-year-old prodigy
15. *Beavis and Butt-head*

1. The French satirical show *Les Guignols de l'info* is very similar to which 1984–96 British series?

2. Created by Fernando Meirelles, which 2009 Brazilian miniseries about a Shakespeare theatre festival was based on the Canadian TV dramedy *Slings and Arrows*?

3. Which 1961–2007 documentary by German film-maker Winfried Junge observed the lives of 18 people in a Brandenburg town?

4. *India: A Love Story* (in 2009), *O Astro* (2012) and *Lado a Lado* (2013) all won the International Emmy for best telenovela. Which country produced them?

5. In 2014, which Bollywood star made his TV drama debut in *Yudh*, playing businessman Yudhisthir Sikarwar?

6. Which RTÉ drama, set in the Dublin criminal underworld, has starred Robert Sheehan in the role of Darren Treacy and Aidan Gillen as John Boy Power?

7. Director Yoon Seok-ho's second 'season drama', which 2002 South Korean TV show was a massive hit throughout Asia and was adapted into a 2009 anime with its stars Choi Ji-woo and Bae Yong-joon as voice actors? Series revenue, thanks to tourism to Nami island where it was shot, is an estimated $27 bn.

8. Directed by Ali Hatami, which 1978–87 Iranian historical drama about the calligrapher Reza Khoshnevis (Jamshid Mashayekhi) was voted the best Iranian TV series ever made?

9. Which 1999–2006 Telecinco *Friends*-inspired sitcom became the longest running show of all time in Spanish TV history?

10. Which French police drama is also titled *Engrenages* ('Cogs')?

11. Which Kenyan soap opera's first season featured future Oscar winner Lupita Nyong'o in the role of student Ayira?

12. Following sleuth Puck Eckstedt and fiancé Einar Bure in the region of Bergslagen, the 1950s-set TV drama *Crimes of Passion* is based on mysteries by which 'Agatha Christie of Sweden'?

13. Which conflict was the setting for the 1963–66 TV series *Thierry la Fronde* (with Jean-Claude Drouot in the title role)?

14. *Tutti Frutti* was the early 1990s German version of which Italian sex game show, involving contestants removing their clothing?

15. Which 2014 TV drama looks at Denmark's post-war cultural history through the tale of dying artist Veronika Grønegaard (Kirsten Olesen) disposing of her immense wealth?

1. *Spitting Image*
2. *Som e Fúria*
3. *The Children of Golzow/Die Kinder von Golzow*
4. Brazil
5. Amitabh Bachchan
6. *Love/Hate*
7. *Winter Sonata*
8. *Hezar Dastan* – named after the character played by Ezzatolah Entezami
9. *7 Vidas*
10. *Spiral*
11. *Shuga*
12. Maria Lang
13. Hundred Years War
14. *Colpo Grosso* ('Big Score')
15. *Arvingerne/The Legacy*

1. In which TV show was the title character, played by Kristen Bell, a private investigator who attended high school in the southern Californian seaside town of Neptune?

2. Who played the role of Ken Miller in *Freaks and Geeks* and then Ron Garner in Judd Apatow's college follow-up *Undeclared*?

3. Patrick Duffy played Mark Harris, who according to the title of a 1970s TV series was *The Man from* . . . where?

4. Which singer was the *Abigail's Party* character Laurence referring to when he said: 'We don't want to listen to that fat Greek caterwauling all night'?

5. What did Henry Winkler, this time in the role of *Arrested Development* lawyer Barry Zuckerkorn, repeat in the episode 'Motherboy XXX' that he had done as Fonzie on *Happy Days*?

6. Who was revealed to be the killer of Laura Palmer in the second season of *Twin Peaks*, though the character was actually possessed by the malevolent spirit known as BOB?

7. Which Canadian actor, also seen in such films as *The Empire Strikes Back* and *Superman*, played Harry Hamilton, the American who orders a Waldorf salad in *Fawlty Towers*?

8. Andy Whitfield was replaced by Liam McIntyre in the title role of which historical action drama, after Whitfield was diagnosed with non-Hodgkin's lymphoma and then died in 2011?

9. Which pop punk band from Santa Barbara composed and performed the theme tune to *Buffy the Vampire Slayer*?

10. What was the first name of the secret agent played by Richard Dean Anderson in *MacGyver*?

11. *Xena: Warrior Princess* was a spin-off of which 1995–99 show starring Kevin Sorbo?

12. In which 1970–72 show did Geoffrey Bayldon, later to play the Crowman in *Worzel Gummidge*, star in the role of an 11th-century wizard who accidentally ends up in the 20th century?

13. Which villain in *The X-Files* was played by William B. Davis?

14. Premiering in 2012, which TV series, based on a DC Comics character, follows billionaire playboy Oliver Queen as he fights crime in Starling City as a secret vigilante using an apparently primitive weapon of choice?

15. Which actor completes this line of succession in *I, Claudius*: Brian Blessed, George Baker, John Hurt, Derek Jacobi and . . . ?

1. *Veronica Mars*
2. Seth Rogen
3. . . . *Atlantis*
4. Demis Roussos
5. Jump the shark – this time he jumped over a dead one
6. Her father Leland
7. Bruce Boa
8. *Spartacus*
9. Nerf Herder
10. Angus
11. *Hercules: The Legendary Journeys*
12. *Catweazle*
13. The Smoking Man
14. *Arrow* – based on the Green Arrow who also uses a bow and arrow
15. Christopher Biggins, who played Emperor Nero, who succeeded Claudius (played by Jacobi)

1. The climactic clash of the civil war known as Robert's Rebellion, which battle saw Robert Baratheon slay Prince Rhaegar Targaryen with a swing from his war hammer?

2. Filming of King's Landing for season two moved to which walled city, using such locations as Lokrum Island, the Knežev dvor and Sponza palaces, Lovrijenac (Fort of St Lawrence) and Fort Bokar?

3. Who are Drogon, Rhaegal and Viserion?

4. Using words and phrases in the novels, which US linguist developed the Dothraki language for the TV series?

5. Series co-creator David Benioff wrote which 2001 debut novel about drug dealer Monty Brogan's last night of freedom before he does a seven-year stretch in prison?

6. In the TV series, who says: 'When you play the Game of Thrones, you win or you die. There is no middle ground'?

7. Which 'red ale', produced by the Cooperstown, New York-based Brewery Ommegang, is named after the motto of House Targaryen?

8. In *A Storm of Swords*, who gives his life to resurrect Catelyn Stark as Lady Stoneheart?

9. The poison-induced demise of a choking King Joffrey Baratheon at his wedding feast was inspired by which son of King Stephen choking to death at a banquet in 1153?

10. Which band's cover of 'The Bear and the Maiden Fair' played during the end credits for the season three episode 'Walk of Punishment'? Hailing from Brooklyn, New York, they released the 2006 album *Boys and Girls in America*.

11. The Northern Irish actor Kristian Nairn plays which character, who can only say his name?

12. The TV depiction of Jaime Lannister's ambush of Ned Stark echoes portrayals of a 1407 incident in which Louis I, Duke of Orleans, was assassinated in Paris by order of which Duke?

13. Rory McCann, who plays Sandor 'The Hound' Clegane, first found fame wearing a vest and kilt in a TV advert for which breakfast cereal?

14. Which character's marriage to Roslin Frey is the event that turns into the infamous 'Red Wedding'?

15. Known as *Taobh Siar Rois* in Scottish Gaelic, which area in the North-West Highlands of Scotland and a part of Ross and Cromarty served as inspiration for a fictional continent?

1. Battle of the Trident
2. Dubrovnik, Croatia
3. Daenerys Targaryen's dragons – coloured black, green and yellow respectively
4. David J. Peterson
5. *The 25th Hour* – made into the film *25th Hour*
6. Cersei Lannister – said to Ned Stark
7. Fire and Blood
8. Beric Dondarrion
9. Eustace IV, Count of Boulogne
10. The Hold Steady
11. Hodor
12. John the Fearless, Duke of Burgundy
13. Scott's Porage Oats
14. Edmure Tully
15. Wester Ross – inspiring the name of Westeros

Arts

1. Whose radical painting *Nude Descending a Staircase* No. 2 caused a sensation at the New York Armory Show of 1913?
2. The Jackson Pollock-esque artwork *Bye Bye Badman* was used for the cover of the Stone Roses' debut LP. Who created it?
3. Which Swiss-born neo-Dada artist created *Untitled (Bread House)* (2004–5), a Swiss-style chalet constructed with loaves of bread? He is also known for his room-size installations *You* and *Death of a Moment* (both 2007).
4. The highly regarded Louisiana Museum of Modern Art is not situated in the USA. It is in fact in which European country?
5. The Italian sculptor Marino Marini (1901–80) was best known for a series of stylised statues based on which animal-related theme (e.g. *Il Pellegrino/The Pilgrim*, 1936, and *Miracolo*, 1959–60)?
6. Portraying surgeons from Dundee's Ninewells Hospital, which acclaimed 2002 painting by Ken Currie is a portrait of Professors R.J. Steele, Sir Alfred Cuschieri and Sir David P. Lane?
7. Which 2006 Turner Prize nominee's work *They Shoot Horses* is a film of a Palestinian disco marathon?
8. Which Turner Prize-winning Official War Artist for the Iraq War created the 'Queen and Country' postage stamp project?
9. Which Kazakh-born 'king of kitsch' painted *The Chinese Girl* (1952), aka 'The Green Lady'?
10. Russian artist Svetlana Petrova inserts her 22-pound ginger pet Zarathustra into famous paintings like the *Mona Lisa* and *American Gothic*. What is the series' three-word title?
11. Cassius Marcellus Coolidge was commissioned to create which set of 11 paintings by Brown & Bigelow to advertise cigars?
12. The original of which studio was on the fifth floor at 231 East 47th Street in Midtown Manhattan?
13. In October 2013, it sold for $23.3 m, setting a record for a work of Asian contemporary art and for a work by a living Chinese artist. Which 2001 painting by Zeng Fanzhi is named after an event in the New Testament?
14. Which US artist directed the feature films *Me and You and Everyone We Know* (2005) and *The Future* (2011), having created such 'live movies' as the 1998 multimedia piece *Love Diamond*?
15. Which pop artist modelled his 1960 sculpture *Painted Bronze* on two Ballantine Ale cans?

1. Marcel Duchamp
2. John Squire – the Stone Roses' guitarist
3. Urs Fischer
4. Denmark – so named after the original property on the site, a country house whose owner's three wives were all called Louise
5. Equestrian/horse and rider/man riding horse
6. *Three Oncologists*
7. Phil Collins
8. Steve McQueen – the Oscar-winning director of *12 Years a Slave*
9. Vladimir Tretchikoff
10. Fat Cat Art
11. *Dogs Playing Poker*
12. The Factory – Andy Warhol's famous studio
13. *The Last Supper*
14. Miranda July
15. Jasper Johns

1. Which artist's 1791 depiction of a key moment in French history, the Tennis Court Oath of 20 June 1789, exists only as a great drawing as the fast-moving events of the Revolution forced him to abandon the work?

2. Originally commissioned for the Four Seasons restaurant in the Seagram Building in New York, which artist gave nine of his *Seagram Murals* to the Tate in the late 1960s?

3. Famous for painting his neighbour Helga Testorf over 240 times, who was, in 1963, the first artist to receive the Presidential Medal of Freedom?

4. Which artist is played by Martin Freeman in Peter Greenaway's 2007 film *Nightwatching*?

5. Painter of *An Experiment on a Bird in the Air Pump* (1768), Joseph Wright was born in and was strongly associated with which English city?

6. Whose nine canvases depicting *The Triumphs of Caesar* (1490) can be seen at Hampton Court Palace?

7. Hanging in Apsley House, one version of *The Waterseller of Seville* by Diego Velazquez was given to which man by a grateful Spanish king?

8. Also known as Paolo Caliari, who painted *The Family of Darius before Alexander* and *The Raising of Jairus's Daughter* (1546)?

9. Lee Krasner was an abstract expressionist painter who marrried which other artist, noted for his style of drip painting?

10. Which Irish artist, the brother of a Nobel laureate, won a silver medal in the arts and culture segment of the 1924 Summer Olympics in Paris, with his painting *The Liffey Swim*?

11. Who created the *ukiyo-e* series *Ten Studies in Female Physiognomy* and *Great Love Themes of Classical Poetry*?

12. Parts having been stolen at various times, whose 12-panel *Ghent Altarpiece* (1432) is also known as *The Adoration of the Mystic Lamb*?

13. Which painter (1471–1528) died from a fever caught while investigating a stranded whale on Denmark's Zealand coast?

14. Who painted his own likeness on the flayed skin of Saint Bartholomew in *The Last Judgement* in the Sistine Chapel?

15. How is designer Celia Birtwell described in the title of a famous David Hockney painting of 1971?

1. Jacques-Louis David
2. Mark Rothko
3. Andrew Wyeth
4. Rembrandt
5. Derby – he is generally known as Joseph Wright of Derby
6. Andrea Mantegna – the Mantegna Gallery
7. Duke of Wellington
8. (Paolo) Veronese
9. Jackson Pollock
10. Jack Butler Yeats
11. Kitigawa Utamaro
12. Jan Van Eyck
13. Albrecht Dürer
14. Michelangelo
15. Mrs Clark – the painting is *Mr and Mrs Clark and Percy*

1. The Farnese Hercules sculpture, signed by an otherwise unknown Glykon, is thought to be an enlarged Roman copy from an original by which Classical Greece era sculptor?

2. Which 4th-century BC stone bust was discovered in 1897 at the archaeological site L'Alcúdia, about two kilometres south of a city in the Spanish autonomous community of Valencia?

3. Also known as the 'Venus Pudica' (modest Venus), which 4th-century BC female nude statue by Praxiteles was called the greatest statue in the world by Pliny the Elder?

4. The gold burial mask of which pharaoh, the third king of the 21st Dynasty who ruled from Tanis between 1047 and 1001 BC, was discovered in 1940 by Pierre Montet?

5. Yielding a hoard of Bactrian gold, which archaeological site in the Afghan province of Jowzjan was excavated in 1978 by a team led by Greek-Russian archaeologist Viktor Sarianidi?

6. Found in Corinthia, which four panels are the only surviving panel paintings (c.540–530 BC) from Archaic Greece?

7. Named after Rafael _____ Herrera, which Lima museum of pre-Columbian art has a collection that includes the Paracas Mantle, Pacopampa Stela and some naughty Huaco pottery?

8. Object 35 in *A History of the World in 100 Objects*, the bronze *Meroë Head* is famed for its staring eyes. It depicts which man?

9. The Hoxne hoard was found in which county in 1992?

10. The Tokyo National Museum's Standing Buddha (1st–2nd century BC) is a fine example of Greco-Buddhist art from which ancient region in the Swat and Kabul river valleys in northern Pakistan and north-eastern Afghanistan?

11. The Sarpedon krater (515 BC) is the only complete example of the surviving 27 vases by which 'Pioneer Group' painter?

12. Discovered by Heinrich Schliemann, the funerary mask from Tomb V at Mycenae has been called the mask of which king?

13. Discovered in the Stadel Cave in 1939, which 40,000-year-old ivory figure is the world's earliest figurative sculpture?

14. Acquired by the Louvre in 1821, which half-nude statue was called 'Our Lady of Beauty' by Henri Heine?

15. 'Can you see anything?' 'Yes, wonderful things' – who responded to Lord Carnarvon's question and what was he describing?

Answers to Ancient Art: Arts Quiz 3

1. Lysippos
2. The Lady of Elche/Lady of Elx
3. Aphrodite of Knidos
4. Psusennes I
5. Tillya Tepe
6. Pitsa Panels/Pitsa Tablets
7. Larco Museum
8. Roman Emperor Augustus
9. Suffolk
10. Gandhara
11. Euphronios
12. Agamemnon, the mythical King of Mycenae
13. Ulm's *Lion Man*
14. Venus de Milo
15. Howard Carter, on finding the collection of Egyptian antiquities in Tutankhamun's tomb

1. *The Torment of St Anthony* (c.1487–88) is the earliest known painting by which artist?

2. Her 1556 *Self-portrait with Easel* is one of the first showing a woman at an easel, while *The Chess Game* portrays her sisters Lucia, Minerva and Europa. Which Italian painter (*c.1532–1625*) was rated by Vasari above all other female artists?

3. In 1421, the (supposed) first ever patent was granted to which Florentine architect, for a barge crane to transport marble?

4. Who painted the *Last Judgement* frescoes in Orvieto Cathedral?

5. In Lorenzo Lotto's late-1520s painting of *Venus and Cupid* in New York's Metropolitan Museum of Art, what is the latter figure seen doing to symbolise fertility?

6. Titian's last finished painting, *The Flaying of Marsyas* (1570–76), is housed in the National Museum of which Czech city, whose nickname is the 'Athens of Hanakia'?

7. The 'Ascension Relief' (1428–30) and the 'Chellini Madonna' are works in the V&A by which sculptor?

8. Commissioned by the Medici, which 1482–85 work by Botticelli is the first example in Tuscany of a painting on canvas?

9. The Louvre's portrait of Sigismondo Pandolfo Malatesta (*c.1450*) is the only picture in France by which Umbrian painter?

10. Noted for its elder subject's age-worn face, *An Old Man and his Grandson* (*c.1450*) was acquired by the Louvre in 1886. Which Florentine contemporary of Botticelli painted it?

11. According to Vasari, which painting was placed at the head of the dead Raphael – 'the sight of his dead body and this living painting filled the soul of everyone looking on with grief'?

12. What is the surname of Pedro (d.1504), the first great Renaissance painter in Spain, and his son Alonso (d.1561), the most important Spanish sculptor of the Renaissance?

13. Sassetta, Matteo di Giovanni, Taddeo di Bartolo and Giovanni di Paolo belonged to which school of painting?

14. Which name was given to the painter Giovanni Antonio Bazzi (1477–1549)? His works include a 1525 *St Sebastian* in the Uffizi and the *Sacrifice of Abraham* in the choir of Pisa Cathedral.

15. Nicknamed after the colour of his hair, who sculpted the monument of Infante James Coimbra, cardinal of Portugal, in the Basilica di San Miniato al Monte, Florence (1461–67)?

1. Michelangelo
2. Sofonisba Anguissola
3. Filippo Brunelleschi
4. Luca Signorelli
5. He is urinating
6. Kroměříž
7. Donatello
8. *The Birth of Venus*
9. Piero della Francesca
10. Domenico Ghirlandaio/Domenico di Tomaso Bigordi
11. *Transfiguration* (1516–20)
12. Berruguete
13. Sienese school
14. Il Sodoma
15. Antonio Gamberelli, nicknamed Antonio Rossellino

1. How many spires will Barcelona's Basílica de la Sagrada Família have when it is completed in 2026?
2. Commissioned by Henry III in the 13th century, where will you find the Cosmati pavement?
3. Which sculptor and architect's reputation was seriously damaged when a commission for Pope Urban VIII to build two bell towers for St Peter's went disastrously wrong?
4. In which city is the Selimiye complex, regarded by Ottoman architect Mimar Sinan as his masterpiece?
5. Although it was to prove financially and technically impossible, what was first proposed by the Ottoman sultan Abdulmecid I, who contracted a French architect to draw up plans in 1860?
6. Derived from communication theory and used in building design, which curve shows the likelihood of two people in the same office speaking to each other as the distance between them increases?
7. What, in ancient Egyptian architecture, were hypostyles?
8. The iconic Ennis House, on a hill above Hollywood, was built by which architect in 1924 from about 27,000 concrete blocks featuring 24 Mayan designs?
9. Which Japanese Pritzker Prizewinner is noted for his disaster-zone relief structures made from huge paper tubes?
10. In 2011, just 25 years after completion, what building in the City of London became the youngest ever to be granted a Grade 1 listing?
11. Which architect's proposed Plan Voisin (1925) involved razing an area in the centre of Paris and replacing it with 18 vast cruciform skyscrapers?
12. The designer of Castle Howard and Blenheim Palace, whose epitaph reads 'lie heavy on him, Earth, for he laid many a heavy load on thee!'?
13. Including St Malo, Belle-Île, Besançon citadel and a fort in Briançon, France has submitted 14 citadels and fortifications built by which 17-century military engineer for a place in the UNESCO list of World Heritage Sites?
14. Who, in 2006, became the first woman to win the Pritzker Prize?
15. Who designed the Orangery at Kensington Palace, Christ Church (Spitalfields), All Souls College (Oxford), The Queen's College (Oxford) and added the west towers to Westminster Abbey?

1. Eighteen. i.e. twelve disciples, four evangelists, Mary and Jesus
2. Westminster Abbey – it's a decorated mosaic floor on which coronations have taken place for the past 900 years
3. Gian Lorenzo Bernini
4. Edirne
5. A tunnel under the Bosporus
6. Allen Curve
7. Pillars holding up the roof
8. Frank Lloyd Wright
9. Shigeru Ban
10. Lloyds Building
11. Le Corbusier
12. Sir John Vanbrugh
13. Marshal Vauban – Vauban built about 150 fortified sites across France
14. Zaha Hadid
15. Nicholas Hawksmoor

Science

1. Which statistical average is calculated by finding out the middle value in a set of data arranged in order?

2. Russian mathematician Grigori Perelman proved which of the Millennium Prize problems in 2003, although turned down the prize of $1 million for doing so?

3. The statistician William Sealy Gossett developed a *t*-distribution and a *t*-test under what pseudonym?

4. Wolfgang Haken and Kenneth Appel solved which mathematical problem using computers in 1976?

5. What adjective is given to a pair of numbers each of which is the sum of the divisors of the other?

6. Which former Cambridge mathematician who discovered the theory called monstrous moonshine with Simon Conway is the subject of Alexander Masters' biography *The Genius in My Basement*?

7. Srinivasa Ramanujan famously identified which number as the smallest number to be the sum of two cubes in two different ways in conversation with G.H. Hardy?

8. Which famous argument was used by Georg Cantor to prove that the set of real numbers is larger than the set of integers?

9. What two-word name is given to the top mathematics graduate at Cambridge University in a given year, past winners having included *Ascent of Man* presenter Jacob Bronowski?

10. According to the Tom Lehrer song, what did Nicolai Lobachevsky say was the secret of success in mathematics?

11. What sporting object could be best described geometrically as a truncated icosahedron?

12. He proved his namesake theorem in his paper 'On a Problem of Formal Logic'; which mathematician, brother of a future Archbishop of Canterbury, died in 1930 aged just 26?

13. Which famous logician would only eat food prepared by his wife and died in 1978, six months after she had been admitted to hospital, following which he starved himself?

14. What name is given to the problem of finding the path of shortest descent from one point to another?

15. The Riemann hypothesis conjectures that all non-trivial zeros of the Riemann zeta function have a real part equal to what amount?

1. Median
2. The Poincaré conjecture
3. Student
4. The four colour theorem (i.e. that four colours is the maximum needed to colour in a map on a planar surface)
5. Amicable
6. Simon Norton
7. 1729
8. Diagonal argument or diagonal slash argument
9. Senior wrangler
10. 'Plagiarize!'
11. A football
12. Frank Ramsey
13. Kurt Gödel
14. Brachistocrone
15. One-half

1. In 1979 at the Jet Propulsion Laboratory, what was NASA *Voyager* Flight Engineer Linda Hyder the first person to see when viewing images of Io?

2. Deriving from the Greek for 'star wound', what ten-letter word is given to meteorite impact craters on the earth's surface?

3. Which moon orbits its planet at distances just over 9,000 kilometres, the closest of any known moon in our solar system?

4. In 2009, for the first time, an asteroid was tracked all the way from space, with fragments duly retrieved from the desert at Almahata Sitta in which country?

5. What is made up of the Perseus, Norma, Scutum–Centaurus, Scutum–Sagittarius and the Outer (an extension of the Norma)?

6. Which element is the heaviest to be created in the collapse of a red giant star?

7. The world's largest radio telescope, the SKA, is likely to cost £1.3 billion and will be split between Western Australia and the Northern Cape of South Africa. What do the letters SKA stand for?

8. Named after a Lahore-born Indian-American Nobel laureate and flying more than 200 times further above the earth than Hubble, what is NASA's premier X-ray observatory?

9. What was discovered in 1964 by Arno Penzias and Robert Wilson?

10. On 11 November 1572, Tycho Brahe spotted a supernova in which constellation?

11. NASA's Kepler Observatory was designed to search for extra-solar planets. It is in orbit around which body?

12. The celebrated Hubble Ultra Deep Field image was taken in a tiny area of sky lying in which constellation?

13. In 1918, which US astronomer studied Cepheid variables and established that the centre of our galaxy lies far away in the direction of the constellation Sagittarius and nowhere near our sun?

14. In 1671, Ole Rømer made an early accurate measurement of the speed of light by detailed study of which moon?

15. In the 1600s, who proposed three laws of planetary motion sometimes described as the Law of Ellipses, the Law of Equal Areas and the Law of Harmonies?

Answers to Astronomy: Science Quiz 2

1. Active extraterrestrial vulcanism
2. Astrobleme
3. Phobos (it orbits Mars)
4. Sudan
5. The Milky Way – they are the main spiral arms of the galaxy
6. Iron
7. Square Kilometre Array
8. Chandra (X-Ray Observatory) after Subrahmanyan Chandrasekhar
9. The CMB – Cosmic Microwave Background
10. Cassiopeia
11. The sun
12. Fornax – a million-second shutter speed
13. Harlow Shapley
14. Io
15. Johannes Kepler

1. Who published the hugely influential paper 'A Mathematical Theory of Communication' (1948)?

2. Which Russian mathematician, a winner of the Stalin Prize, set up Russia's most famous maths school in Moscow, which awards just 200 places a year using a nationwide competition?

3. In the 1950s, which American developed a method of measuring levels of carbon dioxide in the air with a namesake graph indicating that these levels have increased steadily for decades?

4. What was the main subject of Albert Einstein's 1905 paper 'On a Heuristic Viewpoint Concerning the Production and Transformation of Light'?

5. In 1930 Wolfgang Pauli confessed to a colleague, 'I have done a terrible thing . . . I have postulated a particle that cannot be detected.' Which particle?

6. Which US microbiologist developed 8 of the 14 vaccines routinely recommended in current vaccination programmes?

7. Awarded the Nobel Prize in Chemistry in 1964, who pioneered the use of X-ray techniques to establish the structures of compounds such as insulin, cholesterol and penicillin?

8. In 1912, who proposed the concept of continental drift, after studying similar fossils from both sides of the Atlantic?

9. In 1900, which Norwegian, now featured on a 200-kroner banknote, was the first to formulate a theory explaining the Northern Lights?

10. What two-word name was given to transposons investigated by Barbara McClintock?

11. Which physicist's key scientific paper was originally rejected in 1965 because it 'was of no obvious relevance to physics'?

12. In 1910, Paul Ehrlich announced his discovery of Salvarsan, a substance which killed the bacterium associated with which disease?

13. In the early 20th century, which scientist worked at his Wardenclyffe Tower research station on Long Island, experimenting with high-voltage and high-frequency electromagnetic waves?

14. Edward O. Wilson's eyesight was damaged in childhood making it easier for him to study small rather than large organisms. He became a leading authority on which creatures?

15. From 1907 Charles Walcott travelled to British Columbia to investigate 'stone bugs' found by railway workers and discovered what?

1. Claude Shannon
2. Alexander Kolmogorov
3. Charles Keeling – the Keeling Curve
4. The photoelectric effect
5. The neutrino
6. Maurice Hilleman
7. Dorothy Hodgkin
8. Alfred Wegener
9. Kristian Birkeland. The first complete map of the magnetic 'Birkeland currents', as they came to be known, was made in 1974 by Alfred Zmuda and James Armstrong some 57 years after Birkeland's death
10. Jumping genes
11. Professor Peter Higgs
12. Syphilis
13. Nikola Tesla
14. Ants
15. The Burgess Shale

1. Which solar system body is the target of the planned NASA TiME mission?

2. Born in Ukraine, which man was retrieved from the Gulag and became the anonymous 'Chief Designer' of the Soviet space programme until his unexpected death in 1966?

3. Translating as 'snowstorm', what was the name of the Soviet Union's ill-fated equivalent of the Space Shuttle?

4. Which catastrophic explosion at the Baikonur cosmodrome in 1960 took the lives of 126 Soviet space and military personnel, including a namesake Marshall?

5. In 2012, which entrepreneur announced that he had located the long-submerged F-1 engines that blasted the Apollo 11 moon mission into space deep in the Atlantic Ocean?

6. What was the name of the Soviet programme one of whose vehicles became, in 1968, the first spacecraft to circle the moon and return to land on earth?

7. Which Apollo mission of 1968 involved the first manned launch of a Saturn V rocket?

8. Which country's national space agency launched a 'space yacht' from Tanegashima in May 2010 which was the first spacecraft to successfully demonstrate solar-sail technology in interplanetary space?

9. Of the 12 men to walk on the moon, 6 were born in which year?

10. In July 1963, in *Vostok* 6, who became the first woman to travel in space?

11. Which astronaut was the first person to orbit the moon alone (Apollo 10), the ninth man to walk on the moon (Apollo 16) and the commander of the Space Shuttle's maiden flight in 1981?

12. Who, in 1961, became the first man to spend a day in orbit?

13. Who was the only astronaut to take part in the Mercury, Gemini and Apollo programmes?

14. Scheduled to launch in 2018, the JSWT will be a large infrared successor to the Hubble Space Telescope. It is named after which former NASA administrator?

15. Ahead of his time, which US professor, physicist and inventor is credited with building the world's first liquid-fuelled rocket 'Nell', which he successfully launched on 16 March 1926?

1. Titan – Titan Mare Explorer. Titan is Saturn's largest moon. A vessel would land and 'sail' on Titan's vast lakes of methane
2. (Sergei Pavlovich) Korolev
3. Buran
4. (Marshall Mitrofan) Nedelin – the Nedelin Catastrophe
5. Jeff Bezos
6. Zond (Zond V specifically)
7. Apollo 8
8. Japan – JAXA
9. 1930
10. Valentina Tereshkova
11. John Young
12. Gherman Titov
13. Wally Schirra
14. James Webb (Space Telescope)
15. Robert Goddard

1. After giving his neighbour a form of absorbent clay to help with a pet problem in 1947, Ed Lowe built a half-billion-dollar business out of which invention?

2. Ettore Steccone simplified window cleaning with the invention of which T-shaped device?

3. The first purpose-built ski lift, where skiers were propelled along in chairs suspended from an aerial rope-way, was designed by Jim Curran and built for which Idaho resort in 1936?

4. In 1973, US engineer Nathaniel Wyeth invented which recyclable plastic to contain carbonated beverages?

5. Invented in 2001 when surgeon Michael Gagner in New York operated on a woman's gall bladder in Strasbourg, which form of long-distance surgery is performed with the help of robots?

6. In 1970, which firm produced the first wrist-worn timepiece to tell the time digitally, a gold watch called the 'Pulsar'?

7. The Busicom LE-120A, or 'Handy-LE', was the first truly pocket-sized example of which device?

8. Conceived and implemented (in its first version) by McGill University postgraduate Alan Emtage, which tool for indexing FTP archives is considered to be the first internet search engine?

9. First created by Samuel Stephens Kistler in 1931, which synthetic porous ultralight material has such nicknames as 'frozen smoke', and has been called the world's lightest solid?

10. Sometimes referred to as the first smartphone, the Simon Personal Communicator was first released in 1994 by which company?

11. Which Canadian computer scientist invented the programming language Java at Sun Microsystems in 1994?

12. Developed by a business consortium led by Bill Lear of the Lear Jet fame, which 1964 invention arose from the desire to produce a magnetic tape playback system for use in cars?

13. True porcelain was manufactured in northern China from the start of which dynasty in the 7th century?

14. Which portable device was invented in 1954 by Robert Borkenstein of the Indiana State Police?

15. Which Russian vice-admiral, who died in 1904 when the *Petropavlovsk* was sunk during the Russo-Japanese War, designed the *Yermak*, the first true icebreaker able to ride over and crush pack ice?

Answers to Inventions: Science Quiz 5

1. Kitty litter/Cat litter
2. Squeegee
3. Sun Valley – on the resort's Proctor and Dollar Mountains
4. Polyethylene terephthalate (PET)
5. Telesurgery/remote surgery
6. Hamilton Watch Company
7. Calculator
8. 'Archie'
9. Aerogel
10. IBM
11. James Gosling
12. Eight-track audiotape/Stereo 8
13. Tang dynasty
14. Breathalyzer
15. Stepan Makarov

Lifestyle

1. Business guru Charles Handy and politician Vince Cable both began their business careers at which Anglo-Dutch multinational company?

2. What name did the Bank of England give to its policy, introduced in 2013, of giving the markets an indication of its likely future attitude to monetary policy?

3. The subject of a 2014 IPO, which UK property website was founded by Alex Chesterman, a serial internet entrepreneur who had earlier founded LoveFilm?

4. Which Franciscan friar is known as the father of double-entry bookkeeping after he published the first description of that system in 1494?

5. *Liar's Poker*, *The Big Short* and *Flash Boys* are among the business-themed works of which US writer?

6. Which Chinese company briefly became in 2007 the world's first company to be valued in excess of $1 trillion?

7. Which UK plc has a former Conservative MP as chairman and a former head of the Football Association as chief executive?

8. Which toy company was founded in Rhode Island in 1923 by Henry and Helal Hassenfeld?

9. Associated with Occidental Petroleum, which US industrialist was said to have been named after the logo of the Socialist Labor Party of America?

10. In business jargon, what kind of manager is said to fly in, make a lot of noise, dump on everyone, and then fly out?

11. Bought by Apple in 2014, which US manufacturer of audio products such as headphones was co-founded by rapper Dr Dre?

12. If K is Klynveld and G is Goerdeler, what are the middle two?

13. Which financial institution, founded in 1968 and part of the Alliance & Leicester Group when it ceased trading in 2003, uniquely had its own non-geographical postcode?

14. Sold by Nokia in 2012, which Hampshire-based mobile telephone company specialises in making luxury mobile telephones with prices starting at over £3,000?

15. The name of which Japanese sports equipment manufacturer is an acronym of a Latin phrase meaning 'healthy mind and healthy body'?

Answers to Commerce and Finance: Lifestyle Quiz 1

1. Royal Dutch Shell
2. Forward guidance
3. Zoopla
4. Luca Pacioli
5. Michael Lewis
6. Petrochina
7. ITV (Archie Norman and Adam Crozier)
8. Hasbro
9. Armand Hammer
10. A seagull manager
11. Beats
12. Peat and Marwick (in the name of accountancy firm KPMG)
13. Girobank
14. Vertu
15. Asics ('anima sana in corpore sano')

1. The noodle soup *pho* is the national dish of which country?

2. The Chinese city of Yulin holds a one-day summer solstice festival involving the slaughter of 10,000 of which creatures? Residents then indulge in mass consumption of hotpot featuring the animals served with lychees and strong grain liquor.

3. Which Hong Kong-based food company was founded by _____ _____ Sheung in 1888 in Nanshui, Guangdong, when he invented the first oyster sauce to gain worldwide popularity?

4. Which Mongolian dish is prepared by cooking a whole Tarbagan marmot from inside out? The animal is cooked with hot rocks inside its own skin, which is tied up to make a bag.

5. Which terrifying Greenlandic dish is is made by seasoning 300-500 auks with seal fat and sticking them (beaks, feet, feathers and all) inside a seal skin, which is buried for 3–18 months? It is a winter/birthday/wedding treat for Inuits.

6. Which one-word Arabic name is given to a popular sandwich of sliced lamb or chicken, usually wrapped in pita bread with tahini? It is akin to the Turkish doner kebab and Greek gyros.

7. *Unagi* is the Japanese sushi term for which fish?

8. G.K. Chesterton wrote 'Yet this high cheese, by choice of fenland men, / Like a tall green volcano rose in power' in a sonnet to what? Daniel Defoe called it the 'English Parmesan'.

9. *Kummerspeck*, meaning 'grief bacon', describes excess weight gained from emotional overeating in which language?

10. Known in Gaelic as *marag dubh*, which meat product from Stornoway holds EU 'Protected Designation of Origin' status?

11. A white stock thickened with white roux, which sauce is enriched with egg to become allemande sauce?

12. The South African dish bunny chow is a hollowed-out loaf of bread filled with what?

13. The traditional Faroese dish *tvøst og spik* consists of potatoes and which type of meat?

14. Which boiled meat features in the classic Viennese dish *Tafelspitz*?

15. As well as a lobster dish, the grandiose game pie *oreiller de la belle Aurore* was named after Claudine-Aurore Récamier. She was the mother of which chef, lawyer and author (1755–1826)?

Answers to Savoury Food: Lifestyle Quiz 2

1. Vietnam
2. Dog
3. Lee Kum Kee – founded by Lee Kum Sheung
4. Mongolian *boodog*
5. *Kiviak* or *Kiviaq*
6. *Shawarma*
7. Freshwater eel, especially the Japanese eel (Anguilla japonica)
8. Stilton cheese
9. German
10. (Highland) black pudding
11. Velouté sauce
12. Curry
13. Pilot whale meat and blubber
14. Beef
15. Jean Anthelme Brillat-Savarin

1. What is unique about the beans grown by the Madagascar coffee species *Mascarocoffea vianneyi*?
2. Absinthe's infamy and its subsequent banning in many countries can be attributed to it containing which wormwood-derived hallucinogenic compound?
3. Nicknamed 'Black Death' thanks to its notorious reputation, the clear, unsweetened schnapps Brennivín ('burning wine') has been called the national liquor of which country?
4. Which phrase, meaning 'with worm', refers to the said creature that is famously found in bottles of Mexican spirit mezcal, though it is actually the larva of two moths that live on the agave plant?
5. Fujian's Tie Guan Yin, Hangzhou's Dragon Well, Yunnan's pu-erh and Taiwan's Don Ding oolong are among the many varieties we can apparently thank Emperor Shennong for. He reputedly made which discovery in 2737 BC?
6. Portón is an ultra-premium brand that is made at the Hacienda La Caravedo in Ica, Peru, the oldest distillery (founded 1684) in the Americas. Fifteen pounds of the grape varieties Quebranta, Albilla and Torontel go into a Portón bottle of which white spirit?
7. Named after a Pacific nation, which brand of water is bottled at the source, the Yaqara Valley on Viti Levu?
8. In 1767, which British scientist made the first glass of potable artificially carbonated water?
9. What is the official beverage of the US state of Indiana?
10. Guinness describes its beer as a dark shade of which red colour?
11. When is the Swedish soft drink, Julmust, usually consumed?
12. The full name of the liqueur Anisette features which French city, the home of the drink's maker Marie Brizard since the company's founding in 1755?
13. Which South American country has been the world's largest producer of coffee for the last 150 years?
14. What is the indentation in the base of a wine bottle called?
15. A trusted hangover remedy, which Mexican *cerveza preparada* (beer cocktail) is made with light beer and lime juice, and can include Maggi, chilli powder, Worcestershire sauce, soy sauce or tomato juice? Salt is generally placed on the rim of the pint glass, and the name comes from a phrase meaning 'my beer, ice cold'.

Answers to Liquid Refreshment: Lifestyle Quiz 3

1. It is naturally decaffeinated
2. Thujone
3. Iceland
4. *Con gusano*
5. Tea
6. Pisco
7. Fiji Water
8. Joseph Priestley
9. Water
10. Ruby
11. Christmas
12. Bordeaux
13. Brazil
14. Punt
15. *Michelada*

1. In Bolivia, the women of the Quechua people have worn which style of hat ever since the 1920s, when British railway workers introduced them there?

2. Created by the Florentine fashion house Gherardini, the Pretiosa handbag is based on a drawing by which artist?

3. Associated with the art deco movement of the 1920s and '30s, the Russian-born fashion illustrator and designer Romain de Tirtoff was known by which one-word name?

4. Traditionally, people from the Aran Islands wore things called 'pampooties' where on their bodies?

5. Who played the US model Gia Carangi, who died of AIDS in 1986 aged 28, in the HBO film *Gia*?

6. Naming it after her third husband Andreas Kronthaler, which British designer commissioned her own tartan 'MacAndreas'?

7. Which US department store began in 1861 when brothers Joseph and Lyman G. started selling hoop-skirts in their Ladies Notions' Shop on Manhattan's Lower East Side?

8. Harry Leuckert was the husband of which fashion designer, who was described as the 'Chanel of England'?

9. Tony Hawk and which *My Name is Earl* star were the first two skateboarders to receive a signature shoe with Airwalk?

10. Which French fashion label was founded in 1983 by Jean-Lou Tepper, Jacques Nataf and Philippe de Hesdin?

11. Which luxury perfumes/cosmetics brand, owned by L'Oréal since 1964, was started by Armand Petitjean in 1935, the same year its first five perfumes – Tendre Nuit, Bocages, Conquete, Kypre, Tropiques – were launched at the World's Fair in Brussels?

12. Sold for $2.4m to New York uber-dealer Josef Mugrabi, which artwork by Maurizio Cattelan is a trophy-style, nude upper-body wax sculpture of the supermodel ex-girlfriend of Axl Rose?

13. Manufactured by Generra Sportswear Company of Seattle, which T-shirts reached peak popularity in c. 1991 thanks to the thermochronic (heat-sensitive) pigment, that changed between two colours – one when warm, another when cold?

14. Which euphemism for 'toilet' is the name of a wire framework hairpiece of the late 15th and early 16th centuries? The finished product was known in France as a *frontange* (tower).

15. What is Daura-Suruwal?

1. Bowler hats
2. Leonardo da Vinci
3. Erté
4. On their feet – they were rawhide shoes similar to American moccasins
5. Angelina Jolie
6. Vivienne Westwood
7. Bloomingdale's
8. Jean Muir
9. Jason Lee
10. Kookai
11. Lancôme
12. *Stephanie*, depicting Stephanie Seymour and nicknamed 'Trophy Wife'
13. Global Hypercolor/Generra Hypercolor/Generra Hypergrafix – the pigment was made by Matsui Shikiso Chemical of Japan
14. Commode
15. Traditional national costume worn by Nepalese men as formal dress (also worn in neighboring Sikkim and Darjeeling in India, the top is Daura, the trousers are Suruwal)

1. Boasting the colours of the French flag, with blue feet, white feathers and a red crest, which is the only variety of chicken in Europe with the Controlled Designation of Origin label?

2. With which country would you most associate the hangi method of cooking meat underground in a pit oven?

3. In which town is the prestigious Jack Daniel's World Invitational Barbecue Challenge held annually?

4. Which soup, a favourite of Nelson Mandela, is known as *umsila wenkomo* in South Africa?

5. Migrant worker Kadir Nurman (1933–2013) is credited with inventing what food item, initially priced at DM 1.50, at his snack-bar opposite the Zoologischer Garten S-Bahn and main-line station in Berlin in 1972?

6. The deglet noor variety makes up the majority of California's crop of which fruit?

7. *Surströmming* is a fermented product, the cans often bulging because of continuing putrefaction. Only 16,000 of 800,000 cans produced annually in Sweden are exported. What is the raw ingredient?

8. The coco de mer is the world's biggest nut and comes from a palm which is endemic to which island nation?

9. Australia's oldest continuously operating example, in which state capital will you find Cascade Brewery?

10. The Quely (pronounced Kelly) is a savoury biscuit produced on which island since 1853?

11. Usually eaten at Christmas and New Year, panettone is a cupola-shaped sweet bread loaf packed with dried fruits and citrus bits which originated in which Italian city?

12. Which US chef's several successful restaurant ventures include the highly acclaimed Napa Valley establishment the French Laundry?

13. Which spice is obtained from the fruit of the *Illicium verum*, a native evergreen tree of south-western China?

14. Now opening branches worldwide, in which country was the US-style fast food restaurant chain Jollibee founded in the 1970s?

15. The former professional boxer Toshio Tanabe specialises in using which somewhat unlikely ingredient at his Tokyo restaurant?

Answers to Food and Drink: Lifestyle Quiz 5

1. Bresse
2. New Zealand – Maori
3. Lynchburg, Tennessee
4. Oxtail
5. Doner kebab/Shawarma/Gyro
6. Date
7. Herring
8. The Seychelles – *Lodoicea Maldivica*
9. Hobart
10. Majorca/Mallorca
11. Milan
12. Thomas Keller
13. Star Anise
14. The Philippines – (aka JFC – Jollibee Foods Corporation)
15. Soil/Dirt/Earth

Miscellaneous III

1. Which Danish architect is the PH in the name of a PH-lamp?
2. Begun in 1997 in Sallanches, Haute-Savoie, by Christian Ollier, which mountain sports, apparel and equipment brand won an IDEA industrial design award for its instant 2 Second Tent?
3. The most famous design associated with Piaggio was the Vespa, designed by which aeronautical engineer (1891–1981)?
4. Who designed the Tiger Moth light aircraft in 1925?
5. Its first export, the TR-55 transistor radio (1955), was the first product to use which company's logo, a branding feature further developed by Yasuko Kuroki and further revised in 1973?
6. While working as a bookkeeper, who persuaded his employer, Liverpool-based meat importer David Elliott, to provide capital for his educational construction toy?
7. In 1957, who co-founded with Tom Geismar the New York-based branding and graphic design firm that created the logos for Mobil Oil, MoMA, Xerox, NBC and *National Geographic*?
8. The forerunner of modern fitted kitchens, which Austrian architect designed the Frankfurt Kitchen for Ernst Mayr's social housing project New Frankfurt in 1926?
9. Which designer's trademarked signature appeared on more than 250 million pieces of Steubenville Pottery's American Modern (1939–59), the most widely sold US ceramic dinnerware in history?
10. In 1963, the Daleks first appeared in *Doctor Who* in shells designed by which BBC employee?
11. Which company's definitive 'Golden Arches' was created in 1968 by the D'Arcy Advertising agency?
12. Which French domestic appliance company was founded by vegetable shredder designer Jean Mantelet in 1932?
13. Which US industrial designer, American Motors' chief stylist, was responsible for such unique automotive designs as the AMC Pacer, Gremlin and Matador Coupe, as well as the Jeep Cherokee?
14. Which architecture and design magazine was founded in 1928 by the architect Gio Ponti and Barnabite father Giovanni Semeria?
15. The subject, in 1946, of MoMA's first exhibit devoted to contemporary ceramics and an individual female designer, which Budapest-born woman narrated her own story of escape from both the USSR and Nazi-annexed Austria in the 2002 documentary *Throwing Curves*?

1. Poul Henningsen
2. Quechua
3. Corradino D'Ascanio
4. Geoffrey de Havilland
5. Sony
6. Frank Hornby – to pay for Meccano
7. Ivan Chermayeff – co-founder of Chermayeff & Geismar, now Chermayeff & Geismar & Haviv
8. Margarete Schütte-Lihotzky
9. Russel Wright
10. Raymond Cusick
11. McDonald's
12. Moulinex/Moulin-Légumes Company – *moulin à légumes* meaning vegetable shredder
13. Richard A. Teague
14. *Domus*
15. Eva Zeisel

1. Which US television presenter claims to have been born in East Finchley Tube station during an air raid in 1944?

2. Which is the only London Underground station to share its name with a station on the Paris Metro?

3. The River Westbourne passes over the tracks of which station on the District and Circle lines, encased in a large metal pipe?

4. The name of which London district is common to the two remaining deep-level stations with island platforms?

5. Of the five underground stations located outside the M25, which is the only one not on the Metropolitan Line?

6. Which now-closed station is just perceptible on the Central line between Tottenham Court Road and Holborn stations?

7. Which 1998 novel by Geoff Ryman is said to be named after the number of seats on a Tube train (including the driver)?

8. Government clerk Arthur Cadogan West is found dead on the tracks near Aldgate station in which Sherlock Holmes story?

9. Which civil engineer who worked on the London Underground improved Marc Isambard Brunel's design for a tunnelling shield to create a shield which is still used today?

10. Edward Johnston designed what important element of the London Underground brand, which is named after him?

11. Which Metropolitan line station is still signed with the additional name '(Swakeleys)' on its roundels, having borne that name in the mid-20th century?

12. Which Bayswater street contains a false front of a house to shield the road from the noise of the Circle and District lines running behind it?

13. The London Underground's highest point above ground level is on the Northern line when a viaduct carries the line nearly 60 feet above which waterway?

14. In 2010, which London Underground station opened the shortest escalator on the tube, one of only two going *up* to the platform?

15. Which architect designed the London Underground headquarters at 55 Broadway as well as some of the network's finest stations, such as Arnos Grove and Gants Hill?

Answers to London Underground:
Miscellaneous III Quiz 2

1. Jerry Springer
2. Temple
3. Sloane Square
4. Clapham (North and Common)
5. Epping
6. British Museum
7. 253
8. 'The Adventure of the Bruce–Partington Plans'
9. James Greathead
10. The typeface used for signage, station names etc.
11. Hillingdon
12. Leinster Gardens (numbers 23 and 24)
13. Dollis Brook
14. Stratford
15. Charles Holden

1. Following the overthrow of its leader in 2011, which country's 1949 flag of three horizontal stripes of red, black and green, and a white crescent and star, was reinstated as its national flag?

2. In a new flag of Lesotho hoisted to honour the 40th anniversary of its independence in 2006, which central symbol is depicted as a black silhouette?

3. The four stars on New Zealand's flag depict what?

4. Which US state flag consists of alternating horizontal stripes of white, red and blue, with the Union Jack in the canton?

5. The motto 'L'Union fait la force' features on the coat of arms in the centre of which country's flag?

6. What colour are the three horizontal stripes, from top to bottom, on the flag of Burma?

7. Which creature featured on the imperial banner of the Holy Roman Empire, from 1401 to 1836?

8. The flag of which Baltic state consists of a crimson background (field) divided horizontally by a narrow white stripe, with a width-to-length ratio of 1:2?

9. What is the inscription, in green-coloured Kufic script, in the centre of the flag of Iraq?

10. Which flag's arc of six white stars was said to stand for the country's six predominant ethnic groups: Albanians, Bosniacs, Gorani, Roma, Serbs and Turks?

11. In 1816, which symbol for Brazil was added behind the shield of Portugal's royal arms featured on the country's then white flag? It represented a navigational instrument.

12. Which state flag features a yellow disc bearing the silhouette of a black swan?

13. While still a French territory in 1963, which Indian Ocean country chose a distinctive local flag designed by heraldist Suzanne Gauthier? Its four white stars represented islands in the archipelago, including Anjouan and Mohéli.

14. At the fly end, which country's flag features a crimson rectangle with a sword-wielding lion and four bo leaves?

15. Which African country hoisted a new flag on 31 December 2001, with the aim of promoting national unity? The design represents the nation's lush vegetation, bathed in the yellow light of the (24-rayed) sun.

1. Libya
2. The traditional Sotho straw hat
3. The constellation/Southern Cross/Crux
4. Hawaii
5. Haiti
6. Yellow, green, red (overlapped by a central white star)
7. A double-headed black eagle (on a yellow field)
8. Latvia
9. 'Allāhu akbar' ('God is great')
10. Kosovo
11. Armillary sphere
12. Western Australia
13. Comoros
14. Sri Lanka
15. Rwanda

1. Known as 'Japan's Le Pen', which far-right politician and author – winner of the 1955 Akutagawa Prize for *Season of the Sun* – became governor of Tokyo in 1999? He also co-wrote *The Japan That Can Say No* with Sony chairman Akio Morita.

2. The paulownia flower pattern (*go-shichi-no-kiri*) is the *mon* (symbol) of which office?

3. What is the concept or philosophy of: a) *kaizen*, b) *gaman*, c) *wabi-sabi*?

4. Known as the 'father of lolicon', which *mangaka* told of the times he deserted civilisation and became a tramp, a pipe-layer and went into rehab in *Disappearance Diary* (2005)?

5. Japan won every men's Olympic swimming title in 1932, except for which event?

6. Meaning 'insert ink', what word refers to a Japanese form of tattooing? And which word, meaning 'carving' or 'engraving', may also describe traditional Japanese tattoos?

7. Protecting against evil, which Japanese supernatural being devours dreams and nightmares? It resembles a tapir.

8. What is the smallest of Japan's four main islands?

9. Which Fukuoka-born 'empress of pop' has sold over 53 million records in Japan since the release of her 1998 debut single 'Poker Face' and debut album *A Song for XX* (1999)?

10. Which 1980s TV show aired in Italy as *Mai dire Banzai* ('Never Say Banzai'), *Humor Amarillo* ('Yellow Humour') in Spain, and *Hullut japanilaiset* ('The Crazy Japanese') in Finland?

11. Resembling a net-less badminton, which traditional New Year's game is played with a wooden paddle called *hagoita*?

12. Meaning 'sitting right on the ground', which word for an element of Japanese manners that shows deference to highly revered people translates into English as 'prostration' or 'kowtow'?

13. Considered the original heir to Hayao Miyazaki's Studio Ghibli throne, which animator died of a brain aneurysm at the age of 47 after directing his only feature, *Whisper of the Heart*?

14. Cocorobo is a trilingual vacuuming robot that was launched in 2012 by which electronics maker?

15. Mentioned in the *Nihon Shoki*, the second oldest book of classical history, the traditional sweet, low-to-non-alcohol drink *amazake* is made from fermented what?

Answers to Japan: Miscellaneous III Quiz 4

1. Shintarō Ishihara
2. Prime Minister
3. a) The continuous improvement in every aspect of life; b) to persevere, to endure pain and suffering with dignity, and suffer in silence; c) the beauty of imperfection and impermanence
4. Hideo Azuma
5. 400 m freestyle – won by Buster Crabbe, who played Tarzan the very next year
6. *Irezumi*; *horimono*
7. *Baku*
8. Shikoku
9. Ayumi Hamasaki
10. *Takeshi's Castle*/*Fūun! Takeshi-jō* ('Operation! Takeshi Castle')
11. *Hanetsuki*
12. *Dogeza*
13. Yoshifumi Kondo
14. Sharp
15. Rice

1. Who took off from Augsburg on 27 May 1931 in a pressurised gondola, becoming, with his assistant, Paul Kipfer, the first person to reach the stratosphere at over 50,000 feet?

2. Which English polymath and explorer produced an unexpurgated translation of *One Thousand and One Nights* and, with John Hanning Speke, was one of the first Europeans to visit the Great Lakes of Africa in search of the source of the Nile?

3. On Sunday, 5 April 1722, the Dutch explorer Jacob Roggeveen was the first recorded European visitor to which island?

4. How is Ma He, born in 1371 and singled out by the Emperor Yangli for his intelligence and courage, better known?

5. Sharing the same surname as Bartolomeu Dias, who reached the westernmost point of mainland Africa in 1444 and named it Cape Verde?

6. Carried by Portuguese explorers, what were *padrões* used for?

7. He disappeared in 1925 during an expedition to find it; what name was given by Col. Percy Harrison Fawcett, a British surveyor, to a city that he thought existed in the jungle of the Mato Grosso region of Brazil?

8. Which navigator and buccaneer from Somerset was the first man to circumnavigate the world three times?

9. Who was the first man to reach both the North and South Poles?

10. Which Spaniard was, in 1513, the first European to lead an expedition to have reached the Pacific from the New World?

11. With a 104-year-old example coming up for auction in 2011, what did Reading-based company Huntley & Palmers provide to expeditions led by Ernest Shackleton and Captain Scott?

12. In 1969, who led the British Trans-Arctic Expedition on the first surface crossing of the Arctic Ocean?

13. Which man, dispatched by the Royal Navy, led an expedition on the ships *Erebus* and *Terror* that explored much of the coastline of Antarctica between 1839 and 1842?

14. In which treaty of 1529 did Spain and Portugal address their competing interests in the east concerning the contentious 'Moluccas issue'?

15. Captain William Anderson (d.2007) served four terms in Congress but is best known for commanding which vessel in a feat of August 1958 dubbed 'the American answer to the Sputniks'?

1. Auguste Piccard
2. Sir Richard Burton
3. Easter Island/Rapa Nui. It was Easter Sunday
4. Zheng He (*zheng* = 'harmony')
5. Dinis Dias
6. Staking territorial claims. They were large stone crosses inscribed with the coat of arms of Portugal
7. Lost City of Z
8. William Dampier
9. Roald Amundsen
10. (Vasco Nunez de) Balboa
11. Biscuits
12. Sir Wally Herbert
13. James Clark Ross
14. Treaty of Zaragoza
15. *Nautilus* – the first submarine to complete a submerged transit to the North Pole

History and Politics

Ancient World: History and Politics Quiz 1

1. Which ruler fought King Porus of the Hindu Paurava kingdom on the east bank of the Hydaspes (Jhelum) River in 326 BC?

2. Which empire in South Asia (30–375) was formed under Kujula Kadphises and had Bactrian for its official language?

3. Landing on the southern coast in 495, Cerdic is the traditional founder of which Anglo-Saxon kingdom?

4. In 1st-century AD Rome, the *Veneta* (Blue) and the *Prasina* (Green) emerged to rival the established *Albata* (White) and *Russata* (Red) factions. They competed in which sport?

5. The University of al-Qarawiyyin is the world's oldest continuously operating degree-granting university, having been founded as a mosque in 859 in which city?

6. Which king of the Persian Achaemenid Empire, who ruled the empire at its peak, authored the Behistun Inscription on Mount Behistun in Iran's Kermanshah Province?

7. What links Cassius Chaerea, Agrippina the Younger, Julia Flavia's steward Stephanus, Narcissus the wrestler and Martialis?

8. Using only sticks and the shadows they cast, which 3rd-century BC Greek mathematician calculated the earth's circumference to be 25,000 miles, very close to the actual circumference?

9. Stricken with an eye disease, Aristodemus was ordered home before the last stand. Pantites went to recruit more troops in Thessaly and did not return until after all was lost. Therefore, they were the only two Spartan survivors of the 300 sent to fight which 480 BC battle?

10. The Lia Fáil (Coronation Stone) and Hill of Tara, the traditional seat of the High Kings of Ireland, is in which county?

11. Which King of the English was stabbed to death in 946 at a St Augustine's Day mass by an exiled thief named Leofa?

12. Which Chinese peasant revolt broke out in 184 during the reign of Eastern Han Emperor Ling? It is the opening event in Luo Guanzhong's classic novel *Romance of the Three Kingdoms*.

13. Ammianus Marcellinus thought it to be so important that he ended his history of the Roman Empire with this event. Eastern Emperor Valens was killed at which 378 battle?

14. Ctesibius invented which pre-cursor to the pipe organ?

15. Established by Augustus in 27 BC, what were the *classis Misenensis* and *classis Ravennas*?

Answers to Ancient World: History and Politics Quiz 1

1. Alexander the Great/Alexander III of the Macedon
2. Kushan Empire
3. Wessex
4. Chariot racing
5. Fes, Morocco
6. Darius I/Darius the Great (*c.*550–486 BC)
7. They all allegedly assassinated a Roman Emperor – Caligula, Claudius, Domitian, Commodus, Caracalla
8. Eratosthenes of Cyrene
9. Thermopylae
10. County Meath
11. Edmund I
12. Yellow Turban Rebellion/Yellow Scarves Rebellion – it ended in 205 with a Han victory
13. Battle of Adrianople or Battle of Hadrianopolis – Adrianople is modern Edirne in Turkey
14. Hydraulis or hydraulic organ – this water organ was invented in the 3rd century BC by the said engineer of Alexandria
15. The first and second most senior fleets of the Imperial Roman Navy

1. Which man who served as Japanese Prime Minister from 1964 until 1972 shared the 1974 Nobel Peace Prize with Sean McBride?

2. Which man became the first Prime Minister of Singapore in 1959, serving in that post for over 31 years?

3. Born to an Aymara family, in 2006 Evo Morales became the first indigenous democratically elected President of which country?

4. In 1986, which European nation's Prime Minister was assassinated while walking home from the cinema with his wife?

5. Ema Solberg and Gro Harlem Bruntland have (at different times) both been elected Prime Minister of which country?

6. Serving from the declaration of the Republic on 18 June 1953 to 14 November 1954, who was the first President of Egypt?

7. The massive riots that followed the assassination in Bogotá of which Colombian Liberal leader on 9 April 1948 were known as the Bogotazo?

8. In 1986, who succeeded Ferdinand Marcos to become the first woman President of the Philippines?

9. The first Premier of the People's Republic of China, who served in that office from 1949 until his death in 1976?

10. With 22 years in office, which Liberal, nicknamed Rex by friends and family, was the longest-serving Prime Minister in Canadian history?

11. Who was both the last President of Czechoslovakia (1989–92) and the first President of the Czech Republic?

12. The first Sikh to hold the office, which Indian economist served as the 14th Prime Minister of India from 2004 to 2014?

13. Concerned about a possible EU ban on menthol cigarettes, which former German Chancellor (1974–82) reportedly hoarded 38,000 of them?

14. Born in Amsterdam, which leader was assassinated by Dmitri Tsafendas in Cape Town in 1966?

15. Which 20th-century Prime Minister was born in Kiev in 1898 and died in Jerusalem in 1978?

1. Eisaku Sato
2. Lee Kuan Yew
3. Bolivia
4. Sweden (Olof Palme)
5. Norway
6. Muhammad Naguib
7. Jorge Eliécer Gaitán
8. Corazon Aquino
9. Zhou Enlai/Chou En-lai
10. William Lyon Mackenzie King
11. Vaclav Havel
12. Manmohan Singh (Kohli)
13. Helmut Schmidt
14. Hendrik Verwoerd – South African PM 1958–66
15. Golda Meir

1. Which future Prime Minister was appointed President of the Board of Trade in 1947 aged just 31?

2. Which district of east London gives its name to the 1981 declaration by the 'Gang of Four' which led to the formation of the Social Democratic Party?

3. Roy Jenkins, Tony Benn, Bobby Sands and Bernadette Devlin have been holders of which unofficial political title since World War II?

4. What role was played by Gillian Duffy during the 2010 general election campaign?

5. There were no ethnic minority MPs from the 1920s until which post-war general election, which saw Diane Abbott, Paul Boateng, Keith Vaz and Bernie Grant elected?

6. What was the title of the important 1969 government paper on industrial relations?

7. In what year was the first Scottish Parliament election held, with Donald Dewar becoming the inaugural First Minister?

8. Margaret Thatcher made her infamous observation that 'there is no such thing as society' in a 1987 interview with which publication?

9. Which 1954 scandal over agricultural land in Dorset led to the introduction of principles for ministerial accountability for civil servants?

10. In 1964 Harold Wilson appointed which trade unionist as the first Minister of Technology, even though he was not (at the time) sitting in Parliament?

11. Which MP for Clwyd North West challenged Margaret Thatcher for the Conservative Party leadership in 1989?

12. In which post-war general election, which it lost, did the Labour Party receive more votes than it has done in any election before or since?

13. Which politician uniquely sat in the House of Commons for the Conservatives, Labour and the SDP?

14. In which British city did Enoch Powell deliver his intensely controversial 1968 'Rivers of Blood' speech?

15. Although he used slightly different words, who in 1990 became the first Cabinet minister to resign to 'spend more time with his family' (truthfully in his case)?

Answers to British Post-War Politics:
History and Politics Quiz 3

1. Harold Wilson
2. Limehouse
3. 'Baby of the House' (i.e. youngest MP in the House of Commons)
4. Gordon Brown called her 'a bigoted woman'
5. 1987
6. 'In Place of Strife'
7. 1999
8. *Woman's Own*
9. Crichel Down
10. Frank Cousins
11. Anthony Meyer
12. 1951
13. John Horam
14. Birmingham
15. Norman Fowler

1. 'Beau Sabreur' ('handsome swordsman') was first a sobriquet for which French cavalry officer and brother-in-law of Napoleon I?

2. Which French king's army was defeated mainly due to English and Welsh archers at the 1346 Battle of Crécy?

3. After costly victories at Heraclea and Ausculum, which king of Epirus went home to Greece after a final drawn battle with Rome at Beneventum in 275 BC?

4. What did the Duke of Wellington call 'the nearest run thing you ever saw in your life'?

5. Which 'cradle of Basque culture' was bombed by the German Condor Legion on 26 April 1937?

6. Which city went to war with Modena in 1325 over a stolen wooden bucket? Beaten at the Battle of Zappolino the bucket remains in Modena's Torre del Ghirlandina.

7. Which one-eyed Hussite general (c.1360–1424) requested that his body be skinned and his skin be made into drums that would lead his followers into battle?

8. Enrolling in the Serbian army, Flora Sandes was the only British woman to officially serve as a soldier in which war?

9. Which April 1522 Italian War clash, north of Milan, saw the French army's Swiss mercenaries driven off by the Imperial forces' arquebusiers, making it arguably the first battle in which firearms were decisive?

10. The Spanish *tercio* formation of pikemen and arquebusiers was developed by Gonzalo de Cordoba, who beat the Swiss at which 1503 battle, arguably the first to be won by musketry?

11. One of the least known yet grimmest World War II battles, it was the longest battle fought by the US Army and perhaps their worst in the European theatre. 'Passchendaele with tree bursts' was Hemingway's description of which 1944–45 'green hell'?

12. The 1279 Battle of Yamen put China under whose control?

13. Nicknamed 'Mad Jack', which kilt-wearing World War II soldier was the last person in recorded military history to kill an enemy with a longbow?

14. Huamachuco (1883) was the last major battle of which war?

15. The final resting place of Prince Henry the Navigator, the Dominican Abbey of Santa Maria de Vitoria at Batalha was built to celebrate João I's historic victory at which 1385 battle?

1. Joachim Murat, king of Naples ('the Dandy King') from 1808 to 1815 and husband of Caroline Bonaparte
2. Philip VI
3. Pyrrhus of Epirus, who gave his name to a pyrrhic victory
4. Battle of Waterloo
5. Guernica
6. Bologna – Alessandro Tassoni based his 17th century mock-heroic epic *La Secchia rapita*/The stolen bucket on the events of the war of the Oaken bucket
7. Jan Žižka
8. World War I
9. Battle of Bicocca
10. Battle of Cerignola
11. Battle of Hürtgen Forest
12. Kublai Khan – the founders of the Yuan dynasty ended the rule of the Song dynasty
13. Jack Churchill, who shot a German NCO with his bow and arrow in 1940 and also captured 42 Germans armed only with his sword. His motto was 'any officer who goes into action without his sword is improperly dressed.'
14. War of the Pacific (1879–83) – Chilean forces decisively defeated those of Peru, who were allied with Bolivia
15. Battle of Aljubarrota

1. Multimillionaire Andrew Carnegie was so concerned by which British Prime Minister's lack of funds that he endowed him with an annuity of £2,000 in 1919?

2. Who was sentenced to life for shooting Roland Legrand in the chest in the Place Pigalle on 26 March 1930, a charge he always denied?

3. In 1951, which was the first African country to gain independence?

4. In either of the world wars, Oberleutnant Gunther Plüschow was the only German to do what?

5. Created by Abdullah al Asnag and active in the 1960s, what did the letters 'SY' stand for in the name of the military organisation FLOSY?

6. Also known as the Revolution of 1911 or the Chinese Revolution, what name is given to the revolution that ended the Imperial era in China?

7. Who led the military junta which siezed power from Isabel Perón in Argentina in 1976?

8. What was Operation True Blue, which took place in London on 17 April 2013?

9. Signed in 1997, the banning of what, essentially, is the concern of the Ottawa Treaty?

10. What was formed as a successor to the Organisation of African Unity with the Sirte Declaration in 1999?

11. At which World War II battle of 1944 did Wojtek, a Syrian bear, achieve legendary status carrying munitions to troops under fire?

12. Devised by Britain and France after the collapse of the Ottoman Empire, which agreement of 1916 drew up a map for the region with the various tweaks and biases therein contributing to problems and tensions that persist to this day?

13. What name (in English) has been given to the vicious battle between oligarchs for control of natural resources in 20th- and early-21st-century Russia?

14. In 1965, Charlie Perkins became the first Australian Aborigine to do what?

15. Reflecting vehicles that played a major part, what informal name was given to the last phase of the Chadian–Libyan conflict, which took place in 1987?

1. David Lloyd George
2. Papillon/Henri Charrière
3. Libya. The UN handed power to King Idris in 1951, having governed since Italy's defeat in World War II
4. Escape from an English POW camp and make it home to Germany – in World War I, he escaped from Donington Hall, Derbyshire
5. South Yemen – the Front for the Liberation of South Yemen
6. Xinhai or Hsin-hai Revolution
7. General Jorge Videla
8. Margaret Thatcher's funeral
9. Anti-personnel mines/landmines
10. African Union
11. Monte Cassino
12. Sykes–Picot Agreement
13. The Aluminium Wars
14. Graduate from an Australian university
15. The Toyota War

Film

1. What role in the *Lord of the Rings* films is played by the actor who plays Will Turner in the *Pirates of the Caribbean* series?

2. Which actor has played real-life figures with the forenames Michael (1996) and Alfred (2004) before winning an Oscar for portraying a man with the forename Oskar in a 1993 film?

3. James Cameron directed which actor as Kyle Reese in *The Terminator* (1984) and as Corporal Dwayne Hicks in *Aliens* (1986)?

4. Playing the title character in the *Machete* series of films, which actor has also starred in *Heat* (1995) and *Con Air* (1997)?

5. Who played astronaut Wally Schirra in *The Right Stuff* (1983), Detective Hal Vukovich in *The Terminator* (1984) and the android Bishop in *Aliens* (1986) and *Alien³* (1992)?

6. Which two times Oscar-winning actor co-starred with Ethan Hawke in *Training Day* (2001), Chris Pine in *Unstoppable* (2010) and Gene Hackman in *Crimson Tide* (1995)?

7. He once represented the UK in diving; which Derbyshire-born actor is now noted for a succession of all-action film roles in pictures such as *The Transporter* (2002) and *Crank* (2006)?

8. Who starred in *Mesrine* (2008) and with his wife Monica Bellucci in both *Irreversible* (2002) and *Secret Agents* (2004)?

9. Which Swiss actor played Adolf Hitler in *Downfall* (2004)?

10. Who played Jesus in *The Last Temptation of Christ* (1988) and the Green Goblin in *Spider-Man* (2002)?

11. Who made his name as Stringer Bell in *The Wire* and has since played the title role in *Mandela: Long Walk to Freedom* (2013)?

12. Which Oscar-winning actor has played Richard I in *The Lion in Winter* (1968), William Bligh in *The Bounty* (1984) and Richard Nixon in *Nixon* (1995)?

13. Appearing in *The Deer Hunter* (1978), *True Romance* (1993) and *Pulp Fiction* (1994), which New York actor memorably danced in the video for Fatboy Slim's 'Weapon of Choice' (2000)?

14. Which great Japanese actor made 16 films with the director Akira Kurosawa, including *Rashomon* (1950), *Seven Samurai* (1954) and *Yojimbo* (1961)?

15. For his role in which 1999 film did Kevin Spacey win a Best Actor Oscar for playing Lester Burnham, a middle-aged magazine writer going through something of a crisis?

Answers to Actors: Film Quiz 1

1. Legolas (Orlando Bloom)
2. Liam Neeson (Michael Collins, Alfred Kinsey and Oskar Schindler respectively)
3. Michael Biehn
4. Danny Trejo
5. Lance Henriksen
6. Denzel Washington
7. Jason Statham
8. Vincent Cassel
9. Bruno Ganz
10. Willem Dafoe
11. Idris Elba
12. Anthony Hopkins
13. Christopher Walken
14. Toshiro Mifune
15. *American Beauty*

1. Starring in *The Girl with the Dragon Tattoo* (2009), which Swedish actress played Dr Elizabeth Shaw in *Prometheus* (2012)?

2. On television she played Ling Woo in *Ally McBeal* and Joan Watson in *Elementary*. Which actress has appeared in both *Kill Bill* (2003) and *Charlie's Angels* (2000)?

3. Director Jean-Pierre Jeunet directed which actress in lead roles in *Amelie* (2001) and *A Very Long Engagement* (2004)?

4. Which English actress played Ava Gardner in *The Aviator* (2004) and the vampire Selene in the *Underworld* series of films?

5. Winning an Oscar for her role in *The Piano* (1993), who voiced Helen Parr in *The Incredibles* (2004) and played Grace Hanadarko in the TV series *Saving Grace*?

6. Which Beijing actress has had leading roles in *Crouching Tiger, Hidden Dragon* (2000), *House of Flying Daggers* (2004) and *2046* (2004)?

7. Who played both Isabella of France in *Braveheart* (1995) and the oil heiress Elektra King in *The World is Not Enough* (1999)?

8. Which actress played the lead in *Run Lola Run* (1998) and Marie Helena Kreutz in *The Bourne Supremacy* (2004)?

9. She played Mallory Knox in *Natural Born Killers* (1994) and Danielle Bowden in *Cape Fear* (1991). Who has also fronted a rock band called the Licks and released her own solo material?

10. Who played the cheerleader Claire Bennet on the NBC series *Heroes* (2006–10) and Juliette Barnes in the TV series *Nashville*?

11. An Indan winner of Miss World in 1994, who became a hugely successful Bollywood actress and married Indian actor and TV host Abhishek Bachchan in 2007?

12. Who starred as Jen in *Dawson's Creek* before picking up Oscar nominations for roles in *Brokeback Mountain* (2005), *Blue Valentine* (2010) and *My Week with Marilyn* (2011)?

13. Born with the forename Susan, which actress has played Dr Grace Augustine and Ellen Ripley in major sci-fi films?

14. She won an Oscar nomination for playing Briony Tallis, the complex child in *Atonement* (2007). Who played a highly trained teenage assassin in *Hanna* (2011)?

15. Noted for playing Sue Storm/Invisible Woman in the *Fantastic Four* films, who reprised her role as dancer Nancy Callahan in *Sin City: A Dame to Kill For*, the sequel to *Sin City*?

1. Noomi Rapace
2. Lucy Liu
3. Audrey Tautou
4. Kate Beckinsale
5. Holly Hunter
6. Zhang Ziyi
7. Sophie Marceau
8. Franka Potente
9. Juliette Lewis
10. Hayden Panettiere
11. Aishwarya Rai
12. Michelle Williams
13. Sigourney Weaver – *Avatar* and *Alien* (plus sequels)
14. Saoirse Ronan
15. Jessica Alba

1. What is the surname of siblings Garry and Penny who have individually directed films including *Big* (1988), *Pretty Woman* (1990) and *The Princess Diaries* (2001)?

2. Which highly distinctive British director has made films including *The Draughtsman's Contract* (1982), *A Zed and Two Noughts* (1985) and *The Cook, the Thief, His Wife and Her Lover* (1989)?

3. Almost sharing both names with a famous explorer, who directed *Mrs Doubtfire* (1993) and the first two *Harry Potter* films?

4. Which director won Best Picture Oscars for *Brokeback Mountain* (2005) and *Life of Pi* (2012) and the Best Foreign Language Film Oscar for *Crouching Tiger, Hidden Dragon* (2000)?

5. For which 2007 film did brothers Joel and Ethan Coen share three Oscars – Best Picture (with Scott Rudin), Best Director and Best Screenplay?

6. Which Japanese director made 30 films including *Kagemusha* (1980) and *Ran* (1985)?

7. What nationality is film director Abbas Kiarostami, who won the Cannes Palme d'Or in 1997 with *Taste of Cherry*?

8. Which American has directed or co-directed film series including *Spy Kids*, *Machete* and *Sin City*?

9. *Klute* (1971), *All the President's Men* (1986) and *Sophie's Choice* (1982) were all directed by which New Yorker?

10. With the forenames Jeffrey Jacob, which director has made multiple films in both the *Star Trek* and *Mission: Impossible* franchises?

11. Directed by Katherine Bigelow, in which 1991 film does Johnny Utah (Keanu Reeves) pursue a group of Californian surfers suspected of robbing banks to fund their beach lifestyle?

12. Which director has acted in his own films playing Jimmie in *Pulp Fiction* (1994) and Mr Brown in *Reservoir Dogs* (1992)?

13. Born in Tokyo, which animator and film director co-founded Studio Ghibli and made noted films including *Princess Mononoke* (1997), *Spirited Away* (2001) and *Howl's Moving Castle* (2004)?

14. *Wadjda* is a 2012 film written and directed by Haifaa al-Mansour and is regarded as the first feature-length film made by a female director from which country?

15. Which US director won an Oscar for directing *Out of Africa* (1985) and was Oscar-nominated for *They Shoot Horses, Don't They?* (1969) and *Tootsie* (1982)?

1. Marshall
2. Peter Greenaway
3. Chris Columbus
4. Ang Lee
5. *No Country for Old Men*
6. Akira Kurosawa
7. Iranian
8. Robert Rodriquez
9. Alan J. Pakula
10. J.J. Abrams
11. *Point Break*
12. Quentin Tarantino
13. Hayao Miyazaki
14. Saudi Arabia
15. Sydney Pollack

1. The 1969 drama *The Night of Counting the Years* concerns a late-19th-century hunt for a gang of tomb-robbers. It is widely seen as one of which country's most important films?

2. Telling the story of five Lebanese women struggling against social taboos in war-ravaged Beiruit, what is the English title of Nadine Labaki's 2007 directorial debut?

3. Djibril Diop Mambéty's 1992 film *Hyènes*, adapted which play?

4. Which Clint Eastwood western was remade in Japan as a 2013 *jidaigeki* (period drama) film with Ken Watanabe in the lead role of Jubee Kamata?

5. Quentin Tarantino's *Reservoir Dogs* borrowed heavily from scenes and plot in which 1987 Hong Kong film, directed by Ringo Lam and starring Chow Yun-fat?

6. Who directed the 2000 Taipei-set film *A One and a Two*?

7. Marketed as the first 'ramen western', which 1985 gastronomic comedy by director Juzo Itami is named after the Japanese word for dandelion?

8. Who played Valentina in *La Notte* (1961), Assunta in *The Girl with the Pistol* (1968), and Dea in *Stardust* (1973)?

9. Which Pedro Almodóvar film features a stage production of *A Streetcar Named Desire* that has tragic consequences for Manuela (Cecilia Roth)?

10. Which 1989 song by the Pixies has lyrics based on Luis Buñuel and Salvador Dalí's shocking surreal short film *Un Chien Andalou*?

11. Which Swede directed the 2013 film *We Are the Best!* – a tale of three teenage girls who form a punk band in 1980s Stockholm?

12. The leader of the *Magnificent Seven* was a gunman called Chris, but what was the equivalent swordsman character's name in the Japanese original *Seven Samurai*?

13. Which critically acclaimed female director has been a key figure in the 'New Argentine Cinema', with such films as *The Holy Girl* (2004) and *The Headless Woman* (2008)?

14. Re-released on the big screen in 2014, this 1948 domestic drama, directed by Fei Mu and starring Wei Wei and Li Wei, is often cited as one of the greatest Chinese films. Give its English title.

15. *Utu* is a 1983 New Zealand film set amidst the British–Maori conflicts of the 1870s, a 'Maori western', restored and recut as *Utu Redux* for its 30th anniversary. What does *Utu* mean?

1. Egypt – the film is alternately titled *The Mummy*/Arabic: *al-Mummia*
2. *Caramel*
3. *The Visit/Der Besuch der alten Dame* by Swiss playwright Friedrich Dürrenmatt
4. *Unforgiven*
5. *City on Fire*
6. Edward Yang/Yang Dechang – it is also known by the title *Yi Yi*
7. *Tampopo*
8. Monica Vitti
9. *All About My Mother/Todo sobre mi madre*
10. 'Debaser'
11. Lukas Moodysson
12. Kambei
13. Lucrecia Martel
14. *Spring in a Small Town*
15. Vengeance

1. Which Bond girl was played by Ursula Andress in a 1967 non-canonical Bond film, and in 2006 by Eva Green?

2. Which Kentucky location is the setting for the denouement of *Goldfinger*?

3. Miss Moneypenny was only given a forename in *Skyfall*. What was it?

4. Which Swedish actress was a Bond girl in both *The Man with The Golden Gun* and *Octopussy*, and also appeared as an extra in *A View to a Kill*?

5. Who was the youngest actor to play James Bond in the Bond films?

6. 'London Calling' by the Clash makes a slightly incongruous appearance in the soundtrack of which Bond movie, the last in which Bond is played by Pierce Brosnan?

7. The non-canonical Bond film *Never Say Never Again* was a remake of which early canonical Bond film?

8. He made his name directing the sequels to the classic documentary *Seven Up* but who also directed *The World is Not Enough*?

9. In the 2006 remake of *Casino Royale*, in which European country is the title casino said to be located?

10. Which Puerto Rican actor played the villainous Dario in *Licence to Kill*, becoming one of the youngest actors to play a Bond villain?

11. In which Bond film did Margaret Thatcher impersonator Janet Brown make a brief appearance as the Iron Lady at the film's conclusion?

12. Said as he opens a bottle of champagne, which recurring character's only line of dialogue in the Bond films was 'Well, here's to us'?

13. What is the name of the deranged industrialist memorably played by Christopher Walken in *A View to a Kill*?

14. Who is the first character to say the words 'shaken, not stirred' in a James Bond film?

15. One of only three actors to play a Bond baddie and a Bond ally in different films, who played Brad Whitaker in *The Living Daylights* and the CIA agent Jack Wade in *Goldeneye* and *Tomorrow Never Dies*?

1. Vesper Lynd
2. Fort Knox
3. Eve
4. Maud Adams
5. George Lazenby
6. *Die Another Day*
7. *Thunderball*
8. Michael Apted
9. Montenegro
10. Benicio del Toro
11. *For Your Eyes Only*
12. Jaws
13. Max Zorin
14. Dr (Julius) No
15. Joe Don Baker (the other actors are Charles Grey and Walter Gotell)

Nature

1. The fattest and most southern of all seals, what is the only seal that can give birth to twin pups and the only seal that stays in Antarctica 365 days of the year?
2. 'Benjamin' died in 1936. He was the last known survivor of his species and ended his days in Hobart Zoo. What animal was he?
3. What name links a beagle and pug 'designer dog', first bred by Wallace Havens in the 1980s, and a baby monotreme (echidna or platypus), in the period between hatching and weaning?
4. Also called the Indian bison, what is the largest extant bovine?
5. Prized as one of the lightest and warmest wools in the world, qiviut is the soft underfur of which Arctic mammal?
6. Starting in the Bering and Chukchi Seas and arriving in the warm-water of Mexico's Baja Peninsula in a round trip that is over 12,000 miles long, which whale's migration route is said to be the longest known mammal migration?
7. Droughtmaster, Murray Grey and Belmont Red are Australian breeds of which farm animal?
8. The ape rescue centre Monkey World is located near Wareham in which county?
9. With over 40 English variations out of 64 that are cited, which big cat has held the Guinness World Record for the animal with most names?
10. Which social pack animal is the largest African canid?
11. Which invasive species was introduced to Hawaii and various Caribbean islands by sugar cane farmers in the 1880s because they were overrun by another invasive species – the rat? They have driven at least seven species of animal to extinction in Puerto Rico and a further five in Jamaica. Ironically, it is facing extinction in its own natural environment.
12. Which Great Dane dog, owned by Norman Scott, was shot dead during the 1970s Jeremy Thorpe scandal?
13. In 1864, Édouard Lartet discovered a woolly mammoth engraving on a piece of mammoth ivory in which cave in Dordogne?
14. The Greater Madagascar hedgehog, lowland streaked and Tailless, also known as the common, are species of what?
15. Which animal – *Felis silvestris lybica* – is considered the ancestor of all domestic cats?

1. Weddell seal – named after the British sealing captain who also gave his name to the Weddell Sea
2. Thylacine/Tasmanian tiger
3. Puggle
4. Gaur / *Bos gaurus* – the tallest species of wild cattle, its domesticated form is named gayal or mithun
5. Muskox/*Ovibos moschatus*
6. Gray Whale/*Eschrichtius robustus*/Eastern Pacific Gray Whale
7. Cattle
8. Dorset
9. Puma/Cougar/Mountain lion/Catamount/*Puma concolor*
10. Painted dog/*Lycaon pictus*/African wild dog/Cape hunting dog
11. Small Asian mongoose / *Herpestes javanicus* or western subspecies Small Indian mongoose / *Herpestes auropunctatus*
12. Rinka
13. Abri de la Madeleine (the Magdalene shelter)
14. Tenree
15. African wildcat/Near Eastern wildcat

1. Its Indonesian name, *malu malu*, means 'shy one'. It is known for its large eyes and stores its toxin in an elbow patch. What is the world's only poisonous primate?

2. Which warbler (*Seiurus aurocapillus*) is the title subject of a 1916 Robert Frost poem?

3. Native to New Guinea and north-east Australia, what is the third largest and the second heaviest living bird?

4. Which passerine birds form the genus *Bombycilla*? Noted for their soft, silky plumage, there are three species: Bohemian, Japanese and Cedar.

5. Which small, ugly scorpaeniform fish of the Triglidae family are also known as 'sea robins'?

6. Which botanist began his 'Expert' book series with *Be Your Own Gardening Expert* in 1958?

7. The bodega El Carpicho, near León in Spain, serves what *Time* magazine has called 'the perfect steak'. It is a huge *chuletón* taken from the central rib section of which ox breed?

8. Known by the binomial name *Macrocheira kaempferi*, when fully grown its leg span can reach 4 metres, with a body size of up to 37 cm. What is the largest known arthropod?

9. The leaves are used to make filé powder, a spice used in making various types of gumbo. The roots of which plant were used to flavour root beer, until it was banned by the FDA?

10. What are the ampullae of Lorenzini?

11. *Hydrurga leptonyx* is said to be the most dangerous pinniped and the only species with a reputation for making apparently unprovoked attacks on people. What is its common name?

12. Which rare species of Andean bromeliad is the largest herb, with a trunk that is up to 4 metres high? It also takes around 150 years to bloom, making it the slowest plant to flower.

13. Which creature gave its name to the WW II project, later Project Orcon (for 'organic control'), that was behaviourist B.F. Skinner's attempt to develop an 'organic' guided missile?

14. Also called the weasel cat or otter cat, which short-legged agile climber of the *Puma* genus has an unspotted coat and short, rounded ears? It ranges from south Texas to southern Brazil.

15. Used for cordage, what stiff fibre of the Mexican agave is named after the Yucatán port from which it was exported?

Answers to Animals and Plants: Nature Quiz 2

1. Slow loris
2. Ovenbird – the poem is called 'The Oven Bird'
3. Southern cassowary (*Casuarius casuarius*) – only the ostrich and emu are bigger
4. Waxwing
5. Gurnard
6. Dr D.G. Hessayon (as in David Gerald)
7. *Rubia Gallega* ('Galician Blond')
8. Japanese spider crab
9. Sassafras
10. Electroreceptors, which enable sharks, rays and other cartilaginous fish to detect electromagnetic fields and temperature gradients
11. Leopard seal
12. Puya
13. Pigeon, as in Project Pigeon
14. Jaguarundi/*Puma yagouaroundi*
15. Sisal/*Agave sisalana*

1. Extremely hard to spot, which bird may be seen at twilight performing a distinctive 'roding' display flight?
2. In 2014, Lisa One was hatched from a crushed egg bringing the number of surviving specimens of which bird (the heaviest surviving parrot and the only flightless one) to 125?
3. The near-flightless kagu is an endangered bird restricted in the wild to which island in the Pacific Ocean?
4. *Otis tarda* is probably the heaviest of all flying birds. Once native to Great Britain, efforts have been made to reintroduce which bird that features on Wiltshire's coat of arms?
5. From which species is the oldest British bird ever recorded with an 'adult' ringed on Bardsey Island in 1957 being recaptured in the same location 50 years and 11 months later, in 2008?
6. Which tern-like bird (family Rynchopidae) is noted for having a lower mandible significantly longer than the upper, which enables a spectacular method of feeding at the water's surface?
7. A substantial fraction of the world's population of which seabird, Europe's biggest, nest on Boreray in the St Kilda archipelago?
8. There are five species of Cinclidae worldwide. Which birds, that forage for small animal prey in and along the margins of fast-flowing freshwater streams and rivers, are these?
9. Although not kosher, which bird has been chosen to be the national bird of Israel?
10. The yellow-browed, chestnut, Japanese, Gila and great spotted are among the many species of which bird?
11. Thought to assist with camouflage, what name is given to the inconspicuous plumage worn by some adult male birds for a short period after the breeding season is over?
12. Found on many birds, in which general area of their bodies are the stiff, hair-like rictal bristles to be found?
13. *Eudyptes chrysolophus*, the world's most common penguin, gets which English name from its crest of yellow plumes?
14. Which American nightjar is the only bird in the world known to hibernate for extended periods, reacting to cold weather by entering a state of torpor?
15. Which large sea eagle, *Haliaeetus pelagicus*, takes its English name from a German naturalist (1709–46) who also gave his surname to other creatures including a sea cow and a sea lion?

1. (Eurasian) woodcock – *Scolopax rusticolam*
2. Kakapo
3. New Caledonia
4. Great bustard
5. Manx shearwater – *Puffinus puffinus*
6. Skimmer – black, African and Indian
7. (Northern) gannet – *Morus bassanus*
8. Dippers
9. Hoopoe – *Upupa epops*
10. Woodpeckers – Picidae
11. Eclipse plumage
12. The bill/beak/mouth. With insect-eating birds they may provide protection against struggling prey and may detect the movements of their victims
13. Macaroni penguin
14. Common poorwill – *Phalaenoptilus nuttali*
15. Steller's sea eagle (Georg Wilhelm Steller)

1. Highly prized as a food delicacy in Japan, which creatures are known to scientists as holothurians?

2. Which living things make up the kingdom Rhodophyta?

3. Gaining energy by repeatedly crossing the boundary between air masses of significantly different velocities, which two-word term describes a flying technique which enables oceanic birds such as the albatross to glide just above the waves for hours at a time?

4. In Japanese fishermen's lore, the slender oarfish (*Regalecus russelii*) is known as the 'Messenger from the Sea God's Palace', as their appearance both in the sea and washed up on shore is thought to be a portent of what?

5. Reaching 18 metres and weighing up to 50 tonnes, which is by far the largest of the toothed whales?

6. Which animals (c. 15,000 species) make up the phylum Porifera?

7. Which fish, *Prionace glauca,* is believed to be the widest-ranging of all vertebrates in the world?

8. Landlady's wig, Neptune's necklace and oyster thief are examples of which marine life form?

9. There are two species in the rare genus *Latimeria* or coelacanth. One is found off the south-east of Africa. The other, *Latimeria menadoensis*, is found in which nation's waters?

10. Which island is noted for the enormous populations of a namesake red land crab which make spectacular annual mass migrations to the sea to spawn?

11. Jellyfish, anemones and corals all belong to which phylum of the animal kingdom?

12. With six species in the family, which are the only surviving cephalopods with a true external shell?

13. Which island is named 'Talamh an Eisc' (Land of Fish) in Irish Gaelic?

14. Certain limpets repeatedly return to precisely the same spot on a rock just before the tide ebbs, with their shells growing, over time, to perfectly match the rock's contours. What two-word name is given to this location?

15. Who published a Gulf Stream chart in 1770, after investigating the anomaly that mailboats sailing from the US to England were consistently faster than English boats sailing to the US?

Answers to Marine Life: Nature Quiz 4

1. Sea cucumbers/sea slugs/namako/*bêches-de-mer*/sea rats
2. Red seaweeds
3. Dynamic soaring
4. Earthquakes
5. The sperm whale – *Physeter macrocephalus*
6. Sponges
7. Blue shark
8. Seaweed/algae
9. Indonesia – the Indonesian Coelacanth
10. Christmas Island (red crab) – their numbers are threatened by the accidentally introduced yellow crazy ant
11. Cnidarians – from the greek *Knide* meaning 'nettle' because of their ability to sting
12. Nautilus
13. Newfoundland
14. Home scar
15. Benjamin Franklin

1. The bandy bandy has alternating black and white or yellowish bands. In which country will you find it?

2. With most of its diet made up of other snakes, what is the world's longest venomous snake?

3. In what country were remains of the giant snake *Titanoboa cerrejonensis* found in a layer of rock at the Cerréjon coal mine?

4. What is the link between the common 'English' names for the snakes *Dendroaspis polylepis* and *Agkistrodon piscivorus* (aka the water moccasin)?

5. Which South American genus of snakes are the longest vipers in the world?

6. Found in the wild on all continents except Antarctica, with 300-plus genera and 1,900-plus species, which is the largest family of snakes?

7. Certain oophagous snakes may have hypapophyses, special adaptations to some of their vertebrae which aid them in eating what items?

8. Which snake, found in Africa, produces the largest litters of any snake with as many as 150 newborns being recorded?

9. On a snake, what is protected by a brille?

10. Which alternative name for the grass snake is indicated by its scientific name *Natrix natrix*?

11. What is the reason for vipers not being found in the wild in Australia?

12. Which heavy and stout viper has the longest fangs of any venomous snake?

13. What name, derived from its very distinctive method of locomotion across sandy ground, is given to the rattlesnake *Crotalus cerastes*?

14. *Eunectes murinus* is the heaviest species of snake in the world. How is it more commonly known?

15. Which of a snake's senses is assisted by its Jacobson's organ?

Answers to Snakes: Nature Quiz 5

1. Australia
2. King cobra – *Ophiophagus hannah*
3. Colombia
4. Both names arise from the colour of their gaping mouths. They are the black mamba and the cottonmouth – black and white mouths respectively
5. Bushmaster – *Lachesis*
6. Colubrids/colubridae
7. Eggs – having swallowed a large egg, the spines are used to cut it open. 'Oophagous' means 'egg eating'
8. Puff adder – *Bitis arietans*
9. The eye – it's a transparent protective layer
10. Water snake – *Natrix* means swimmer
11. Continental drift – a timing issue: Australia was 'on the move' before vipers evolved, and could populate it
12. Gaboon viper – *Bitis gabonica*
13. Sidewinder
14. (Green) Anaconda
15. Smell – the flicking tongue wafts odour-laden air to the roof of the mouth

General Knowledge: Fiendishly Difficult

1. What is the first element mentioned in Tom Lehrer's humorous song 'The Elements'?
2. Which Hungarian horse of the 19th century won every one of the 54 races she ran?
3. It was unusual because he is white: Guy Scott was appointed Vice-President of which southern African nation in 2011?
4. The 5th-century BC Greek philosopher Diagoras of Melos was an early adherent of what school of thought?
5. Which Norwegian writer has won acclaim for his controversially titled six-volume autobiographical series of works *My Struggle*?
6. X is a border town in the Netherlands. A sizeable chunk of its territory is a Belgian exclave called X-Hertog, while the Dutch bits are called X-Nassau. Name X.
7. The title of which famously unsuccessful BBC television show of the early 1980s referred to Felixstowe, Gothenburg and Amsterdam?
8. Which 29-letter word was used in 2012 by Jacob Rees-Mogg in a House of Commons debate about the EU, becoming the longest word to feature in 'Hansard'?
9. Which Japanese architect designed the notorious Pruitt–Igoe housing project in St Louis which was demolished in 1972, almost 30 years before an even more famous work of his was destroyed in very different circumstances?
10. What constant did Einstein add to the theory of general relativity to achieve a static universe, describing it as his 'biggest blunder' once it became clear the universe was expanding?
11. Which Italian composer's 1782 comic opera *The Barber of Seville* was comprehensively eclipsed over 30 years later by Giaocchino Rossini's version?
12. The CCR, the CCX and the Agera are models of car made by which Swedish manufacturer of hypercars?
13. Eleanor of Aquitaine was married to Henry II of England, and which King of France?
14. Which film won most Academy Awards without winning Best Picture?
15. The herb *Mentha pulegium*, which is used in infusions but in high doses can be highly toxic, is known by what ten-letter name?

Answers to General Knowledge:
Fiendishly Difficult Quiz 1

1. Antimony
2. Kincsem
3. Zambia
4. Atheism
5. Karl Ove Knausgård
6. Baarle
7. *Triangle* (it was about a ferry operating between those ports)
8. Floccinaucinihilipilification
9. Minoru Yamasaki (the other work was the World Trade Center)
10. Cosmological constant
11. Giovanni Paisiello
12. Koenigsegg
13. Louis VII
14. *Cabaret*
15. Pennyroyal

1. Bulgur, parsley, mint, tomato and spring onion, and a seasoning of lemon juice and olive oil are the common ingredients of which Middle Eastern salad?

2. Which Quebec-born singer with an English stage surname is one of the highest selling French-language acts of all time?

3. Which spoken greeting, common in India, is usually accompanied by a slight bow made with hands pressed together?

4. Executed at the age of 33 in 1936, which Spanish lawyer and politician founded the Falangist party?

5. Robert Shields, who died in 2007, created one of the longest examples of what between 1972 and 1997, when he had a stroke?

6. Thought to be named after a chemical element mined locally, which Colorado town plays host to an international film festival?

7. Which Swedish ski-jumper is noted for popularising the 'V' style of ski-jumping?

8. In 1832, which French caricaturist and painter was imprisoned for a caricature of King Louis Philippe?

9. Which French noble and diplomat (1728–1810) spent the final 33 years of his life claiming to be a woman, although at death was certified anatomically male?

10. Consisting of cities including Amsterdam, Rotterdam, The Hague and Utrecht, which conurbation is one of the larger European cities when taken in totality?

11. Starring Steven van Zandt as relocated mobster Frank Tagliano, what was the first drama series produced by Netflix?

12. What was the surname of the father and son musicologists John and Alan, who between them collected thousands of examples of folk music from around the world?

13. John F. Kennedy's '. . . ask not what your country can do for you; ask what you can do for your country' is an example of which figure of speech, where elements of a clause are reversed for effect?

14. Thought to be a now-extinct variety of the genus *Ferula*, which plant was used in antiquity as a seasoning and a medicine?

15. What name is given to the region of Mars which includes various interesting hill and valley formations, and most famously a rock formation in the shape of a human face?

Answers to General Knowledge:
Fiendishly Difficult Quiz 2

1. Tabbouleh
2. Mylène Farmer
3. Namaste or namaskar or namaskaram
4. José Primo de Rivera
5. A diary
6. Telluride
7. Jan Boklöv
8. Honoré Daumier
9. (Charles), Chevalier d'Éon (de Beaumont)
10. Randstad
11. *Lilyhammer*
12. Lomax
13. Chiasmus
14. Silphium or Silphion
15. Cydonia

1. Which German choreographer died in 2009 of cancer in Wuppertal, having been associated with the Tanztheater in that city?

2. Which 'living fossil' found in the Namib Desert only ever has two leaves, each of which grow up to 9 metres in length, and typically fray into many smaller strands?

3. Which US soprano (1868–1944) was famous for her complete lack of singing ability?

4. Which word was coined by humorist H.L. Mencken to mean a stripper?

5. Which uninhabited Pacific coral island is a territory of the US, and best known as the destination Amelia Earhart never reached?

6. The two-word name of which chain of holiday resorts has both words misspelt in British English?

7. Which 1960s television series concerned a teenage girl originally from Belgrade called Julia, who moves to a stud farm in the country?

8. Which town near Moscow was from 1956 home to the Soviet bloc's Joint Institute for Nuclear Research, and gives its name to a chemical element?

9. Which Catholic priest (1891–1979) broadcast to more than 30 million Americans each week in the 1930s, although eventually his career disintegrated after he veered in an anti-Semitic direction?

10. Which San Diego-born rugby player is by some margin the all-time leading points scorer in the Heineken Cup?

11. Which US rock band broke the record for most weeks on the Billboard Hot 100 with their 2012 hit 'Radioactive'?

12. Which cartoon character, a 6-year-old boy, gets extremely defensive whenever an undescribed earlier event called 'the Noodle Incident' is mentioned?

13. When asked why he robbed banks, he apocryphally said, 'Because that's where the money is.' Which US bank robber gives his name to a rule of focusing on areas with likely high returns, or ruling out obvious explanations first?

14. Which 2013 made-for-TV B-movie about a waterspout that deposits certain sea creatures in Los Angeles went viral on Twitter?

15. What was found in 1991, just inside Italian territory, by two German tourists, and is now displayed in a museum in the Italian town of Bolzano?

Answers to General Knowledge:
Fiendishly Difficult Quiz 3

1. Pina Bausch
2. Welwitschia
3. Florence Foster Jenkins
4. Ecdysiast
5. Howland Island
6. Center Parcs
7. *The White Horses*
8. Dubna
9. Charles Coughlin
10. Ronan O'Gara
11. Imagine Dragons
12. Calvin (from *Calvin and Hobbes*)
13. Willie Sutton
14. *Sharknado*
15. The body of Ötzi

1. In 2011 which US singer earned notoriety with her famously bad song 'Friday', which went viral on YouTube?

2. Which of the Aleutian Islands was the site of the only World War II battle fought on an incorporated territory of the United States?

3. Which African mammal of the genus *Madoqua* is named after its alarm call?

4. Along with Mauritania, which is the only country whose currency unit is not subdivided into a power of ten subunits?

5. Which artist is also known by the name Bob and Roberta Smith?

6. Which fictional airline has been used as the stock airline in many television shows and films (most notably *Lost*), to circumvent the problem that no real airline wishes to be associated with fictional crashes and disasters?

7. In 1953, which French politician founded the Union de Défense des Commerçants et Artisans (UDCA), which believed in low taxes and the protection of small owner-managed businesses?

8. What two-word English term is given to the mystery addressee of a love letter written by Ludwig van Beethoven in 1812?

9. What Ancient Greek name is given to the act of acting against one's better judgement through being weak-willed?

10. Which professor at the Institute of Advanced Studies, Princeton became in 1990 the only physicist to be awarded a Fields Medal?

11. Which Irish-American Harvard student became the first Olympic champion since the 4th-century AD (probably) when he won the triple jump, the first event in 1896?

12. Which town in Bosnia-Herzegovina, close to the Croatian border, became from 1981 a site of pilgrimage for Catholics following a reported apparition of the Virgin Mary?

13. What name is given to the Japanese abacus, operation of which is learnt by all Japanese schoolchildren?

14. Until 2009, an elusive 'toaster' left a half-drunk bottle of cognac and three roses at the grave of which US writer on that writer's birthday every year?

15. Which English film actor killed himself in 1972 in Spain, leaving a suicide note beginning, 'Dear World, I am leaving because I am bored'?

Answers to General Knowledge:
Fiendishly Difficult Quiz 4

1. Rebecca Black
2. Attu
3. Dik-dik
4. Madagascar
5. Patrick Brill
6. Oceanic
7. Pierre Poujade
8. Immortal beloved
9. Akrasia
10. Edward Witten
11. James Connolly
12. Medjugorje
13. Soroban
14. Edgar Allan Poe
15. George Sanders

1. Although other flights take longer, the longest scheduled flight by distance is from Sydney to which US airport?

2. Examples include ketchup: what name is given to a fluid which is viscous when static but flows more easily when shaken?

3. Which Yemeni World Heritage Site is known as 'the Manhattan of the Desert' for containing about 500 'tower houses' of about 5 to 11 storeys in height?

4. Which US war correspondent is best known for his 1977 work *Dispatches*?

5. Which Norwegian-American is remembered for his invention of the outboard motor for boats?

6. A performer of Estonia's winning entry in 2001, which singer was the first and so far only black winner of the Eurovision Song Contest?

7. What was the name of the sports and popular culture website Bill Simmons set up in 2011, taken from the forename of an early-20th-century US sportswriter?

8. What is Swiss explorer Johann Ludwig Burckhardt known for rediscovering in 1812?

9. Which US pianist earned fame in 1958 aged 23 when he won the International Tchaikovsky Piano Competition in Moscow?

10. Which character in *Breaking Bad* uses the restaurant chain Los Pollos Hermanos as a front?

11. Contrasted with mutualism (where both organisms benefit) and parasitism (where one organism is harmed), what type of symbiosis where one organism benefits and the other is left neutral?

12. He died aged just 52; which British film director directed the classic Ealing comedy *Kind Hearts and Coronets* but is now almost forgotten?

13. Which suburb of Johannesburg gives its name to the trial which saw leading members of the African National Congress, including Nelson Mandela, sentenced to life in prison?

14. Which temple, originally built 15 kilometres south of Aswan, was in 1968 moved in entirety to Madrid?

15. The paradox that people prefer a lottery with known probabilities to one with unknown probabilities is named after which economist, better known for leaking the Pentagon Papers?

Answers to General Knowledge:
Fiendishly Difficult Quiz 5

1. Dallas/Fort Worth
2. Thixotropic
3. Shibam
4. Michael Herr
5. Ole Evinrude
6. Dave Benton or Efrén Eugene Benita
7. Grantland
8. The ruins of Petra
9. Harvey 'Van' Cliburn
10. Gustavo 'Gus' Fring
11. Commensalism
12. Robert Hamer
13. Rivonia
14. Temple of Debod
15. Daniel Ellsberg

1. Which three-word phrase is used in US television to describe an episode of a drama dealing with a controversial social issue?
2. Also called the Manchurian incident, what is the name of the 1931 incident which provided a pretext for Japan's invasion of Manchuria?
3. Which 2001 US musical film is about a fictional rock band fronted by Hansel Schmidt, an East German transgender singer?
4. The concepts of the 'role model' and the 'self-fulfilling prophecy' were all devised by which US sociologist?
5. Who in 1987 wrote the organ piece *As Slow As Possible*, a performance of which began in Germany in 2001 and will last for 639 years?
6. Which British modern artist is the first person in the world to have an antenna built into his skull?
7. Which fish is the subject of lurid stories that it is able to swim up an arc of urine and into a man's urethra?
8. Which Latin writer is perhaps best known for his bawdy prose narrative *The Golden Ass*?
9. An example is 'ex-patriot' for 'expatriate' – what term is given to a substitution of word(s) for word(s) that sound similar or identical but retain a plausible meaning?
10. Which Englishman was the only Test cricketer whose Test batting average never dropped below 60?
11. In June 2014 what new Indian state was carved out of Andhra Pradesh, with the two states sharing Hyderabad as capital for an interim period?
12. The second-largest city in Mauritania, which Atlantic port has become the world's largest ship graveyard, with over 300 derelict ships sitting in its bay?
13. In robotics, who gives his name to the paradox that the apparently simplest human skills such as face recognition require vastly more computational resources than high-level analytical skills?
14. In the plural it is the surname of a Formula One driver who competed until 2011 – what name is given to traditional drystone huts with a conical roof found in Apulia, Italy?
15. The Dane Thomas Vinterberg was one of the co-founders of which avant-garde movement in 1995?

Answers to General Knowledge:
Fiendishly Difficult Quiz 6

1. Very special episode
2. Mukden Incident
3. *Hedwig and the Angry Inch*
4. Robert K. Merton
5. John Cage
6. Neil Harbisson
7. Candiru
8. Lucius Apuleius
9. Eggcorn
10. Herbert Sutcliffe
11. Telangana
12. Nouadhibou
13. Hans Moravec
14. Trullo (trulli in the plural)
15. Dogme '95

1. Which desert rodent does not drink water at all in the wild, getting sufficient moisture from the food it eats?

2. Which British architect designed a number of important British houses including the remodelling of Cragside in Rothbury, Northumberland?

3. What French name is given to a pinnacle of ice caused by inter-secting crevasses on a glacier?

4. Which 1507 map, named after its creator, was the first to use the name 'America'?

5. Occurring seven weeks after Passover, which Jewish festival celebrates God's handing down of the Torah on Mount Sinai?

6. Which fictional Alaskan town was the setting for the drama series *Northern Exposure*?

7. Which 1971 winner of *Opportunity Knocks* became the following year the youngest person to have a UK number one album aged 12, a record he still holds?

8. In 2010, which actor and his wife sought asylum in Canada, claiming that they were in danger of being killed by 'Hollywood star whackers' were they to remain in the US?

9. Which soldier, with the title Duke of Addis Ababa, succeeded Mussolini as Italian Prime Minister in July 1943, although remained in power less than a year?

10. Which member of the US House of Representatives was the only congressperson to vote against the US entry into both world wars?

11. Which song cycle by Gustav Mahler is based on poems written by Friedrich Rückert on the death of two of his children?

12. Which Nobel Prize-winning physicist joined up with his son to develop the idea that an asteroid impact caused the extinction of the dinosaurs?

13. Canadian Kyle MacDonald began a series of trades, beginning with a small object, and eventually ended up with a house. What was the object he began the series with, and also the name of the website he created to publicise his exploits?

14. Which thief in Shakespeare's *The Winter's Tale* was a 'snapper-up of unconsidered trifles'?

15. Which US baseball team have not won the World Series since 1908, their trophyless drought since then being the longest in US professional sports?

1. Jerboa
2. (Richard) Norman Shaw
3. Serac
4. Waldseemüller map
5. Shavuot
6. Cicely
7. Neil Reid
8. Randy Quaid
9. Pietro Badoglio
10. Jeanette Rankin
11. *Kindertotenlieder* or *Songs on the Death of Children*
12. Luis Alvarez
13. *One red paperclip*
14. Autolycus
15. Chicago Cubs

1. Mentioned in a Neutral Milk Hotel album title, on which Louisiana inland island is all the world's Tabasco sauce created?
2. What name is given to the pastime of rolling downhill in a transparent inflatable ball?
3. This Japanese actress survived the bombing of Hiroshima, but eventually died 18 days later. Who was the first person officially to be certified as dying of radiation poisoning?
4. Which Bangladeshi political party went into abeyance after the 1975 killing of Sheikh Mujibur Rahman, but has since 1990 re-emerged under the leadership of Sheikh Hasina?
5. When he tied for fourth in the PGA Championship in 1972, who became the first golfer to record top-ten finishes in the golfing majors in five different decades?
6. Which Romanian-born Hungarian composer wrote his only opera, *Le Grand Macabre,* in the mid-1970s?
7. Played by Ralph Bates, who was the chief baddie in 1970s BBC drama series *Poldark*?
8. Which US writer of novels including *Anywhere But Here* discovered in her 20s that she was the biological sister of Steve Jobs?
9. What name is given to the effect by which incompetent people make mistakes, but lack the self-perception to realise it?
10. Which is the only country to depict the Bible on its flag?
11. The four extant families in the order Crocodilia are true crocodiles, alligators, caimans and what family of reptiles?
12. Bencivieni di Pepo, who died in 1302 and according to Vasari taught Giotto, is regarded as one of the earliest great Italian painters – under what name is he best known?
13. Located on the border between Alaska and the Yukon, which mountain is the second highest in both Canada and the US?
14. What type of chemical reaction involves two chemicals swapping bonds, for example salt and silver nitrate forming silver chloride and sodium nitrate?
15. Which 2005 crime comedy film shares its name with a 1968 work of film criticism by Pauline Kael and a song from the soundtrack of the James Bond film 'Thunderball'?

Answers to General Knowledge:
Fiendishly Difficult Quiz 8

1. Avery Island
2. Zorbing
3. Midori Naka
4. Awami League
5. Sam Snead
6. Györgi Ligeti
7. George Warleggan
8. Mona Simpson
9. Dunning–Kruger Effect
10. Dominican Republic
11. Gharials or gavials
12. Cimabue
13. Mount Saint Elias
14. Metathesis or double decomposition or double replacement
15. *Kiss Kiss Bang Bang*

1. Which Belgian-born French novelist's works include *Alexis* and *Mémoires d'Hadrien*, before becoming the first woman elected to the Académie française in 1980?

2. Which 2000 number one hit single was written by Kirsty Bertarelli, who, following her marriage to a Swiss businessman, became one of Britain's richest women?

3. Ben Silbermann is a co-founder and the CEO of which website which allows users to post items related to their lifestyle interests such as fashion, cooking or home decoration?

4. Who composed the memorable theme of ITV's *South Bank Show* taken from his album, *Variations*?

5. What name roughly translating as 'those who confront death' is given to armed Kurdish fighters, in operation since the 1920s?

6. Oklo, a mine located in Gabon, was in 1972 shown to be the only known location in the world where which chemical process had occurred spontaneously?

7. Puppetry, chanted narration, and the playing of the *shamisen* are the key elements of which type of Japanese puppet theatre?

8. Which Tibetan peak is the source of the Sutlej, Indus and Brahmaputra rivers and is sacred to Buddhists, Hindus and Jains?

9. The name of which ancient Slavic alphabet, is also used in the name of a 1926 choral work by Leoš Janáček?

10. Rottnest Island, off the coast of Perth, Australia, is the principal home for which small marsupial of the genus *Setonix*?

11. In a morbid context, what forms a set of four with pallor, algor and livor?

12. Which Scottish boxer became WBA World Lightweight Champion when he defeated Panamanian Ismael Laguna in 1970?

13. Which man led the Praetorian Guard under the Roman emperor Tiberius, and from was de facto ruler of Rome between Tiberius' withdrawal to Capri and this mans death in AD31?

14. Which Briton is the only person to win a Supporting Actor or Actress Academy Award for playing the title role in a film?

15. Which French Jesuit priest and philosopher set forth a sweeping account of the unfolding of the cosmos which set aside the account in the Book of Genesis in his posthumously published *The Phenomenon of Man*?

1. Marguerite Yourcenar
2. 'Black Coffee' (by All Saints)
3. Pinterest
4. Andrew Lloyd Webber
5. Peshmerga
6. Nuclear fission
7. *Bunraku*
8. Mount Kailash
9. Glagolitic
10. Quokka
11. Rigor (stages of 'mortis')
12. Ken Buchanan
13. Lucius Aelius Sejanus
14. Vanessa Redgrave (for *Julia*)
15. Pierre Teilhard de Chardin

1. The Satin Dolls go-go bar provided the location for what venue in a multi-Emmy-winning HBO series?

2. In which city has Estrella Damm pilsner beer been produced since 1876?

3. In Japanese cuisine, *gari*, served as a pink sushi tray garnish, consists of thin slices of which root that have been marinated in sugar and vinegar?

4. Who serves a five-year term as Yang di-Pertuan Agong ('He who is made lord')?

5. Haida artists are noted for producing argillite carvings. Argillite is an extremely rare variety of black slate that is only found in which Canadian archipelago?

6. In 1869, while studying pus-stained bandages, Friedrich Miescher identified traces of what substance which he named nuclein?

7. Exenatide, a key ingredient in a new diabetes drug named Byetta, was first found in the saliva of which North US creature?

8. Who is the *Fifth Queen* in Ford Maddox Ford's trilogy of historical novels of that name?

9. Part of the US Department of Defense, what is the purpose of JPAC?

10. Which three words complete the name of the Whistler painting of 1875 which attracted Ruskin's ire, leading to a famous court case: *Nocturne in Black and Gold:_____ _____ ____*?

11. The 'Guizer Jarl' leads proceedings in which Scottish festival?

12. Born in Iowa, Paul Edward Yost (1919–2007) is often referred to as the 'father of . . .' which sport?

13. In 2006, ten-year-old Guiseppe Mangano took 55 minutes and 30 seconds to become the youngest ever swimmer of which 2.3-mile-wide body of water?

14. A co-chief council in the Watergate investigation, he served as a Tennessee senator (R) from 1994-2003. Which actor starred in *The Hunt for Red October* and *Die Hard 2*?

15. Two full-sized submarine replicas used in *Raiders of the Lost Ark* were previously used in which 1981 film?

Answers to General Knowledge:
Fiendishly Difficult Quiz 10

1. Bada Bing – in *The Sopranos*
2. Barcelona
3. Ginger
4. The King of Malaysia
5. Queen Charlotte Islands
6. DNA – deoxyribonucleic acid
7. Gila monster (*Heloderma suspectum*)
8. Catherine Howard
9. Joint POW/MIA Accounting Command. It searches worldwide for Americans listed as MIA or as POW
10. *The Falling Rocket*
11. Up-Helly-Aa (Shetlands)
12. Hot-air ballooning
13. Strait of Messina
14. Fred Thompson
15. *Das Boot*

1. In 2009, whose *Theatre of Death* show was banned on 'religious grounds' in Tampere, Finland's third city, and moved on to Espoo?

2. Released in 2011, the album *Lulu* was a collaboration between the heavy metal band Metallica and which musician?

3. What very dangerous activity is pursued by men known as *zama zama* in South Africa?

4. On which island is the Washington Slagbaai National Park, created to protect some of the Caribbean's last desert habitat?

5. In which city is the Grand Île, the first city centre to be classified in its entirety as a UNESCO World Heritage Site?

6. A fungal disease, Fusarium wilt, is killing which iconic Los Angeles trees?

7. The Karl Jordan Medal is a significant international prize awarded for outstanding contributions to the scientific study of which order of creatures?

8. Which country's 'Golden Age' reached its height under the reigns of David the Builder and his granddaughter Tamara in the 11th and 12th centuries?

9. What did the submarine *Seraph* drop in the Atlantic Ocean off Spain in World War II?

10. How are Isabel de Velasco and Maria Agustina Sarmiento collectively known in a painting of 1656?

11. Most having being destroyed in the Dissolution or by Puritans, what was portrayed on an English medieval painting known as a doom board?

12. To the displeasure of Bolivia, Colombia and Ecuador, FIFA have enforced which maximum altitude above sea level (in metres) for international soccer games?

13. Who was the third batsman to score two Test match triple centuries after Sir Donald Bradman and Brian Lara?

14. Which 1980 epic western film was loosely based on the Johnson County War, a grim episode in 1890s Wyoming?

15. A popular gift for graduating US students, whose last book was *Oh, the Places You'll Go!* (1990)?

Answers to General Knowledge:
Fiendishly Difficult Quiz 11

1. Alice Cooper
2. Lou Reed
3. Mining – they invade disused tunnels and work underground in extremely dangerous conditions for months
4. Bonaire
5. Strasbourg
6. Palms – many are Canary date palms
7. Lepidoptera (inc. moths and butterflies)
8. Georgia
9. The Man Who Never Was – 'Captain William Martin' – real name Glyndwr Michael
10. *Las Meninas* – Maids of Honour – Diego Velazquez
11. The Last Judgement
12. 2,500 m
13. Virender Sehwag
14. *Heaven's Gate*
15. Dr Seuss (Theodor Geisel)

1. The TV series *Karen Sisco* was a spin-off from which 1998 film directed by Steven Soderbergh?

2. The annual week-long Sziget rock festival is held on an island in the Danube in which city?

3. The Pershore Yellow Egg is a cooking variety of which fruit?

4. Sagatiba Pura is an ultra-premium brand of which Brazilian spirit?

5. Which is the only one of the United Arab Emirates to have coastlines on two distinct seas?

6. *Billy Ruffian* by David Cordingly is a much-praised history of which Royal Navy ship?

7. Armadillo Aerospace is led by which man, a key designer of the *Doom* and *Quake* computer games?

8. The Russian word Krysha was a crimimal slang term for protection in turbulent 1990s Russia. What is its literal translation?

9. Sun Yaoting, who died on 17 December 1996, was China's last surviving what?

10. Turner's various *Blue Rigi* paintings show Mount Rigi rising 1,800 metres above which lake?

11. Where would you wear a Malory band?

12. The subject of a lawsuit in 17th-century England over a fake example led to the principle of *caveat emptor*. Which stones found in the stomachs of ruminants were once viewed as a cure for depression and as antidotes to poison?

13. Which footballer sang and played bass for the reggae band Revelation Times on their 1984 single 'Not the Dancing Kind'?

14. Which Canadian wrote *The Penelopiad*, a play that retells Odysseus's 20 years of wandering from the viewpoint of Penelope?

15. Baz Luhrmann's films *Strictly Ballroom*, *Romeo & Juliet* and *Moulin Rouge!* make up which trilogy?

Answers to General Knowledge:
Fiendishly Difficult Quiz 12

1. *Out of Sight*
2. Budapest
3. Plum
4. Cachaca
5. Sharjah – Persian Gulf and Gulf of Oman/Arabian Sea
6. HMS *Bellerophon*
7. John Carmack
8. A Roof
9. Imperial eunuch
10. Lucerne
11. Around your waist – it's a piece of cord worn to discourage overeating – a primitive external gastric band
12. Bezoars
13. Ruud Gullit
14. Margaret Atwood
15. *Red Curtain*

1. The Harajuku Girls, backing dancers nicknamed Love, Angel, Music and Baby, appeared in several of which New York singer's music videos including 'The Sweet Escape'?

2. Johnny Gomez and Nick Diamond were the primary commentators/presenters of which TV series?

3. What did John Maynard Keynes denigrate as 'a barbarous relic'?

4. A special train named the Pink Express used to deliver which harvest from the Leeds–Wakefield–Pontefract triangle to London in the 1950s?

5. Hank Johnson beat Republican Cynthia McKinney in Georgia to become one of the first two members of the US Congress of which faith?

6. Although actually a ria, it has been described as southern Europe's deepest fjord. In which country is the Bay of Kotor?

7. Opened in 1913, Subte is South America's oldest underground mass transit system and is found in which city?

8. Based on studies of pianists and violinists, what 'rule' was proposed by Anders Ericsson of Florida State University?

9. In tribute to her opposition to Mussolini's invasion of 1935, in which capital city is the suffragette Sylvia Pankhurst buried?

10. Which country's biggest hydroelectric power plant is the Karahnjukar, built to power a new Alcoa aluminium smelter?

11. What anatomical criticism was voiced by commentators on Ingres' painting *La Grande Odalisque* (1814)?

12. *Freedom's Fury*, a documentary produced by Quentin Tarantino and Lucy Liu, is about a highly charged 1956 Olympics match between Hungary and the Soviet Union in which sport?

13. Although she was to return from retirement and play in 2010 and 2011, which woman said: 'This is the end of a child's dream,' as she became, in 2008, the first woman to retire at the top of the tennis rankings?

14. Which Texan Oscar-winning actor who turned down a place at West Point has a tenor voice which won him a scholarship at UCLA in the early 1980s?

15. Sharlto Copley plays the central character Wikus van de Merwe in which 2009 film directed by Neill Blomkamp?

Answers to General Knowledge:
Fiendishly Difficult Quiz 13

1. Gwen Stefani
2. *Celebrity Death Match*
3. The Gold Standard
4. Rhubarb – mild winters are putting the entire 'indoor rhubarb' industry at risk
5. Buddhism
6. Montenegro
7. Buenos Aires
8. The 10,000-hour rule – needed to achieve expertise
9. Addis Ababa
10. Iceland
11. She appears to have three extra vertebrae
12. Water polo
13. Justine Henin
14. Forest Whitaker
15. *District 9*

1. Because his young daughter Alexandria was a huge fan, David Bowie voiced the character Lord Royal Highness in an episode of which animated series?
2. Which two hard rock bands combined in the 2009 NINJA tour?
3. What, popular with thrifty Japanese, is Happoshu?
4. In which capital city does the world's largest luxury fur auction take place?
5. In 1959, Sir Seewoosagur Ramgoolam became the first Prime Minister of which independent island nation?
6. With depths of up to 1,500 metres, the Wadi Nakhr Gorge is, effectively, which country's 'Grand Canyon'?
7. In the context of astronomy, what does the CfDS campaign for?
8. What sort of bird is a Simon's emerald, named after a French ornithologist, Eugene Louis Simon, who spent his life studying them?
9. Who was the only US President to have been born on Independence Day?
10. The US artist and photographer William Wegman is particularly noted for compositions featuring dogs of which breed?
11. Who, between AD 42 and AD 62, founded the Coptic Church in Alexandria?
12. Ryoko Tani, a Japanese Olympic champion, won a record seventh under-48 kg world title in which sport after the birth of her son?
13. The Dru, Matterhorn, Eiger, Piz Badille, Tre Cima de Laverado and the Grandes Jorasses are collectively regarded as the six classic Alpine ascents of which type?
14. Which auteur director cooked and ate his own shoe after losing a bet with documentary-maker Errol Morris?
15. How many copies of *Moonfire: The Epic Journey of Apollo 11*, published in 2009, have been printed?

Answers to General Knowledge:
Fiendishly Difficult Quiz 14

1. *SpongeBob SquarePants*
2. Nine Inch Nails and Jane's Addiction
3. A cheap low-malt beer
4. Copenhagen
5. Mauritius
6. Oman
7. Dark skies (Campaign for Dark Skies)
8. A hummingbird
9. Calvin Coolidge
10. Weimaraner
11. St Mark the Evangelist
12. Judo
13. North Face (ascents)
14. Werner Herzog
15. 1969

1. Launched in 2004, *Plus belle la vie* (aka *PBLV*) is a very successful soap on French TV and is centred on Roland Marci's bar in the Le Mistral district of which city?

2. The life and death of Anna Nicole Smith, the glamour model who married an oil tycoon 63 years her senior, was turned into an opera by which British composer?

3. Which root vegetable (*Helianthus tuberosus*) is also called sunroot, sunchoke, earth apple or topinambour?

4. What is the name of the process charged with halting the trade in blood diamonds?

5. Which Swiss climber has innumerable records to his credit including the speed record 2:47:33 for a solo ascent of the Eiger north face, Heckmair route in 2008?

6. Which is the 'widest' country to use just one time zone?

7. Five of the original 'Mercury Seven' astronauts were immortalised as characters in the *Thunderbirds* TV series. Who missed out?

8. *Pteropus voeltzkowi* is a species of megabat and is endemic to which African island, where conservation measures have diminished fears for its extinction?

9. In which 2003 Glasgow *Herald* contest did Wee Jimmy Krankie emerge triumphant with Craig and Charlie Reid (the identical Proclaimer twins from Auchtermuchty) finishing joint fifth?

10. What nickname has been applied to the 8830 international model of the BlackBerry?

11. Which photographer created the important exhibition People of the 20th Century?

12. In cricket, what name is given to the graphic which shows the bowlers' deliveries in the air about the batsman?

13. A term also used to describe certain training jumps for horses, what is the Italian name for the rigging that supports a tightrope walker's rope?

14. *Tough Without a Gun* is a biography of which actor, the quote being a Raymond Chandler description of him?

15. Subsequently playing Uncle Fester in *The Addams Family*, who is regarded as having been Hollywood's first major child star, being picked, aged six, by Charlie Chaplin to play the 'Kid'?

Answers to General Knowledge:
Fiendishly Difficult Quiz 15

1. Marseilles
2. Mark-Anthony Turnage
3. Jerusalem artichoke
4. The Kimberley Process
5. Uli Steck
6. China
7. Deke Slayton and Wally Schirra
8. Pemba – The Pemba flying fox
9. Most Scottish Person in the World
10. BarackBerry
11. August Sander
12. Beehive
13. Cavaletti
14. Humphrey Bogart
15. Jackie Coogan

1. Nelly Uvarova plays the lead role in *Ne Rodis Krasivoi* 'If you're not born beautiful, be born lucky' – the Russian version of which TV programme?
2. The composer Vic Mizzy died in 2009. Although he composed numerous works his fortune was made by the theme tune to which comedy series which first aired in 1964?
3. In 1933, which Lyon chef, who would subsequently train Paul Bocuse, was the first woman to have a three-Michelin-star restaurant?
4. Carlo Petrini founded the Slow Food movement in 1986 as a reaction to the arrival of a McDonald's near which Roman landmark?
5. The Odintsovo district is one of the most exclusive suburbs of which city?
6. Considered one of the best preserved of all Andean mummies, *La Doncella* is another name for which 15-year-old girl?
7. Which warbler, originally a Mediterranean bird but breeding in Britain since 1972, is reckoned to have the loudest song of any British bird and to be extraordinarily difficult to view?
8. Larimar is an opaque blue stone found only in which country?
9. What was the very specific source of the wood from which Nelson's coffin was made?
10. Which model from Yongzhou, possibly China's most successful model ever, was the first Chinese model to be signed by Estée Lauder and the first Asian on the catwalks of Victoria's Secret?
11. 'Diamond fibre' is a top-class variety of which fabric?
12. What does the NGS publication *The Yellow Book* list?
13. Who became the first Chinese to win an Olympic athletics gold medal when he won the 110 metres hurdles at Athens on 2004, equalling Colin Jackson's world record of 12.91 seconds?
14. Who promised gladiatorial contests in Central Park in his failed 1969 bid for the post of New York mayor?
15. What is the essential characteristic of the Japanese culinary practise of *Ikizukuri*?

Answers to General Knowledge:
Fiendishly Difficult Quiz 16

1. *Ugly Betty*
2. *The Addams Family*
3. Eugenie Brazier
4. The Spanish Steps
5. Moscow
6. The Llulaillaco Maiden
7. Cetti's warbler
8. The Dominican Republic
9. The mast of *L'Orient*. In the Battle of the Nile, a large chunk of *L'Orient's* mast landed on a British ship
10. Liu Wen
11. Cashmere
12. Gardens in England and Wales
13. Liu Xiang
14. Norman Mailer
15. The eating of live creatures

1. As echoed in the title of a 2006 film, the three components of a magician's trick are the Pledge, the Turn and . . . ?

2. The ten Italian Cristiani siblings made up a celebrated circus act. What was their speciality?

3. Katsuhiro Nakamura was the first Japanese chef to do what?

4. Dominique Pierru was hailed as a gastronomic genius after creating what delicacy?

5. What, eaten by the Inca, was *charki*?

6. At a height in excess of 2,260 metres, the T'izi n' Tichka Pass is the highest in which country?

7. The Cat Ba leopard gecko, which was discovered in 2009, is found on only one small island off the north of which country?

8. In which lake will you find the Ngamba Island Chimpanzee Sanctuary, aka 'Chimp Island'?

9. President Abraham Lincoln wrote a celebrated letter of condolence to which mother of five sons believed to have died fighting for the Union in the American Civil War?

10. In World War II, HMS *Pembroke* V was a cover name for which facility?

11. Canadian photographer Edward Burtynsky has taken numerous striking photographs of which specific type of working location?

12. Which Parisian prison is the largest in France?

13. Used in early golf balls, from which tree is gutta-percha obtained?

14. Built on the site of the former Fruitlands Nursery, which famous sporting venue was opened in 1933?

15. The Oscar-nominated documentary *Waste Land* by Lucy Walker is about the 'pickers' or 'catadores' who scavange Jardim Gramacho, an enormous dump in which city?

Answers to General Knowledge:
Fiendishly Difficult Quiz 17

1. The Prestige
2. Bareback riding with associated stunts
3. Win a Michelin star
4. Snail caviar
5. Dried llama meat
6. Morocco – it's in the High Atlas
7. Vietnam
8. Lake Victoria
9. Mrs Lydia Bixby
10. Bletchley Park
11. Quarries
12. La Santé
13. Sapodilla
14. Augusta National Golf Club
15. Rio de Janeiro

1. Riley Bluckett, a blind guitarist, is credited with being the first to fuse which singing style with country music in 1924?

2. Okean is a chain of shops being opened in Russia which will sell which iconic British dish?

3. What measure has been coined by risk analysts to denote a 'one-in-a-million chance of dying'?

4. To what was Napoleon referring when he said, 'Six for a man, seven for a woman and eight for a fool'?

5. Khadijeh Saqafi, 'Mother of the Revolution', died in 2009 at the age of 93. She was the widow of which famous figure?

6. Used as a slogan in Lyndon B. Johnson's 1964 presidential campaign against Barry Goldwater, 'We must love each other or die' is a quotation from which poet's poem 'September 1', 1939?

7. Launched in 2008, which internet online game for kids was invented by Michael Acton Smith?

8. In 1699, working for the Royal Mint, who brought an end to the successful career of British counterfeiter William Chaloner?

9. In World War II, the so-called 'Cockleshell Heroes' of Operation Frankton entered occupied Europe via which estuary?

10. Eugenius Birch, the 'Brunel of the British seaside', was particularly noted for the design of which type of structures?

11. Which city holds the annual *Su e Zo per i Ponti*, or Up and Down the Bridges event where thousands walk all around the city and cross 45 bridges?

12. Mike Wells (39) set a record of 395 feet (120 metres) when he swam through Fish Rock Cave (Australia's longest ocean cave) on a single breath. This cave lies south of which city?

13. Which holder of numerous world boxing titles played Captain Ballard in *The Matrix Reloaded* (2003)?

14. In 2009, which film became the first ever animated feature to open the Cannes Film Festival?

15. Shakespeare's *The Tempest* is believed to have been inspired by an account by a survivor, William Strachey, of the 1609 wreck of the Sea Venture off which island?

Answers to General Knowledge:
Fiendishly Difficult Quiz 18

1. Yodelling
2. Fish and chips
3. Micromort
4. Hours of sleep in a night
5. Ayatollah Khomeini – she died in Tehran
6. W.H. Auden
7. Moshi Monsters
8. Sir Isaac Newton. Chaloner was hanged, drawn and quartered.
9. Gironde estuary
10. Seaside piers
11. Venice
12. Brisbane
13. Roy Jones Jr
14. *Up*
15. Bermuda

1. Grown on the slopes of Mount Elgon, the arabica coffee Bugisu is regarded as the finest coffee from which African country?

2. A member of Carsten Borchgrevink's Southern Cross Expedition, which Norwegian zoologist became the first person to be buried in Antarctica when he died on 14 October, 1899?

3. Nicknamed 'the artist' by his army comrades, whose earliest surviving war picture, from December 1914, is of the ruined church of St Nicholas in Messines (now Mesen, Belgium), where he was quartered in the crypt?

4. Who so disliked modernism in art that he told his painter friend Alfred Munnings if he ever saw Picasso in Piccadilly he would 'kick him up the arse'?

5. What is the oldest commercial corporation in North America?

6. Which company owns Jack Daniel's and Southern Comfort?

7. Who links Reed, Newley, Kass, Holm and Gibson?

8. In India, an *Aṅkuśa* is normally used to handle, train and sometimes goad which animals?

9. Named after a villain in *David Copperfield*, which English rock band had a massive hit in Germany in 1977 with 'Lady in Black', a song off their fourth album *Salisbury* (1971)?

10. Nicknamed the 'city of chairs', which Italian town of chair-makers, near the Slovenian border, has the world's largest chair in its piazza (it is seven storeys tall and weighs almost 23 tons)?

11. Famed for its Sea Shells praline, which Belgian chocolate-maker created the largest ever chocolate easter egg (8.32 m tall) in 2005, using at least 50,000 bars?

12. Which 1836 opera, composed by Nicola Vaccai, was based on the final days of a nine-day queen of England?

13. The largest book ever published is a 133-pound tome that measures 5 by 7 feet and needs a gallon of ink for printing and costs $2,000 to buy. Written by MIT scientist Michael Hawley, it has which Asian Kingdom for its title?

14. In 1988, Barry Davies was commentating on which sport when he made the famous remark: 'Where were the Germans? But frankly, who cares?'?

15. Present at General Robert E. Lee's surrender at Appomattox, which cavalry leader became, at the age of 23, the youngest general in the Union Army in June 1863?

Answers to General Knowledge:
Fiendishly Difficult Quiz 19

1. Uganda
2. Nicolai Hanson - he apparently died of an intestinal disorder
3. Adolf Hitler
4. Winston Churchill
5. Hudson's Bay Company founded in 1670
6. Brown-Forman Corporation based in Louisville, Kentucky
7. Joan Collins, who married Maxwell Reed, Anthony Newley, Ronald S. Kass, Peter Holm, and is still married to Percy Gibson
8. Elephants
9. Uriah Heep
10. Manzano
11. Guylian
12. *Giovanna Gray* – based on the last days of Lady Jane Grey
13. *Bhutan: A Visual Odyssey Across the Last Himalayan Kingdom*
14. (Olympic) field hockey
15. George Armstrong Custer

1. The *Thebaid* is a Latin epic by which 1st-century poet?
2. Featured in a *Wolf of Wall Street* dancing scene, which song was first recorded by Umberto Tozzi in 1979, and later reworked with English rather than Italian lyrics, became an international hit in 1982–83 for Laura Branigan?
3. Created by Australian Lindsay Fleay in 1985–89, *The Magic Portal* was the first ever stop-motion film made using which toys?
4. Home to the Ahmed Baba Institute, which city on the southern edge of the Sahara Desert is known as the 'City of 333 Saints'?
5. Which letter refers to a vitamin group of eight fat-soluble compounds that includes tocopherols and tocotrienols?
6. In 1989, Barack Obama met his future wife Michelle while working as a summer associate at which award-winning Chicago law firm? For the fourth straight year, it was revealed in November 2013 to have more first-tier national rankings in the *U.S. News – Best Lawyers* law firm rankings than any other US law firm.
7. Which men are known as the *papabili*?
8. Rati, the goddess of desire or passion, is the consort of which Hindu god of love?
9. Which dictator, in power between 1954 and 1989, was South America's longest-lived cold war tyrant?
10. In which 1881 work by Pierre-Auguste Renoir, painted at the Maison Fournaise along the Seine River, is the artist's future wife, Aline Charigot, seen holding a dog and the painter Gustave Caillebotte found seated in the lower right?
11. Sunk in July 1914, what is the 'Adriatic's Titanic'?
12. Famed for its synth-drum intro and the sound of its title being intoned in a deep voice rumble, which 1985 song by Yello was featured to memorable effect in *Ferris Bueller's Day Off*?
13. With at least 590 people killed, the deadliest ever disaster at a sporting event was caused by a temporary terrace collapse and fire at which Hong Kong racecourse on 26 February, 1918?
14. Who used the aliases Anne de Breuil, Comtesse de la Fère, Baroness of Sheffield, Lady Clarick and Charlotte Backson?
15. In a treaty of 1959, which geographical name is missing: 'In the interest of all mankind that _____ shall continue forever to be used exclusively for peaceful purposes and shall not become the scene or object of international discord'?

Answers to General Knowledge:
Fiendishly Difficult Quiz 20

1. Statius/Publius Papinus Statius
2. 'Gloria'
3. Lego bricks, it is known as a 'brickfilm'
4. Timbuktu
5. (Vitamin) E
6. Sidley Austin
7. Candidates/cardinals likely to be elected Pope
8. Kama/Kāmadeva
9. Alfredo Stroessner of Paraguay
10. *Luncheon of the Boating Party/Le déjeuner des canotiers*
11. *Baron Gautsch*, an Austro-Hungarian steamboat that went down with 240-390 lives lost
12. 'Oh Yeah' – also heard in that other '80s classic, *The Secrets of My Success*
13. Happy Valley Racecourse
14. Milady de Winter – in *The Three Musketeers*
15. Antarctica – from the Antarctic Treaty

1. Which Congolese leader was played by Chiwetel Ejiofor in a 2013 Young Vic production of the Martinique poet Aimé Césaire's play *A Season in the Congo*?

2. The *koru* ('loop') is a spiral shape based on a new unfurling silver fern frond. Symbolising new life, growth and peace, it is an integral part of which Polynesian people's art and tattoos?

3. In 2001, which Latina became the first ever person to have a US number one album and a number one film in the very same week?

4. Which 1870 painting by Peter Nicolai Arbo depicts King Harald Hardrada of Norway getting hit in the neck by an arrow?

5. The site of a 1950 invasion and battle, which Asian city has the second largest tidal range of any port, with up to a 10 m difference between high and low tides?

6. 'Sacrifices must be made!' were the last words of the first man to make repeated, successful glider flights. Which German 'Glider King' died in 1896 after breaking his neck in a fall?

7. Deriving its name from the Latin for 'sausage', what is the most acutely lethal toxin known to man?

8. Named after the Boston Celtics legend, Larry is the bird logo of which online microblogging service?

9. Which Japanese Robin Hood was publicly boiled alive in 1594, with his young son Gobei, for a failed assassination attempt on warlord Toyotomi Hideyoshi?

10. Danes call it *tommermaend* ('carpenter'), the Swedes *baksmalla* ('a whack on the ass'), while the Spanish say *resaca* ('backwash') and Mexicans are *cruda* ('raw'). Turks use *aksamdan kalmalık* ('evening remainder') and the Vietnamese, *dụ'ng xiên* ('built cockeyed'). What is the English equivalent?

11. The *devşirme* system was used by the Ottoman Empire to recruit Christian children into which elite fighting force, who were wiped out by Sultan Mahmud II in the Auspicious Incident of 1826?

12. What is the largest living land carnivore?

13. 'Trust yourself. You know more than you think you do' is the opening line of which manual, first published in 1946?

14. Which golfer was the first Australian winner of the US Masters?

15. Which French–Italian clothing brand, founded in 1952 by René Ramillon, is known for its down jackets and sportswear? Its name is an abbreviation of a mountain village near Grenoble.

Answers to General Knowledge:
Fiendishly Difficult Quiz 21

1. Patrice Lumumba
2. The Maori
3. Jennifer Lopez – film: *The Wedding Planner* album: *J-Lo*
4. *Battle of Stamford Bridge/Slaget ved Stamford Bridge*
5. Incheon or Inchon, South Korea
6. Otto Lilienthal
7. Botulinum toxin ('sausage poison')
8. Twitter
9. Ishikawa Goemon – Nezumi Kozo (the rat kid), aka Nakamura Jirokichi was another (18th-century) Robin Hood type
10. Hangover
11. The Janissaries (Ottoman Turk: 'New Soldier')
12. Kodiak bear/Alaskan grizzly bear/*Ursus arctos middendorffi*
13. *The Common Sense Book of Baby and Child Care* by Benjamin Spock, MD
14. Adam Scott – Masters Champion in 2013
15. Moncler – from Monestier-de-Clermont

1. What completes this sequence: Hydra, Kerberos, Nix, Styx, _____?
2. Which ruthless Zhou dynasty empress (reign: 690–705) is the only woman in Chinese history to rule in her own right?
3. Thought to depict a *fravashi* (guardian angel), the *Faravahar* is a symbol of which religion?
4. Steve 'Doc' Nemeth played the bawdy Bixby Snyder, star of the TV smutfest *It's Not My Problem*, who often tells viewers that he would 'buy that for a dollar' in which 1987 movie?
5. The discoverer, in 1912, of an eponymous law of X-ray diffraction, which 25-year-old winner of the Nobel Prize in Physics became the youngest ever Nobel laureate in 1915?
6. The largest documented catfish species is named after which Asian river? (Guinness World Records has called it the world's largest freshwater fish.)
7. Only 2,000 copies were produced of which US musician's 1993 debut album *Golden Feelings*?
8. Which legendary lumberjack's footprints, together with those of his blue ox Babe, created Minnesota's 10,000 lakes?
9. Rem Koolhaas designed the Amsterdam HQ for which Dutch denim company, whose CEO and founder is Jos van Tilburg?
10. Known as the father of all monsters, which 100-headed creature's conjugal union with Echidna produced Cerberus, the Lernean Hydra, the Chimera and the dragon Ladon?
11. Which Japanese company introduced Nanoblock toy bricks?
12. Only outdone golds-wise by Jesse Owens (who won four to his three), which German gymnast was the most successful Olympian at the 1936 Berlin Games in terms of total medals (six)?
13. Produced since 1972 by Charles Martell & Son at Laurel Farm, Dymock, its distinctive odour comes from its immersion during ripening in perry made from a namesake pear. It was first made from the milk of the Gloucester breed when it only consisted of 68 breed heifers. The Gloucester cattle has been revived to make production of which cheese possible?
14. The oldest group of chemotherapeutics used in fighting cancer today, alkylating agents were originally derived from which wartime weapon?
15. Dubbed 'El Chino Ántrax', José Rodrigo Aréchiga Gamboa (b. 1980) is a jailed leader of which drug trafficking organisation?

Answers to General Knowledge:
Fiendishly Difficult Quiz 22

1. Charon – moons of Pluto in decreasing distance to its surface
2. Wu Zetian/Empress Wu
3. Zoroastrianism
4. *Robocop*
5. William Lawrence Bragg
6. Mekong – the river gives its name to the Mekong giant catfish
7. Beck (Hansen) – *Mellow Gold* features his breakthrough hit single 'Loser'
8. Paul Bunyan
9. G-Star RAW
10. Typhon
11. Kawada Co. – Nanoblocks are soy ink-coloured bricks that come in 11 types and in award winning sets based on Neuschwanstein Castle and the Tokyo Skytree
12. Konrad Frey
13. Stinking Bishop
14. Mustard gas in World War I
15. Sinaloa Cartel – named after the north-western Mexican state, it is said to be the world's most powerful drug trafficking cartel, money laundering and organised crime syndicate

1. Bulgarian Miroslav Barnyashev uses which WWE ring name?
2. Who died at about 1.45 p.m. on 30 November 1900, in a small first-floor room at L'Hôtel d'Alsace, 13 rue des Beaux-Arts, in Paris?
3. Who was the first unsigned artist to have a no. 1 single on the Billboard Hot 100, thanks to a song from the film *Reality Bites*?
4. Founded in 1891 by Artur Hazelius, Skansen, the world's first open-air museum, is in which country?
5. Discovered by Lincoln Ellsworth, which peak in the Sentinel Range of the Ellsworth Mountains is the highest in Antarctica?
6. Which suffragette hid in a Palace of Westminster cupboard over-night on Census night 1911, so she could legitimately give her place of residence on the census form as the 'House of Commons'?
7. Once called 'the Athens of the Americas', which capital city, the third-highest in South America, owns what has been called the largest moorland in the world, Sumapaz Páramo?
8. The 'Pillars of Creation' is a famous photo of elephant trunks of interstellar gas and dust in a nebula taken on 1 April 1995 by the Hubble Telescope. Some 7,000 light years from earth, which nebula shows the process of creating new stars?
9. What is the second most traded commodity on earth?
10. With an average ground-level elevation of 1.5 m/4 ft 11 in above sea level, which country is the lowest on earth, as well as the one with the lowest natural point in the world, at 2.4 m/7 ft 10 in?
11. A week-long slaughter of some 5,000 Italians in September 1943, the Massacre of the 33rd Acqui Infantry Division by Wehrmacht troops took place on which Ionian island?
12. Which cocktail was supposedly created in Florence in 1919 when an Italian count, first name Camillo, asked a Bar Casoni bartender to add gin instead of soda to his Americano?
13. The Black Orlov, Akbar Shah, Archduke Joseph, Lesotho Promise and Moon of Baroda are noted examples of what?
14. The 21-year-old slalom champion at the 1972 Sapporo Olympics, which skier, nicknamed 'Paquito', is known for being the first and only Spaniard to win Winter Olympic gold?
15. What links the bands Dethklok, Mystik Spiral, Timmy and the Lords of the Underworld and Sadgasm?

Answers to General Knowledge:
Fiendishly Difficult Quiz 23

1. African hairy frog/Horror frog/*Trichobatrachus robustus*
2. Oscar Wilde
3. Lisa Loeb – with the 1994 song 'Stay (I Missed You)'
4. Sweden
5. Vinson Massif
6. Emily Davison – who died in 1913 after stepping in front of the King's horse at the Epsom Derby
7. Bogotá
8. Eagle Nebula
9. Coffee – the first is oil
10. Maldives
11. Cephalonia/Kefalonia – the event was depicted in *Captain Corelli's Mandolin*
12. Negroni
13. Diamonds
14. Francisco Fernández Ochoa
15. They are fictional bands that featured in animated TV series (*Metalocalypse, Daria, South Park, The Simpsons*)

1. Clout, field, flight, target, popinjay and gungsul, or gukgung (the traditional Korean type), are forms of which Olympic sport?
2. Exploring the history of sanitation and hygiene, the Sulabh International Museum of Toilets is in which Indian city?
3. Named after a then fortified city in the Ardennes department, which victory for the French in a Thirty Years' War battle of 19 May 1643 marked the decline of Spanish military might and the rise of France as a leading European power?
4. Kanye West claimed that a lamp designed by which Swiss-French architect was the 'greatest inspiration' for his 2013 album *Yeezus*?
5. The last to close, Miranda de Ebro was the site of the largest of the 104 prison camps run by which regime?
6. Director of the Conservatoire de Paris (1871–96) till his death, which French composer is best known for his operas *Mignon* (1866) and *Hamlet* (1868)?
7. Located in the Gulf of Gabes off the coast of Tunisia, what is the largest island of North Africa? Its principal town is Hawmat al-Sūq and the main port is Ajīm.
8. Which train station name completes the title *Leaving the_____ _____*, a 2012 debut novel by Ben Lerner about the young US poet Adam Gordon, who is in Madrid on a prestigious fellowship?
9. Lucky Diamond Rich, aka Gregory Paul McLaren, is 100% what?
10. Described by the *New York Times* as 'the Tabasco of the Lesser Antilles', which company's Soca Hot Sauce is manufactured in the Trinidad town of Arima? Its appeal is said to come from Scotch bonnet peppers which 'taste of the island itself'.
11. Lying 78 light years away, which hot blue-white star is about 3.5 times larger than our sun and marks the heart of the lion?
12. The 1982 death of South Korean boxer Kim Duk-koo, following his fight with Ray Mancini, prompted the WBC to limit a professional bout to a maximum of how many rounds?
13. Famed for it's nut–cracking chimpanzees, the Parc National de Taïis, in which West African country?
14. Site of Napoleon's great victory, the village of Austerlitz – now named Slavkov u Brna – is in which present-day country?
15. Premiering in 2013 on TV Publica, the Argentine miniseries *Combatants* showed 'the human, the pain and the historic' aspects that get 'sidelined' when discussing which conflict?

Answers to General Knowledge:
Fiendishly Difficult Quiz 24

1. Archery
2. New Delhi
3. Battle of Rocroi
4. Le Corbusier/Charles-Édouard Jeanneret-Gris
5. Francoist regime of Francisco Franco of Spain
6. Ambroise Thomas
7. Djerba/Jarbah
8. Atocha Station
9. Salt/sodium
10. Matouk's
11. Regulus – the brightest star in Leo
12. Twelve rounds (a reduction from 15 rounds)
13. Côte d'Ivoire – nut-cracking as in their use of advanced tools
14. Czech Republic
15. Falklands War/*Guerva de las Islas Malvinas*

1. Known as the 'Age of the Mammals', it began 66 million years ago and has a name meaning 'new life'. What is the current and most recent of the three Phanerozoic eras?

2. Named after the Italian for 'little hairs', what is the thinnest type of long rod-shaped pasta? Coiled into nests, it becomes 'angel hair' as in '_____ d'angelo'.

3. Which white crystalline xanthine alkaloid is the most widely used psychoactive drug in the world?

4. In 2013 the 37-year-old Russian Alexander Georgiev won his sixth world championship in which board game?

5. Soviet television produced nine TV films (1979–86) at the LenFilm movie studio in Leningrad starring Vasily Livanov in the greatest role of his career as which detective?

6. Dandi Biyo is which Asian country's national game?

7. Claiming about 6% of the national population as members, what is the world's largest political party?

8. Held every July in Alberta, which 10-day event bills itself as 'the Greatest Outdoor Show on Earth'? Over one million annual visitors watch one of the world's largest rodeos, agricultural competitions, chuckwagon racing and First Nations exhibitions.

9. In January 1924, biochemist Boris Zbarsky and anatomist Vladimir Vorobyov were issued with a political order to stop the natural decomposition of which object?

10. Executive Director of the Academy of Motion Picture Arts and Sciences (AMPAS) from 1945 to 1971, Margaret Herrick was once reminded of an uncle who grew wheat and fruit. What was the first name of that man, a Mr Pierce?

11. Edmond Halley (in 1720) and Jean-Philippe de Cheseaux (1744) both suggested early forms of a paradox described by which German amateur astronomer in 1823? Edgar Allan Poe offered the first plausible solution in his essay *Eureka*.

12. Which Japanese music producer/DJ founded the street wear fashion label A Bathing Ape (BAPE) in 1993?

13. Which group forms the second largest branch of Shia Islam?

14. Cheaper than using the classic Venetian gondola, which name, meaning 'ferry', is given to the affordable gondola ferries?

15. Complete the quote by Nobel laureate Sir Ernest Rutherford: 'All science is either physics or . . .' what? (Clue: a hobby.)

Answers to General Knowledge:
Fiendishly Difficult Quiz 25

1. Cenozoic Era
2. Capellini
3. Caffeine
4. Draughts/checkers
5. Sherlock Holmes – Vitaly Solomin played Dr Watson
6. Nepal – it is played with a stick (Dandi) and a wooden pin (Biyo); the former two feet long, the latter six inches.
7. Communist Party of China (CPC)/Chinese Communist Party/ *Zhōngguó Gòngchǎndzǎng*
8. The Calgary Stampede
9. Lenin's body
10. Oscar
11. Heinrich Wilhelm Olbers – Olbers' paradox argues that the darkness of the night sky conflicts with the idea of an endless universe uniformly populated with luminous stars
12. Nigo/Tomoaki Nagao
13. Nizari Ismailis/Seveners – the longest being the Shia Twelvers
14. *Traghetto*/pl. *traghetti*
15. '. . . stamp collecting'

1. Liege-born Frédéric Collignon (b.1975) retired in 2012 having won more world titles than any other player in history of which game, patented by Harold Searles Thornton in 1923?

2. Which song on the Beatles' *White Album* was inspired by Paul McCartney's Old English Sheepdog?

3. In medieval zoology, the sly and clever ichneumon was said to be which mythical creature's only true enemy?

4. Called 'Switzerland's answer to *The Girl with the Dragon Tattoo*', *The Truth about the Harry Quebert Affair* is the 2012 debut novel by which writer from Geneva?

5. A reference to the attire of protagonist 'Mal' Reynolds, Browncoats are fans of which Joss Whedon sci-fi TV series?

6. In which 2014 film is Joe Pesci played by Joey Russo and the name of his *Goodfellas* character – Tommy DeVito – borne by its real-life inspiration, who is played by Vincent Piazza?

7. Owned by Munich's Alte Pinakothek, the *Saint Columba Altarpiece* (c.1455) triptych was painted for a Cologne church by which Early Netherlandish artist?

8. Which horse, noted for its strength and endurance, was developed by the US singing teacher Justin _____ (1747–98), who owned the stallion, Figure, that founded the breed?

9. Of the 27 moons known to orbit Uranus, which 'shepherd moon' is closest to the planet? It is named after a Shakespearean tragic heroine.

10. Home of KS Tërbuni Pukë, where is the town of Pukë?

11. The Humble Administrator's Garden, the Yunyan Pagoda in Tiger Hill and Changmen Gate are features of which Chinese city on the lower reaches of the Yangtze in Jiangsu Province?

12. Legend has it that peasants threw them into the river to distract fish from eating the body of the beloved poet Qu Yuan, who drowned himself in 278 BC as a protest against corruption. What are *bak chang* or *zongzi*?

13. '*Gun bae*!' is a drinking salute in which Asian language?

14. The Mantova-based firm Pasotti was started in 1956 by owner Eva Giacomini's mother Ernesta Pasotti. It makes 30,000 of which 'DOC'-quality products every year?

15. In 1811, Thomas Manning became the first English national to speak with which religious figure?

Answers to General Knowledge:
Fiendishly Difficult Quiz 26

1. Table football
2. 'Martha My Dear'
3. Dragon
4. Joël Dicker
5. *Firefly*
6. *Jersey Boys* – Piazza plays Tommy DeVito
7. Rogier van der Weyden
8. Morgan
9. Cordelia
10. Ine the Pukë district in the northern Albania
11. Suzhou
12. Glutinous rice dumplings
13. Korean
14. Umbrellas/*ombrelli*
15. Dalai Lama (then the ninth, Lungtok Gyatso) – Manning was also the first Englishman to enter Lhasa

1. Howard Hughes's *Spruce Goose* H-4 Hercules transport plane was almost entirely made of which wood?
2. Which terrorist group assasinated Tsar Alexander II?
3. Used in a namesake test, litmus is obtained from a mixture of which composite organism?
4. Which sportswear company was founded by the first British runner to win the Boston Marathon, in 1970?
5. Produced from Dankowski rye, which Polish vodka was introduced in 1864 and is named after the king who saved Vienna from the Turks in 1683?
6. In 1981, which actor became the youngest performer to have a one-man show in the West End, subsequently returning to the London stage in *The New Revue*, *The Nerd* and *The Sneeze*?
7. The southern boobook or morepork is the smallest, as well as the continent's most widely distributed and common, bird of which type in Australia?
8. Which republic, with its first two capitals at Eraclea (697–742) and Malamocco (742–810), lasted from 697 until 1797?
9. Author of *Glad to Wear Glasses* (his first full-length collection) and the children's poetry book *I am a Poetato*, which Popticians frontman has been called 'comedy's Poet Laureate'?
10. Dubbed 'the king of the one-liner', which Liverpool-born US comedian and violinist performed his classic joke 'Take my wife . . . please!' during his cameo in the film *Goodfellas*?
11. Which RPG-style 'masocore' video game is a sequel designed to be extremely difficult by creative director Hidetaka Miyazaki, who likes 'a really sadistic game'? It centres on an Undead traveller who must find a way to break his curse of 'undeath' in the kingdom of Drangleic.
12. Founded in Brussels in 1829, what is the oldest fine leather luxury house in the world? It shares its name with a Belgian painter of female nudes like *The Sleepy Town* (1938).
13. Named after David Attenborough, *Nepenthes attenboroughii* is a species of which carnivorous plant? The type specimen was collected on the summit of Mount Victoria in Palawan, Philippines.
14. Who had a 1988 no. 3 hit song with *We Call It Acieed*?
15. Around 110 miles north of the Arctic Circle, Levi is, with 43 ski slopes and 27 ski lifts, which country's largest ski resort?

Answers to General Knowledge:
Fiendishly Difficult Quiz 27

1. Birch
2. Narodnaya Volya/People's Will
3. Lichen
4. Ronhill – founded by Ronald Hill
5. Sobieski – named after Jan III Sobieski
6. Rowan Atkinson
7. Owl
8. Repubblica di Venezia/Venice
9. John Hegley
10. Henny Youngman
11. *Dark Souls II*
12. Delvaux – the painter is Paul Delvaux
13. Pitcher plant
14. D Mob
15. Finland

1. Which crab in the genus *Uca* is famed for its sexually dimorphic claws – the male's major claw is much larger than the minor claw; female claws are both the same size?

2. The Hamilton Leather Tote, Selma Satchel and Jet Set Wallet were created by which Long Island-born fashion designer, who was Celine's first-ever women's ready-to-wear designer?

3. Only one known animal, a large rodent with chisel-like teeth called the agouti, can crack open the hard outer coating of its fruit. Which nut tree – *Bertholletia excelsa* – towers at heights of up to 160 feet over the Amazon rainforest?

4. The British Olympic fencer Bob Anderson was one of at least five men who played which role in the original *Star Wars* trilogy?

5. Which Kate Bush song was sampled in the Utah Saints' 1992 hit 'Something Good'?

6. Which Greek letter gives its name to particles that consist of two protons and two neutrons bound together into a particle identical to a helium nucleus?

7. Which team shocked defending champions West Germany by beating them home and away (1–0, 1–2) in qualifying for the 1984 European Championships, but failed to make the finals?

8. Albert IV, Duke of Bavaria, promulgated the *Reinheitsgebot* ('German Beer Purity Law'), which originated on 30 November 1487, by specifying which three ingredients for the brewing of beer?

9. In its modern form, what includes the grind, the spine, the fuller, the ricasso, the guard, the butt, and the lanyard?

10. In which city does the Doge's Palace have an entrance on Piazza Matteotti and another on Piazza De Ferrari?

11. Which Swabian artist painted *The Miraculous Draft of Fishes*?

12. If a beef patty is the savoury part of a 'Luther Burger', what is the sweet component?

13. Which mineral gave its name to the 'Crisis' or 'Revolution' that shook the watchmaking industry in the 1970s and early 1980s, as mechanical watches were replaced by cheaper imports?

14. What is the stage name of the Swiss-born Italian DJ Robert Concina who sold over 5m copies of his 1995 single 'Children'.

15. Which actor is often seen in Adam Sandler films saying, in an inexplicable Cajun accent, the line: 'You can do it!'?

Answers to General Knowledge:
Fiendishly Difficult Quiz 28

1. Fiddler crab/calling crab
2. Michael Kors
3. Brazil nut tree
4. Darth Vader
5. 'Cloudbusting'
6. Alpha (particles)
7. Northern Ireland
8. Water, malt, hops
9. Knife – the other two parts: blade and handle
10. Genoa
11. Konrad Witz – in 1444
12. The two doughnuts that act as replacement hamburger buns
13. Quartz
14. Robert Miles
15. Rob Schneider

1. Often called 'the first Egyptologist' due to his efforts in identifying and restoring historic buildings, temples and tombs, Prince Khaemweset is the best known son of which pharaoh?

2. Created by Shaun T. (for Thompson), which 60-day High-intensity Interval Training product from Beachbody is so named because 'it's going to get you crazy-good results' and calls itself the 'Number One Workout in America'?

3. With the accession of Bulgaria to the European Union on 4 January 2007, what became the third official script of the EU, following the Latin and Greek scripts?

4. Appearing in Chengdu in around the 10th century, the Song dynasty *jiaozi* is known as the world's first paper form of what?

5. Nicknamed 'the Alcatraz of the South' and 'the Farm', Louisiana State Penitentiary is the USA's largest maximum security prison and has earned a reputation as the 'bloodiest prison in the country'. Which penal plantation's popular name comes from its federal post office and not an African country?

6. Reputedly the world's loudest insect, *Thopha saccata* or the double drummer is a species of what?

7. Which AP Press photographer took the Pulitzer-winning picture of a naked, napalm-burned 9-year-old Phan Thi Kim Phuc in 1972?

8. Which rationalist architect designed the Casa del Fascio (1932–36) in Como and the unbuilt Danteum monument to Dante?

9. In 2014, Sarah Hendrickson (USA) achieved what first?

10. The 'dark triad' is a group of negative personality traits: narcissism, psychopathy and which other, named after an Italian Renaissance political philosopher?

11. Retiring as MP for North Antrim in 2010, who founded the Free Presbyterian Church of Ulster? He is now Lord Bannside.

12. Known for such albums as *Bass Culture* and his 1978 debut *Dread Beat an' Blood*, which Jamaican-born recording artist has been called 'the father of dub poetry'?

13. In 1976, which future Labour MP was acquitted of robbing a Barclays bank branch, having been apparently framed by BOSS, South Africa's Bureau of State Security?

14. Which Formula One team founder was killed at Goodwood in 1970 when his Can-Am car crashed on the Lavant Straight?

15. Which female Banksy stencilled 12 *Rude Popes* in London?

Answers to General Knowledge:
Fiendishly Difficult Quiz 29

1. Ramesses II/Ramesses the Great
2. INSANITY
3. Cyrillic
4. Money/banknote
5. Angola
6. Cicada
7. Nick Ut/Huỳnh Công Út
8. Giuseppe Terragni
9. First woman to ski jump in Olympic competition
10. Machiavellianism
11. Reverend Ian Paisley
12. Linton Kwesi Johnson
13. Peter Hain
14. Bruce McLaren
15. Bambi (they depict Benedict XVI doing a V-sign. Bambi is best known for Camden Road's Amy Winehouse mural.)

1. Inspired by TV's Alf Garnett, which pop group's drummer wrote the 1967 hit 'Randy Scouse Git', aka 'Alternate Title'?

2. Featuring a US no.1 hit of 1989, which movie 'tearjerker to end all tearjerkers' was based on a 1986 novel by Iris Rainer Dart?

3. Which Colombian cyclist won the 2014 Giro d'Italia?

4. A famed example of a TV 'breakout character', which ultra-nerd was played by Jaleel White in the US sitcom *Family Matters*?

5. Which edible saltwater bivalve is the largest burrowing clam in the world and has a Lushootseed-(Nisqually-) language name that either means 'dig deep' or refers to its suggestive shape?

6. What is the language of Chennai movie industry Kollywood?

7. A 55,000-year-old cave bear's femur pierced by spaced-out holes was found in 1995 at a site below Šebrelje, and near Cerkno in north-west Slovenia. On show at the National Museum of Slovenia, what is probably the world's oldest known musical instrument has which three-word name?

8. Based in the monastery of San Vittore al Corpo, the Museo della Scienza e della Tecnologia 'Leonardo da Vinci' – Italy's largest science and technology museum – is in which city?

9. Often performed during Chinese New Year, which form of traditional dance, also known as *wǔ lóng*, has teams mimic the sinuous movements of a legendary river spirit? These patterns have names like 'Whirlpool', and 'Looking for Pearl'.

10. Chalcis is the capital city of which island, Greece's second largest?

11. Which newspaper was founded in 1821 as a 7d weekly by cotton merchant John Edward Taylor, who was backed by a group of Nonconformist businessmen?

12. Which *Doctor Who* actor played lifeguard Ben Carpenter, the hero of 2002 cult film *Shark Attack 3: Megalodon*?

13. Later publications included *Thirtyfour Parking Lots* and *Nine Swimming Pools and a Broken Glass*. In 1962, which US pop artist published *Twentysix Gasoline Stations*, possibly the first modern artist's book? He is also known for word paintings like *OOF*, *The End* and *BOSS*.

14. The birthplace of King Henry VII, which castle was built over a large cave known as the Wogan?

15. *Wang* is the Dutch name for which part of the body?

Answers to General Knowledge:
Fiendishly Difficult Quiz 30

1. The Monkees – the drummer being Micky Dolenz
2. *Beaches* – the single is 'Wind Beneath My Wings' by Bette Midler
3. Nairo Quintana who came second to Chris Froome in the 2013 Tour de France.
4. Steve Urkel
5. Geoduck (pronounced 'gooey duck') – *Panopea generosa*
6. Tamil
7. Divje Babe flute – Divje Babe is the name of the archaeological site
8. Milan
9. Dragon Dance
10. Euboea
11. The *Guardian*, founded as the *Manchester Guardian*
12. John Barrowman
13. Ed Ruscha
14. Pembroke Castle
15. Cheek/jowl

1. The first person to be honoured with a second ticker-tape parade, which dodgy polar explorer flew in the aeroplanes *Josephine Ford* and *Floyd Bennett*?

2. Which disposable white-rimmed basic 16 oz red cup is a ubiquitous sight at booze-fuelled house parties in US movies? The original was created in the 1930s by Leo Hulseman.

3. A memorial plaque at the Brighton Centre states that which entertainer gave his last ever public performance there on 10 October 1977? Accompanied by the Gordon Rose Orchestra, his final recorded performance, of the song 'Once in a While', took place at Maida Vale Studios on 11 October.

4. The Nordic Council includes five countries and three territories: Greenland, Faroe Islands and which Swedish-speaking islands?

5. Which valley east of Düsseldorf was named after the German Reformed Church pastor whose most famous hymn, 'Praise to the Lord, the Almighty, the King of creation', was published in 1680?

6. Octavio de Moraes invented which sport on Copacabana beach?

7. In 1967, the Finnish firm Fiskars introduced the world's first plastic-handled scissors in which now trademarked colour?

8. Which six-letter word is missing from the title of Mark Twain's 1880 essay 'The Awful _____ Language'?

9. Played on film by Rex Harrison, which Pope (1443–1513) founded the Swiss Guard?

10. Sweet Adelines International is a worldwide organisation that advances which type of musical art form?

11. 'The Bureaucrat', 'the Avalanche' and 'Fistful o' Dollars' are among the Eight Great Gambits used in which game?

12. Featuring Sir Christopher Lee as the Uruguayan bar owner Manolo, which 1956 Powell and Pressburger war film was retitled *Pursuit of the Graf Spee* for US audiences?

13. Which AD 65 plot against Nero was betrayed by Milichus, a freedman of plotter and praetorian tribune Flavius Scaevinus?

14. Living at 698 Candlewood Lane in Cabot Cove, Maine, who sent the manuscript of her first novel, *The Corpse Died at Midnight*, to publishers after the death of her husband Frank?

15. Introduced in 1996 to compete with Intel's Pentium microprocessor, the K5 was the first x86 processor to be developed entirely in-house by which US semiconductor company?

Answers to General Knowledge:
Fiendishly Difficult Quiz 31

1. Richard E. Byrd
2. Solo Cup
3. Bing Crosby, who died on 14 October while he was in Alcobendas, Madrid, Spain
4. Åland Islands
5. Neandertal Valley/Neander Valley – named after Joachim Neander, the only hymnist with a fossil hominid named after him
6. Footvolley
7. Orange
8. German
9. Julius II/Giuliano della Rovere – 'Sexy Rexy' played him in *The Agony and the Ecstasy*
10. Barbershop harmony
11. Rock-Paper-Scissors/Roshambo/Paper-Scissors-Stone
12. *The Battle of the River Plate*
13. Pisonian conspiracy – the eponymous conspirator was the senator Gnaeus Calpurnius Piso
14. Jessica Fletcher, born Jessica Beatrice McGill – Angela Lansbury's sleuth in TV's *Murder She Wrote*
15. AMD/Advanced Micro Devices

1. 'Warwick the Kingmaker', Richard Neville, 16th Earl of Warwick, was killed at which April 1471 battle?

2. Home to a Musée Gauguin, what is Tahiti's oldest village?

3. Introduced to the US public by Ôlohe Solomon Kaihewalu in 1963, which ancient Hawaiian martial art of breaking bones and dislocating joints is known by a three-letter name?

4. Peter Sellers was the first in April 1964 and in April 2014, Bruno Mars became the 10th. Those who came in between include Burt Reynolds (October 1979), Donald Trump (March 1990) and Seth Rogen (April 2009). They were all bestowed with which 'honour'?

5. Known for its thick, fibrous bark, the woollybutt is a species of which Australian tree?

6. In 2007, it was announced that the computer program Chinook had 'solved' which board game, meaning that it cannot be beaten?

7. 'What, me worry?' is the catchphrase of which US magazine mascot?

8. The dog breed Xoloitzcuintle or *perro pelón mexicano* has which common two-word English name?

9. Sharing its title with a 1980 thriller by Jack Higgins, which 2013 novel opens with our hero celebrating his 45th birthday with a breakfast of scrambled eggs and six rashers of bacon at the Dorchester Hotel in 1969?

10. Desmology is the study of which bands of fibrous tissue, given such riveting names as the inferior glenohumeral?

11. Which vermouth brand dates back to 1757 and the Turin herbal shop of brothers Giovanni Giacomo and Carlo Stefano, who created a 'vermouth Bianco' with a secret 35-ingredient recipe?

12. Which annual event uses the slogan '*Ce n'est pas une course, c'est un monument*'?

13. Referring to a hunting trip he took earlier in the day, who wrote '*rien*' ('nothing') in his diary entry for 14 July 1789?

14. A 2012 and 2013 Prêmio Brasil Olímpico winner, which Brazilian gymnast's gold in the rings exercise at the London Games was Latin America's first ever Olympic medal in artistic gymnastics?

15. Founded by the Byzantine emperor Alexios I Comnenos, Kykkos Monastery is the largest monastery on which island, the setting for Lawrence Durrell's autobiographical book *Bitter Lemons*?

Answers to General Knowledge:
Fiendishly Difficult Quiz 32

1. Battle of Barnet
2. Papeari
3. Lua
4. Men who have posed for the cover of *Playboy* magazine
5. Eucalyptus/*Eucalyptus longifolia*
6. Draughts
7. Alfred E. Neuman of *Mad* magazine
8. Mexican hairless
9. *SOLO* by William Boyd – our hero being James Bond
10. Ligaments
11. Cinzano
12. Prix de l'Arc de Triomphe horse race
13. King Louis XVI – on the day that the Bastille was stormed
14. Arthur Zanetti
15. Cyprus

1. Juicy Couture launched which signature velour item in 2001?

2. Which *Johnny English Reborn* star has co-authored the 2014 sci-fi novel *A Vision of Fire* with thriller writer Jeff Rovin?

3. Who was King of Cambodia in 1941–55 and 1993–2004? He held so many political offices that he is the Guinness World Record holder for 'most state roles held by a modern royal'.

4. Which Woody Allen film and musical is about the making of the play *God of Our Fathers* by David Shayne?

5. Which state was dissolved with the 1933 *Machtergreifung*?

6. Which city is the title of a Carl Sandburg poem; songs by Sufjan Stevens, Groove Armada, Tom Waits and Kiki Dee; a novel by Egyptian author Alaa Al Aswany; plays by Sam Shepard and Maurine Dallas Watkins; and a musical by Kander and Ebb?

7. Also known as Ambras syndrome, what is hypertrichosis?

8. Which Swiss-born naturalist's epoch-making work, *Recherches sur les poissons fossils* (Research on Fossil Fishes), appeared in parts from 1833 to 1843?

9. Which Catalan artist's 1936 surrealist *Object* features a silk-stockinged leg with velvet garter, stuffed parrot, engraved map and bowler hat?

10. So insane that its Cannonball Loop water slide had a complete vertical loop, the infamously dangerous Action Park closed in 1996. It was in which US state?

11. Who did Robert Jenkinson, 2nd Earl of Liverpool, succeed as Prime Minister in 1812?

12. At a 1985 Christie's auction, a bottle of 1787 Château Lafitte was purchased for $156,450. This Bordeaux remains the most expensive bottle of wine ever sold. Which man's initials – 'Th.J' – are etched into this bottle of now undrinkable rotten vinegar?

13. First played in 1971, which football match is nicknamed 'Le Classique'?

14. Which Swiss mathematician introduced many current notations, including $f(x)$ to describe a function; the letter e for the base of the natural logarithm; and a, b and c for the sides of a triangle?

15. It has 1,282 pages, the text pages having two columns of type. Approximately, 180 copies were printed: 40 on vellum, 140 on paper. Taking three years, printing of the copies of which book was completed around 1456?

Answers to General Knowledge:
Fiendishly Difficult Quiz 33

1. Juicy Tracksuit
2. Gillian Anderson
3. Norodom Sihanouk
4. *Bullets over Broadway*
5. Germany's Weimar Republic (*Machtergreifung*, translates as 'seizure of power')
6. *Chicago*
7. Abnormal amount of hair growth over the body, so you resemble a wolf-man (Ambras was the surname of a 17th century family of sufferers from the Canary Islands)
8. Louis Agassiz
9. Joan Miró
10. New Jersey
11. Spencer Perceval, the only assassinated British Prime Minister
12. Thomas Jefferson
13. Paris Saint-Germain versus Olympique de Marseille derby
14. Leonhard Euler – *e* for the base of the natural log is now also known as Euler's number
15. The 42-line Gutenberg Bible – probably the first European printed book using movable type

1. According to Nietsche, which opera is 'Christianity arranged for Wagnerians'?
2. Premiered in 2009, who wrote *Kepler*, an opera about the 17th-century astronomer?
3. How do we better know James Brine, James Hammett, George and James Loveless, Thomas and John Standfield?
4. The Bagrationi dynasty was the ruling family of which country from the early Middle Ages until the early 19th century?
5. The Orda Caves in Russia's Perm region are thought to be the largest in the world to be formed from which crystallised mineral?
6. Used for naval spars that may have given Nelson's fleet an advantage, what tree was declared by Captain Cook's botanist to be 'the finest timber I ever saw'?
7. The Larsen trap is principally used to catch examples of which particular family of birds?
8. What two-word name (in English) is given to France and Belgium's substantial annual haul of unexploded World War I bombs and munitions?
9. Which future British Prime Minister was wounded in the leg by shrapnel at Gallipoli?
10. Due to be restored at a cost of 6 million euros, the Seven Halls is a complex of (nine) cisterns in Rome which supplied water to which major bathing facility in ancient times?
11. One of the earliest sets of what was created in the 15th century by Martin Ketzel in Nuremberg based on painstaking measurements he had made in Jerusalem?
12. The German firm of Marklin is a revered 150-year-old toymaker particularly associated with which type of toy?
13. Noted for a grotesque injury to Wayne Shelford, which French city was host to a rugby union Test match of legendary ferocity between France and New Zealand in November 1986?
14. When the actor Jean Reno was married in 2006, which prominent politician was his best man?
15. Performed by Alicia Keys and Jack White, which was the first Bond film to feature a duet as the title song?

Answers to General Knowledge:
Fiendishly Difficult Quiz 34

1. *Parsifal*
2. Philip Glass
3. The Tolpuddle Martyrs
4. Georgia
5. Gypsum
6. Kauri
7. Corvids (magpies, crows etc.)
8. Iron Harvest. The same term is used for Germany's annual discovery of about 2,000 tonnes of World War II ordnance
9. Clement Attlee
10. Baths of Trajan
11. Stations of the Cross
12. Model trains
13. Nantes – 'the Battle of Nantes'
14. Nicolas Sarkozy
15. *Quantum of Solace*

1. Which rock frontman had 'Kill Bon Jovi' written on the headstock of one of his guitars because Bon Jovi's chopper had inadvertently buzzed the band while they were on-stage at Donnington?

2. Composed entirely of women, in which capital city is the Light and Hope Orchestra based?

3. What is the rather bleak meaning of the acronym 'NINJA' as relating to US borrowers?

4. *Kina* is the Maori name for an edible type of which sea creature?

5. Giuseppe Garibaldi spent his last 27 years on the tiny island of Caprera, which is part of the Maddalena Archipelago which lies just off the north coast of which larger island?

6. Sharing their name with an OMD album of 1983, what were the warships camouflaged with abstract patterning devised by Norman Wilkinson called?

7. 'Queen of the Forest' is a Madagascan nickname for which tree?

8. Who was the last emperor of Byzantium?

9. In which city did the St Scholastica's Day riot begin on 10 February 1355, with opposing forces of town and gown on the rampage for three days?

10. Hajji Firuz, a black-faced character clad in bright red clothes and a red hat, is the traditional herald of which Zoroastrian festival?

11. Referring to a London store, what name was given to the Italian version of art nouveau?

12. In 2014, which 75-year-old announced his entry into the Route du Rhum, a 3,500-mile solo ocean yacht race he had last contested in 1982?

13. Who sired the Derby winners Nijinsky, the Minstrel and Secreto?

14. Dying in 2009, Shih Kien made over 300 films but is best known to Western audiences for playing the villainous Han in which 1973 film?

15. Eighteenth-century Scotsman William Brodie, who was hanged in 1788, was the inspiration for which literary character(s)?

Answers to General Knowledge:
Fiendishly Difficult Quiz 35

1. James Hetfield (of Metallica)
2. Cairo
3. No Income, No Job (and) no Assets
4. Sea urchin
5. Sardinia
6. Dazzle ships
7. Baobab
8. Constantine XI (Palaeologus)
9. Oxford
10. Nowruz/Persian New Year
11. Stile Liberty
12. Sir Robin Knox-Johnston
13. Northern Dancer
14. *Enter the Dragon*
15. Dr Jekyll and Mr Hyde

1. The singer Neil Diamond won a sports scholarship to New York University. Which sport?
2. Ejected from the Vienna choir school when his voice broke, which composer eked out a living as a busker until an Italian composer named Porpora took pity and hired him as a valet?
3. Which Cheshire town has hosted a cheese show for over a century which it claims is the biggest cheese show in the world?
4. In 1855, which French monarch introduced the classification of Bordeaux's best wines?
5. What rare political distinction was achieved by Professor Ralf Dahrendorf, who died in 2009?
6. Under what name did Joseph Wurzelbacher gain national attention during the 2008 US presidential election?
7. Which Irish geologist discovered the outer core of the earth in 1906 and identified the P and S waves caused by earthquakes?
8. Which Berber tribesmen are known as 'the Blue Men' because of their flowing indigo robes?
9. With the temperature falling to minus 14°C (7°F), the parade was cancelled and the ceremony held indoors. Which US President was inaugurated on the coldest day?
10. In which country are there numerous keyhole-shaped burial mounds dating from the Kofun Culture in the 3rd century AD?
11. Which country is served by the Yonhap news agency?
12. Which cyclist won seven successive Paris–Nice classics from 1982 through 1988?
13. Who replied, 'What's Hoover gotta do with it? I had a better year than he did,' on being asked how he felt about earning more than the President?
14. At the 2007 Academy Awards Ceremony he became the first actor from his country to win a Best Supporting Actor Oscar. One year later, she became the first actress from this same country to win a Best Supporting Actress Oscar. They married in due course. Which country?
15. Which Hollywood director, commenting on fame, said, 'One day you are a signature, next day you're an autograph'?

Answers to General Knowledge:
Fiendishly Difficult Quiz 36

1. Fencing
2. Joseph Haydn
3. Nantwich
4. Napoleon III
5. He was, at different times, a member of both the British and German parliaments
6. Joe the Plumber – an exchange with Senator Obama in Ohio made the headlines.
7. Richard Dixon Oldham
8. Tuareg
9. Ronald Reagan – second term in 1985
10. Japan
11. South Korea
12. Sean Kelly
13. Babe Ruth
14. Spain (Javier Bardem – *No Country for Old Men* and Penelope Cruz – *Vicky Christina Barcelona*)
15. Billy Wilder

1. KT Tunstall's song 'Suddenly I See' was inspired by whose cover portrait of Patti Smith on the album *Horses*?
2. He set a world record of 57 cars in 45 seconds. What is the particular skill of Aniket Chindak from Karnataka, India?
3. Which best-selling PDO (Protected Designation of Origin) hard cheese was created nearly 900 years ago by the Cistercian monks of Chiaravalle Abbey?
4. The vegetarian dip *Cervelle de Canut* ('silk worker's brains') is a classic recipe from which French city?
5. *The Troubled Man* is the latest novel to feature which detective?
6. Proving a major source of military intelligence for Britain on German pre-World War I shipbuilding, 'Baby Brookfield' was the 14-year-old daughter of the incumbent British consul at which strategic city?
7. Otto Bock was founded in 1919 by its namesake as a consequence of World War I. It is today a leader in which field producing, amongst other products, the Michelangelo?
8. Now thought to have been a solar observatory, in which country are the 13 Towers of Chankillo?
9. The first version of the SOLAS Convention was adopted in 1914 in response to the *Titanic* disaster. What do the letters SOLAS stand for?
10. Since 1712, in which cathedral have all but one of the Russian Tsars been buried?
11. In 2014, which 1973 French Open champion became a senator?
12. Which F1 driver, born in Germany of a Uruguayan father who was a soloist with the Munich Philharmonic Orchestra, had aspirations himself of becoming a classical concert pianist?
13. According to the rules of golf (R&A and USPGA), what is the maximum volume (ccs) of golf club head allowed?
14. At the 2007 Academy Awards ceremony he became the first actor from his country to win a Best Supporting Actor Oscar. One year later, she became the first actress from this same country to win a Best Supporting Actress Oscar. They married in due course. Which country?
15. The events of the poem 'Casabianca' take place during which battle of 1798?

Answers to General Knowledge:
Fiendishly Difficult Quiz 37

1. Robert Mapplethorpe
2. Limbo-skating
3. Grana Padano
4. Lyon
5. Kurt Wallander (Henning Mankell)
6. Danzig (now Gdansk) – she spoke fluent German and roamed wild and free around the city
7. Prosthetics. The Michelangelo is a sophisticated artificial hand
8. Peru
9. Safety Of Life At Sea
10. Peter and Paul, St Petersburg
11. Ilie Nastase – Romania
12. Adrian Sutil
13. 460 cc (with a tolerance of 10 cc)
14. Spain (Javier Bardem – *No Country for Old Men* – and Penelope Cruz – *Vicky Cristina Barcelona*)
15. Battle of the Nile

1. Which major Italian city has a leading daily newspaper called *Il Secolo XIX* – 'The 19th Century' – indicating it might be behind the times, but it was actually one of the first Italian newspapers to be printed in colour?

2. In 1979, Paul McCartney received from the *Guinness Book of World Records* a disc fashioned from which extremely rare metal, recognising him as the best-selling songwriter/recording artist of all time (gold, silver or platinum being inadequate!).

3. What is the technical term for sound that is lower in frequency than the normal limit of human hearing?

4. In May 2014 Albert Bunjaku scored which country's first official international goal since recognition by FIFA, in a 6–1 loss to Turkey?

5. Leopold von Ranke (1795–1886) a professor at Berlin for nearly 50 years, was highly influential in developing which subject?

6. The Battle of Camerone (1863) holds a central place in the mythology and history of which military organisation?

7. Which pasta shape was invented in the 1960s by an industrial designer and is named for its supposed resemblance to a particular piece of machinery?

8. From 2013 the number of women's major golf championships was increased to five, with the addition of which tournament?

9. Which controversial leader of the far-right Austrian Freedom Party died in a car crash in 2008?

10. What is New Zealand's longest river?

11. A national emblem of Turkmenistan, what is the Akhal–Teke?

12. Which Austro-Hungarian emperor loved the premiere of Cimarosa's 1792 opera *The Secret Marriage* so much that he invited the whole cast and orchestra to dinner, before demanding that they stage the whole thing once again?

13. Which hobby might involve the use of a Black Zulu, an Orange Peril, a Pot Scumbler, a Welsh Partridge and the Butcher?

14. The US developmental biologist James Thomson led the University of Wisconsin School of Medicine team that, in 1998, won the race to isolate and culture which type of cell?

15. When JFK said, 'Victory has a hundred fathers but defeat is an orphan,' in the wake of the 1961 Bay of Pigs disaster, he was quoting which Foreign Minister of Fascist Italy (1936–43)?

Answers to General Knowledge:
Fiendishly Difficult Quiz 38

1. Genoa
2. Rhodium
3. Infrasound – the normal limit being c. 20 Hertz per, or cycles, second
4. Kosovo
5. History
6. The French Foreign Legion – a 'last stand' action fought during the French invasion of Mexico. Spanish name Camaron
7. Radiatori
8. The Evian Championship (previously the Evian Masters)
9. Jorg Haider
10. Waikato
11. Horse breed
12. Leopold II
13. Fly-fishing – they are the names of lures
14. Human embryonic stem cells – which have the ability to develop into any of the 220 cell types in the body
15. Galeazzo Ciano – the original Italian 'nessuno vuole riconoscere l'insuccesso' more accurately translated 'no one wants to recognise failure'

1. Which TV comedy show featured the sketches 'Continental Breakfast', 'East/West College Bowl', 'I Said Bitch', 'Dubstep', and 'McCringleberry's Excessive Celebration'?

2. Demonstrated in the films *Heat* and *Collateral*, what is the 'Mozambique Drill'?

3. Which Cossack began Russia's conquest of Siberia in 1582?

4. Owners of the Ogilvy Group and Cohn & Wolfe, which British firm is the world's largest advertising company by revenue?

5. Which 1931 *Time* magazine Person of the Year was found guilty of high treason and executed by firing squad in October 1945?

6. Which French scientist gave his name to the principle that states how a chemical system in equilibrium will respond to changes in order to establish a new equilibrium?

7. Founded in 2010 by real estate investor Chen Mingjing, which theme park near Kunming, Yunnan province, is a village apparently populated by dwarfs (less than 51 in tall) putting on comic performances?

8. Featured on the cover of the debut album *Killing is My Business . . . and Business is Good!* (1985), Vic Rattlehead is the mascot of which US thrash metal band?

9. Imperial Russia's part in the Scramble for Africa was hilariously brief as they were kicked out of 'New Moscow' by the French after less than a year. In 1889, Russians founded a colony in Sagallo in which present-day country?

10. Telling the story of Dar (Marc Singer), which 1982 cult film used the tagline 'Born with the courage of an eagle, the strength of a black tiger, and the power of a god'?

11. Which English physicist, whose autistic traits led Einstein to say, 'This balancing on the dizzying path between genius and madness is awful', married Margit, the sister of fellow Nobel laureate and colleague Eugene Wigner, after meeting her while she was visiting Princeton from her native Hungary?

12. Hydrogen cyanide is secreted by the 'shocking pink dragon _____' to protect itself. What is the missing word?

13. Which Cairo team is the world's most successful football club in terms of trophy count and by number of international titles won?

14. What nationality is double Oscar nominee Djimon Hounsou?

15. Finn, the dog Jake and the Land of Ooo feature in which show?

Answers to General Knowledge:
Fiendishly Difficult Quiz 39

1. *Key and Peele*
2. A close-quarter shooting technique: double tap centre mass then a kill shot to the head
3. Yermak (Timofeyevich)
4. WPP
5. Pierre Laval, 101st Prime Minister of France
6. Le Chatelier's principle
7. Kingdom of the Little People/*Xiǎo Ǎirén Wángguó* – it has been comdemned by Warwick Davis as a return to the 'freak show'
8. Megadeth
9. Djibouti
10. *The Beastmaster*
11. Paul Dirac
12. Millipede
13. Al Ahly Sporting Club, with – at the time of writing – 126 official trophies (107 domestic, 19 international)
14. Beninese, strictly speaking, now Beninese–American
15. *Adventure Time* (the animated TV series created by Pendleton Ward for the Cartoon Network)

1. Who directed the 1968 Rolling Stones documentary *Sympathy for the Devil*?

2. Which Californian singer (*Closing Time* (1973) and *Swordfishtrombones* (1983)), was praised by the Vatican for 'representing the marginalised and the misunderstood'?

3. Adopting the name of which Far Eastern Russian city, gold miner Peter Hambro Mining changed its name in 2009 to both reflect the names of the founders Peter Hambro and Paul Maslovsky and to emphasise its Russian focus?

4. Which is the only city in the UK with its name protected by a trademark?

5. The name of which large Scottish island is thought to derive from the Norse for 'cloud island'?

6. Reaching a speed of 24,791 mph, what was the fastest ever manned spacecraft?

7. Afred Russel Wallace went to the Malay archipelago to capture and study which creatures, the variation in which ultimately inspired his theories of natural selection?

8. The colours of the rainbow mnemonic Richard Of York Gave Battle In Vain is said to refer to which battle of 1460?

9. Used to neutralise strong odours, what is so-called Garlic Soap actually made of?

10. Two bored cherubim in Raphael's painting *Sistine Madonna* have become a symbol for which city, where the painting hangs?

11. Antoine Watteau's rococo painting *Pilgrimage to Cythera* (1717) is a classic example of which genre, showing the idyllic amusements of the idle rich?

12. Of the five successful 65-yard-and-over field goal attempts in NFL history (up to the end of 2013), four have been achieved in which city?

13. Selling for over $9,000,000 in 2014, what, made in 1856, was discovered in 1873 by L. Vernon Vaughan, a 12-year-old Scottish boy living in South America?

14. Which 2011 film, directed by Alejandro Brugués, was billed as Cuba's first zombie film?

15. Which composer gave Vladimir Nabokov, on the run from the Nazis with his Jewish wife Vera, the money for their passage across the Atlantic?

Answers to General Knowledge:
Fiendishly Difficult Quiz 40

1. Jean-Luc Godard
2. Tom Waits
3. Petropavlovsk (plc)
4. Sheffield
5. Skye – (*Ski* + *Ey'* – Norse)
6. Apollo 10
7. Birds of paradise
8. Wakefield
9. Stainless steel
10. Dresden
11. *Fête galante*
12. Denver – the thin 'mile high' air aids with distance
13. Stamp – the British Guiana one-cent magenta
14. *Juan of the Dead/Juan de los Muertos*
15. Sergei Rachmaninov

1. Which singer played professional wrestler Wendi Richter's manager in the inaugural WrestleMania event?

2. Which rapper with the real name James Todd Smith wrote the book *Platinum 360 Diet and Lifestyle*?

3. Iron Goddess of Mercy and Phoenix Supreme are varieties of which type of tea?

4. What, in France, are *DOM-TOMS*?

5. Charles Darwin visited which place in Cambridgeshire, Britain's oldest nature reserve, to collect the rare crucifix ground beetle?

6. Who/what took the famous photograph of earth known as *The Pale Blue Dot* in 1990?

7. Recently discovered in Madagascar, *Calumma tarzan* is a forest-dwelling variety of which type of lizard?

8. In 2007, which land speed record breaker was buried with wrenches in his hands, accompanied by a jar of Bonneville salt, and the declassified manual to the General Electric J97 jet engine?

9. A massive best seller with 50 editions in its first year, *Eikon Basilike* was whose partly ghost-written spiritual autobiography, published very soon after his death?

10. The Orchard Factory, situated north-west of the Forbidden City in Beijing, was first established in the 15th century to manufacture fine carved artefacts from what substance, obtained from *Toxicodendrum vernicifluum*?

11. *Punto in aria* (stitches in the air) is a Venetian term for what?

12. In 2009, Geoff Allen (36), riding Duke's Touch of Fun, beat Martin Cox in which annual 22-mile event at Llanwrtyd Wells, Powys?

13. In 2014, Maryam Mirzakhani became the first women, after 52 men (since 1936), to receive which major award?

14. Which brother of singer Sinéad O'Connor wrote a trilogy of novels comprising *Star of the Sea* (2003), *Redemption Falls* (2007) and *Ghost Light* (2010)?

15. What is the well-known last line of Philip Larkin's poem 'An Arundel Tomb' (1956)?

Answers to General Knowledge:
Fiendishly Difficult Quiz 41

1. Cyndi Lauper
2. LL Cool J
3. Oolong (Chinese)
4. Overseas territories – Departements de Territoires Outre-Mer
5. Wicken Fen
6. *Voyager 1* – from over 4 billion miles away
7. Gecko
8. Art Arfons
9. Charles I – executed on Jan 30, 1649. The book may have laid some of the ground work for the restoration
10. Lacquer – it is the Chinese lacquer tree
11. Lace
12. Man versus Horse Marathon/man-against-beast hill race
13. Fields Medal (for mathematics)
14. Joseph O'Connor
15. 'What will survive of us is love'

1. Which trumpeter (1933–2012), acclaimed as the 'greatest classical trumpeter of the 20th century', was born in the town of Ales in the Gard region of southern France and attributed his playing stamina to five years digging coal?

2. Who was described as 'the worst threat to American children since polio' by President George W. Bush?

3. Called Mont Blanc in France, what are puréed to make the classic northern Italian dessert Monte Bianco?

4. What was called *nostra chaxa* by Venetians?

5. Prompting fears that a repeat is possible, scientists have uncovered evidence of a disastrous flood in about AD 563 which wiped out which present-day city?

6. What, in India, is the punganur?

7. The Queen was presented with necklaces called *tabuas* by the Paramount Chiefs of Fiji. These are made of the teeth of which creature?

8. Which specific type of weapon was pioneered by the Italians with successful attacks on the British battleships *Valiant* and *Queen Elizabeth* in Alexandria in 1941?

9. Which monarch is credited with introducing the red-legged or French partridge to Britain as a game bird?

10. Which fellow artist was the model for the figure wearing a red headscarf in the foreground of Gericault's *The Raft of the Medusa* (1819)?

11. Who designed the bizarre armadillo shoes which featured in the Lady Gaga video for 'Bad Romance'?

12. Dungeons is a famous surfing reef off which city?

13. Sinclair coefficients are used to compare different weight classes in which Olympic sport?

14. Which writer oversaw the exhumation and reburial of many thousands of corpses during the 1860s rerouting of the Midland Railway through St Pancras?

15. How are David Hare's dramas *Page Eight*, *Turks and Caicos* and *Salting the Battlefield* collectively known?

Answers to General Knowledge:
Fiendishly Difficult Quiz 42

1. Maurice André
2. Eminem
3. (Sweet) chestnuts
4. The Adriatic Sea ('our house')
5. Geneva – a rock fall into Lake Geneva caused a tsunami
6. A dwarf cow which had been facing extinction but has become a very desirable 'pet' partly because it produces three pints of milk a day with twice the fat content of standard milk
7. Sperm whales
8. Manned torpedoes (two-man crews)
9. Charles I
10. Eugene Delacroix
11. Alexander McQueen
12. Cape Town
13. Weightlifting
14. Thomas Hardy
15. *The Worricker Trilogy* – Bill Nighy has played the central character Johnny Worricker on TV

1. Which Looney Tunes rodent was billed as 'the fastest mouse in all Mexico'?

2. What names (both forename and surname) connect both the lead actress from *Last Tango in Paris* (1972) and a Grammy-winning US composer and big-band leader?

3. In Italy, small gangs of pensioners known as *battitori* or 'beaters' set about bushes with a stick when harvesting which fruit?

4. Tungi spirit is distilled in St Helena from what type of plant?

5. In which country will you find Isla Coiba, once an infamous prison island and now a National Park?

6. Hinterstoisser Traverse, Swallow's Nest, Death Bivouac, Traverse of the Gods and White Spider are key climbing landmarks on which mountain?

7. *Dina Robin* is the Arabic name for which island nation?

8. Discovered in Mexico, the small spider *Bagheera kiplingi* is unique in what way?

9. Where does the bitterling (*Rhodeus amarus*) lay its eggs, where the young are protected until ready to swim free?

10. Who, in 2013, was, in accordance with his final wish, finally buried in an unmarked grave next to his mother Ellen in Wangaratta, Victoria?

11. How would we translate *Aaru*, the ancient Egyptians' name for their ultimate heavenly paradise?

12. Carpenter Edward Hurley was Royal Carpenter to Edward II and is best known for which 1342 work, part of the so-called 'Ship of the Fens'?

13. Unparallelled in quality outside China, the British Museum's Percival David Foundation collection consists of 1,752 examples of what from the Song, Yuan, Ming and Qing dynasties (10th century to 20th century)?

14. In Japan, the skin of which creature is used as an under-layer for the cord or leather wrap (*ito*) on Japanese swords (*katanas*), owing to its hard, rough texture?

15. *Pietr the Latvian* was the first novel to feature which detective?

Answers to General Knowledge:
Fiendishly Difficult Quiz 43

1. Speedy Gonzalez
2. Maria Schneider
3. Juniper berry – the juniper tree resists cultivation.
4. Cactus (specifically the *Opuntia* – prickly pear)
5. Panama
6. Eiger (north face)
7. Mauritius
8. It is a vegetarian – the only known species of spider to be so. It lives almost exclusively on leaf buds
9. In freshwater mussels
10. Ned Kelly
11. Reeds (the Field of Reeds or Reed Fields)
12. The Ely Octagon – in Ely Cathedral
13. Ceramics/porcelain/pottery
14. Ray/stingray
15. Jules Maigret (Georges Simenon)

1. The PGA Grand Slam of Golf gathers together the four winners of the season's majors in a 36-hole tournament. Which item of clothing is won by the victor?

2. Dr. Joseph Murray performed which 'first' in Boston in 1954?

3. Which French director co-wrote, directed and starred in the seven-episode miniseries *The House in the Woods* (1971)?

4. The oldest Chinatown in the western hemisphere is in a country where c. 20% of the population has Chinese heritage, Barrio Chino is in the colonial San Felipe district of which capital city?

5. David Megas Komnenos (r. 1459–61) was the last emperor of where?

6. 'The nature island of the Caribbean', which country occupies the most mountainous of the Lesser Antilles and is home to Boiling Lake, the world's second-largest thermally active lake?

7. Packing stadiums with fans, *gushtingiri* has been called Tajikistan's 'national obsession'. What type of sport is it?

8. Apparently named after the Swedish immigrant Peter Gunnarsson Rambo, 'Rambo' is a US variety of what fruit?

9. Which cult sitcom starred both Chevy Chase, as 'moist-towelette millionaire' Pierce Hawthorne, and Donald Glover (rapper Childish Gambino), as plumbing genius Troy Barnes?

10. Mithrim Montes (2 km/1.2 miles high), a mountain range named after the Mithrim Mountains in J.R.R. Tolkien's Middle-Earth, and Doom Mons (1.45 km/0.9 miles), also given a Tolkien-inspired name, are features of which moon?

11. Named after an Irish traveller (1797–1873), the bronze-yellow mineral pentlandite is the principal ore of which metal?

12. Forming a team with his younger sister Olga, Vladimir 'Vova' Galchenko (b.1987) – originally from Penza, Russia – they are known as the greatest ever exponents of the 'club passing' form of which physical skill and competitive activity?

13. Author of the 1723 textbook *La Chirurgien Dentiste*, which 'father of modern dentistry' recommended daily rubbing of the teeth and gums with a small piece of natural sponge?

14. Which author, who died in 2013, is the only person to have won both the Booker Prize and an Oscar?

15. Reigning 309–79, which king of the Persian Sasanian Empire was the longest reigning monarch of the Sassanid dynasty?

Answers to General Knowledge:
Fiendishly Difficult Quiz 44

1. Pink jacket
2. The world's first truly succsessful kidney transplant operation – Ronald Herrick donated a kidney to save the life of his dying twin Richard
3. Maurice Pialat
4. Panama City
5. Empire of Trebizond, the last independent remnant of the Byzantine Empire
6. Dominica
7. Traditional jacket wrestling
8. Apple
9. *Community*
10. Titan – all Titanian mountains are named after mountains in Tolkien's works
11. Nickel
12. Juggling
13. Dr Pierre Fauchard
14. Ruth Prawer Jhabvala
15. Shapur II

1. *Portrait of a Carthusian* (1446), in New York's Metropolitan Museum, was painted by which Netherlandish artist, whose *Portrait of Edward Grimston* is in the National Gallery?
2. Maison Dandoy is a Belgian maker of which food products?
3. Which writer's compendium of 1960s *New Yorker* articles, titled *Business Adventures*, is Warren Buffett and Bill Gates' single favourite book about business?
4. Famed for his work with Justin Bieber and Cara Delevingne, what is the adopted name of Manhattan-based celeb tattooist Keith McCurdy?
5. The disorder trimethylaminuria makes sufferers smell of what?
6. The BBC broadcast the first ever television serial in 1938. Name this story about the growing love between a London couple?
7. Which Japanese art form is concerned with moulding earth and water to create a sphere that is shined up with fine dust particles to resemble a billiard ball? It derives its name from 'mud' and a round dumpling created from pressed rice flour.
8. The beautiful white sand beaches of the Caribbean are mostly composed of the excrement of which fish, whose name derives from the way their densely packed teeth resemble the part of a certain bird?
9. What status links Anser, Antinous, Apis, Argo Navis, Cancer Minor, Cerberus, Phaethon, Solarium, Testudo, Tigris, Triangulum Major, Triangulum Minor and Vespa?
10. The highest peak in Central America at 4,211 metres, the inactive volcano Tajumulco is in which country?
11. Though football is popular, *va'a* is Tahiti's national sport. A variation on an Olympic sport, what is *va'a*'s two-word English name?
12. What links *The Long Goodbye* by Harper Lee, *The Owl in Daylight* by Philip K. Dick, *The House on Value Street* by Stephen King and Kurt Vonnegut *If God Were Alive Today*?
13. Which New South Wales town's name means 'many crows'?
14. Which 1941 book by US psychiatrist Hervey M. Cleckley – subtitled *An Attempt to Clarify Some Issues About the So-Called Psychopathic Personality* – is considered the most influential clinical description of psychopathy in the 20th century?
15. What is the oldest Japanese car manufacturer?

Answers to General Knowledge:
Fiendishly Difficult Quiz 45

1. Petrus Christus
2. Biscuits
3. John Brooks
4. BangBang
5. Rotten fish – it is fish odour syndrome
6. *Ann and Harold*
7. Dorodango (*doro* litterally means mud in Japanese, *dango* is the dumpling part)
8. Parrotfish
9. They are former constellations – they are no longer recognised by the International Astronomical Union for various reasons
10. Guatemala
11. Outrigger canoeing
12. They are unpublished or abandoned or unfinished novels
13. Wagga Wagga – in the language of the Widadjuri, one of the NSW Aboriginal peoples, wagga means crow, repetition signifies the plural
14. *The Mask of Sanity*
15. Daihatsu

1. First bottled in St Galmier, Massif Central, in 1838, which gently carbonated drink is France's best-selling sparkling water?

2. Which 'little reed horses' are reed water craft that have been used by Peruvian fishermen for the past 3,000 years?

3. In 722 BC, who became king of the Assyrian Empire after the death of Shalmeneser V?

4. A concept record about the member of a US political dynasty, what is Benjamin Biolay's 2001 debut album?

5. A diamond's value is calculated according to the 4C criteria: cut, colour, carat and what?

6. The first US woman to earn an Olympic medal in judo (in 2008), which UFC Women's Bantamweight Champion is the consensus world no. 1 pound-for-pound female MMA fighter?

7. Pedro Lascuráin's presidency, lasting 15 minutes to an hour, makes him a contender for shortest tenure as a head of state. Lascuráin became, in 1913, the 34th president of where?

8. Which alliance of top airlines 'working as one' includes British Airways, American Airlines, Qantas, Qatar Airways and Iberia?

9. First performed in 1625, *La liberazione di Ruggiero* is widely considered the first opera by a woman composer – which is this singer, lutenist and poet, nicknamed 'La Cecchina'?

10. The world's shallowest sea, which inland sea was known in classical antiquity as Lake Maeotis? Ports include Mariupol.

11. Thought to be 100,000 years old, two shell beads made from *Nassarius gibbosulus* (sea snail) shells may be the oldest known jewellery. They were found in Skhul Cave/Es Skhul on the slopes of which mountain in the Haifa district of Israel?

12. Arsenal Futbol Club won the Primera Division title in 2012. Nicknamed 'El Arse', it is a football club in which country?

13. Edmund Fairchild founded which 'bible of fashion' in 1910?

14. Regarded as Sweden's funniest man, who plays the title character Allan Karlsson in the 2013 film of Jonas Jonasson's novel *The Hundred-Year-Old Man who Climbed Out of the Window and Disappeared*?

15. The crème fraîche from Normandy is famous and the type that comes from a defined area around which town in the Calvados department is the only cream with AOC status?

Answers to General Knowledge:
Fiendishly Difficult Quiz 46

1. Badoit owned by Groupe Danone
2. *Caballitos de totora*
3. Sargon II
4. *Rose Kennedy*
5. Clarity
6. Ronda Rousey – she also played Luna in *The Expendables 3*
7. Mexico
8. oneworld
9. Francesca Caccini – the opera's full title is *La Liberazione di Ruggiero dall'isola d'Alcina* ('The Liberation of Ruggiero from the Island of Alcina')
10. Sea of Azov
11. Mount Carmel/Mount Saint Elias/Kurmul
12. Argentina – (full name Arsenal de Sarandi) is based in Avallaneda Partido, Greater Buenos Aires
13. *Women's Wear Daily*
14. Robert Gustafsson
15. Isigny-sur-Mer

1. Which Yale Law School student, born in 1984 in Brooklyn, New York, is the top-earning female tournament poker player of all time, with more than $9 million in prize money?

2. Which US chemist – the inventor of both leaded petrol and CFCs – has been called 'the one human responsible for more deaths than any other in history'?

3. In which language is the *Hamlet* quote 'To be or not to be' rendered as '*Esti aŭ ne esti*'?

4. *Black Angels: Thirteen Images from the Dark Land* (1971) is a work by which US composer, who won the Pulitzer Prize in 1968 for his orchestral work *Echoes of Time*?

5. Known to 'shoot faster than his shadow', which cowboy is the creation of Belgian cartoonist Morris (Maurice De Bevere)?

6. Cameroon's best known literary figure, whose novel *The Poor Christ of Bomba* (1956) is a cynical recounting of the failure of a missionary to convert a small village's people?

7. Which sportsman was the dedicatee of the 2010 album *The Joker* by a rock band called Zona B?

8. Which 'cowboys' of the Camargue in southern France ride the famous Camargue horses to herd the wild bulls there?

9. The tradition of ringing church bells at noon in many parts of Europe derives from a papal command, ordering thanksgiving for the successful defence of which capital city in 1456?

10. What is the name of the loose, flowing long robe-like dress, traditionally black and covering all but the hands, face and feet, worn by women in parts of the Muslim world?

11. The DDD was introduced by the World Health Organization, to standardise comparisons of drug usage. DDD stands for what?

12. The photographer and painter born Henriette Markovitch in 1907 is most famous as an artistic muse of Pablo Picasso in the 1930s and '40s. What was her assumed name?

13. Tina Turner became a citizen of which country in 2013?

14. A leading Croatian football team is called Hajduk Split. What is or was a *hajduk*?

15. Mongol forces withdrew from their successful invasion of Europe in 1242 because of the death of their Great Khan back in their heartland and the need to hold a council to elect a new one. What was the deceased's name?

Answers to General Knowledge:
Fiendishly Difficult Quiz 47

1. Vanessa Selbst
2. Thomas Midgley, Jr
3. Esperanto
4. George Crumb
5. Lucky Luke
6. Mongo Beti/born Alexandre Biyidi-Awala
7. Novak Djokovic (Zona B are from Serbia)
8. Gardians
9. Belgrade, which was successfully defended against the Ottoman Turks
10. Abaya (plural abayat)
11. Defined daily dose
12. Dora Maar
13. Switzerland – the singer gave up her US nationality
14. An outlaw or guerrilla fighter (largely 17th–19th century)
15. Ogedei Khan (successor of Genghis Khan)

1. *Before Sunrise* = Vienna, *Before Sunset* = Paris, *Before Midnight* = where?

2. Only two of the 196 winners of the Nobel Prize in Physics up to 2013, only two have been women. One is Marie Curie; the other is which 1963 Katowice-born laureate, who shared her prize with Wigner and Jensen, for her work on nuclear shell structure?

3. What breed of domestic cat is Hello Kitty?

4. Denmark's Peter Madsen co-wrote and co-directed the 1986 animated film of which *Asterix*-style comedic romp through old Norse myths – a series that he helped create?

5. The first historically recognised King of Denmark, who ruled from Jelling, reigning from *c*.936 to his death in *c*.958, and made the oldest of the Jelling Stones in honour of his wife Thyra?

6. Which industrial town was the first parliamentary constituency to be represented by the young Winston Churchill?

7. *The Last Tycoon* is a 1976 film about the Hollywood golden age based on a novel by F. Scott Fitzgerald, which was far from finished at his death in 1940. The film title is an abbreviation of that of the book. What was the book's title?

8. A very influential designer whose work can be seen in many areas of British life, from traffic lights and bus shelters to cutlery design, died in 2009. He shared his name with a sometimes controversial former Tory cabinet minister. What was his name?

9. The site of the Battle of the Boyne, one of the key moments in the history of Ireland, lies at Oldbridge in which county?

10. What is the Spanish word for breakfast?

11. Which term was coined in 1989 to describe films by Luc Besson, Leos Carax and Jean-Jacques Beineix, often dealing with urban alienation in a showy, distinctive visual style?

12. The population of which Asian country officially reached 100 million in late July 2014?

13. Which Labour politician was the first leader of the new devolved Welsh Assembly from 1999, only to resign the following year, being succeeded by Rhodri Morgan?

14. The poem *Pan Tadeusz*, considered Poland's national epic, was published in 1834. Who was the author?

15. Black-, brown-, white- and golden-mantled are species from the *Saguinus* genus of which New World monkeys?

Answers to General Knowledge:
Fiendishly Difficult Quiz 48

1. Kardamyli, Messinia, Greece, and Pylos, Greece (they are the respective settings for the Richard Linklater films starring Ethan Hawke and Julie Delpy)
2. Maria Goeppert-Mayer, nicknamed 'the Onion Madonna'
3. Japanese Bobtail
4. *Valhalla*
5. Gorm the Old/Gorm the Sleepy
6. Oldham
7. *The Love of the Last Tycoon*
8. David Mellor
9. Meath
10. *Desayuno*
11. Cinema du Look
12. Philippines
13. Alun Michael
14. Adam Mickiewicz
15. Tamarin

1. Which French aviator was the top Allied fighter ace of World War I, with 76 kills?

2. The record known as the CET is the oldest continuous measure of temperatures in the world. CET stands for what?

3. Belonging to Iran, what is the largest island in the Persian Gulf?

4. Which 2001 Perrier Award-winner, who played the barman Spencer in *Phoenix Nights*, told Bob Holness he wanted to be a comedian when he was a teenage *Blockbusters* contestant?

5. Which *Daily Express* cartoonist created the character Maudie, Countess of Littlehampton?

6. James Joyce's novel *Ulysses* begins in what specific type of structure, situated near the port of Dun Laoghaire?

7. Which European monarch was the target of an assassination attempt in 1902 by an Italian anarchist as he returned from a ceremony honouring his recently deceased wife?

8. An 1876 novel by Emile Zola featured an artist, who was a thinly-disguised version of Paul Cézanne. It seems to have led to the ending of their long friendship. What is the book's title?

9. Which US composer was aged 103 when he completed his last work, *Epigrams* for piano trio, in 2012?

10. Which Bavarian spa town is famous for the German Federal Police winter sports training centre that has produced such Olympic champions as speed skater Claudia Pechstein?

11. Which Hungarian football manager allegedly cursed Benfica after it turned down his request for a pay rise in 1962? The Portuguese club has lost all of its subsequent European finals.

12. Which African country declared war on Germany in January 1918, and subsequently became the only independent African country to join the League of Nations as a founder member?

13. Which heroine of Greek tragic drama is condemned to death by her uncle King Creon?

14. In 2008 a village in Kent opened a 'Smugglers' Trail', commemorating the activities of one of the largest and most notorious smuggling gangs of the 18th and early 19th centuries. Named after the village, what was the gang called?

15. Two British scientists with the initials A. H. jointly received the Nobel Prize in Medicine in 1963 for their discovery of how plants and animals generate electricity. Name either man.

Answers to General Knowledge:
Fiendishly Difficult Quiz 49

1. René Paul Fonck
2. Central England Temperature (an area bounded roughly by London, Bristol and Lancashire) still continuing today, this meteorological dataset dates back to the mid-17th century
3. *Qeshm/Arabic: JazTrat al-Tawīlah*
4. Daniel Kitson
5. Osbert Lancaster
6. A Martello Tower
7. Leopold II of Belgium
8. *L'Oeuvre* (The Work – although often called *The Masterpiece* in English)
9. Elliott Carter
10. Bad Endorf
11. Béla Guttmann
12. Liberia
13. Antigone
14. The Hawkhurst Gang
15. Andrew Huxley or Alan Hodgkin

1. Known for a bleak ending that was changed in its Hollywood remake, George Sluizer's 1988 film *The Vanishing* was based on which novel by Dutch writer Tim Krabbé?

2. A leader of the Annales school, which French historian wrote *The Mediterranean in the Age of Philip II* (1972) and *Civilization and Capitalism, 15th–18th Centuries* (1979)?

3. The English-born granddaughter of Queen Victoria and Alexander II of Russia, Marie was the last queen-consort of Romania as the wife of which king, who died in 1927?

4. Having dominated her country's pop music scene for three decades, which Turkish singer's 2011 album *Öptüm* was her first international release? Her nicknames include the 'queen of Turkish pop' and *Minik Serçe* ('Little Sparrow').

5. US park ranger Roy Cleveland Sullivan was 71 when he committed suicide over an unrequited love. Between 1942 and 1977, what happened to him on seven different occasions?

6. Which artistic style derives its name from a shop that Siegfried Bing opened at 22 rue de Provence, Paris, on 26 December 1895?

7. *The Romantics* is the 1999 debut novel of which Indian author?

8. Which 1982 TV film, written by Jack Rosenthal, had the thoughts of the cricket-obsessed boy Alan (John Albasiny) voiced by real-life BBC radio commentator John Arlott?

9. The singer Alim Qasimov is considered the finest exponent of which dramatic ancient poetry art form of Azerbaijan?

10. Which MLB team signed the starting pitcher Masahiro Tanaka from the Tohoku Rakuten Golden Eagles in January 2014?

11. What is the largest art deco-style sculpture in the world?

12. Which US mechanical engineer summed up his efficiency techniques in his hugely influential 1911 monograph *The Principles of Scientific Management*?

13. Which US band's 1986 album *To Hell With The Devil* was the first Christian metal LP to achieve platinum status?

14. The last all-Christian community in the West Bank, which Palestinian village has held an Oktoberfest since 2005 and is home to the Middle East's only microbrewery?

15. Awarded a gold medal for *Dolce far niente* at the 1884 St Louis Expo, who was Argentina's first realist painter? He is perhaps best known for *El despertar de la criada*/*The Maid's Awakening*.

Answers to General Knowledge:
Fiendishly Difficult Quiz 50

1. *The Golden Egg*
2. Fernand Braudel
3. Ferdinand I
4. Sezen Aksu
5. He was hit by lightning on each occasion
6. Art nouveau – from Maison de l'Art Nouveau
7. Pankaj Mishra
8. *P'tang, Yang Kipperbang*
9. Mugham
10. New York Yankees
11. *Christ the Redeemer* – in Rio di Janeiro
12. Frederick Winslow Taylor – the 'father of scientific management'
13. Stryper
14. Taybeh
15. Eduardo Sívori

Children's

1. Her surname is Forget-me-Not; who stars on children's television with the Flowertots?
2. What is the name of Old Jack's boat in the children's television programme of the same name?
3. Archie the inventor; Spencer the painter-decorator and Miss Hoolie the nursery teacher are central characters in which children's television programme set in a Scottish namesake village?
4. How many pontipines live *In the Night Garden*?
5. Sportacus, Stephanie and Robbie Rotten inhabit which neighbourhood in a childen's television programme?
6. What is the name of the masked fox who keeps trying to steal stuff in *Dora the Explorer*?
7. What is the name of Rupert Bear's elephant friend in the show of that name?
8. Named after the noise they make, what set of 7 wooden objects live on an island with 'Abney and Teal'?
9. In *Rastamouse*, the title character forms which crime-busting reggae band with Scratchy and Zoomer?
10. In which children's television programme do Cheebies come and play games with the Piplings in the land of Nara?
11. In *Tilly and Friends*, what colour are the walls of the house that the title characters live in?
12. What kind of creatures are Squirt and Sparkie, as seen in *Mike the Knight*?
13. What is the name of the concrete mixer in *Bob the Builder*?
14. What are the steps you need to take to send the spotty bag back to Mr Tumble at the end of an episode of 'Something Special'?
15. To what does the Coconut Clock count down in *ZingZillas*?

Answers to Younger Children's Television:
Children's Quiz 1

1. Fifi
2. The *Rainbow*
3. *Balamory*
4. Ten
5. LazyTown
6. Swiper
7. Edward Trunk
8. The poc-pocs
9. Da Easy Crew
10. *Waybuloo*
11. Yellow
12. Dragons
13. Dizzy
14. Take your finger, touch your nose, blink three times (and off it goes!)
15. The Big Zing

1. Anna Conda, Arthur Sleep, Rapids Johnson and Keith-Fit are all characters in which children's sketch show?
2. Which elf and fairy have a *Little Kingdom* in the title of a children's television programme?
3. B1 and B2 are the title characters in which children's television programme? They live on Cuddles Avenue near teddy bears Amy, Lulu and Morgan.
4. In *Postman Pat*, what is the surname of the title character?
5. What type of bird is Pocoyo's friend Pato?
6. Which town is the setting for *Fireman Sam*?
7. Name either of the two dogs who play with the Tweenies.
8. Osbourne the Owl is one of the two teachers in *Timmy Time*. What species of bird is Harriet, the other teacher?
9. In *Teletubbies*, which is the only Teletubby to carry a bag?
10. Polluto and his sidekick Smogg are constantly trying to battle which superhero title character of a children's television programme?
11. In *Thomas & Friends*, what is the largest town and chief railway centre on the Isle of Sodor?
12. What kind of shop do Carrie and David run in a children's television programme?
13. In *Woolly and Tig*, what kind of creature is Woolly?
14. Scrappz, the Shapes and the cuckoo Tocky assist which creative children's television character?
15. Driver Dan and Raa Raa are what species of large cat?

Answers to Yonger Children's Television II:
Children's Quiz 2

1. *GiggleBiz*
2. Ben and Holly
3. *Bananas in Pyjamas*
4. Clifton
5. A duck
6. Pontypandy
7. Doodles or Izzles
8. Heron
9. Tinky Winky
10. *Tommy Zoom*
11. Tidmouth
12. A pop shop
13. A toy spider
14. Mister Maker
15. Lion

1. In *Despicable Me* (2010), what does Victor 'Vector' Perkins steal and then hide by his residence by painting it pale blue with white clouds so it blends in with the background sky?

2. In *James and the Giant Peach* (1996), which character plays Bach's Partita No. 3 for violin on the peach as it crosses the Atlantic?

3. In which 2009 animated film on a Neil Gaiman novella, does Dakota Fanning voice the title character who visits the Other World at night?

4. In which 2009 film is the wedding of Susan Murphy and local TV weatherman Derek disrupted when she is exposed to quantonium, growing enormously tall as a consequence?

5. Sisters Anna and Elsa feature in which 2013 Disney film, inspired by a Hans Christian Andersen tale, which quickly became the highest-grossing animated film of all time?

6. Voiced by Brad Pitt, who is Megamind's primary foe in the 2010 film of the same name?

7. In *Kung Fu Panda* (2008), what sort of animal is the fearsome Tai Lung, voiced by Ian McShane?

8. In *Spirited Away* (2001), ten-year-old Chihiro Ogino and her parents enter a magical world where her parents are turned into which animals?

9. In which 2009 film does John Travolta provide the voice for the canine title character and Miley Cyrus that of his owner Penny?

10. What sort of creature is Rango, voiced by Johnny Depp in the 2011 animated film of that name?

11. Voiced by David Schwimmer, what sort of animal is Melman in the *Madagascar* animated films?

12. In *Hotel Transylvania* (2012) who is the worried, over-protective father of Mavis?

13. Reanimating his dead dog Sparky using electricity, Viktor is the central character in which 2012 animated film?

14. Which 2005 animated film follows the adventures of Rodney Copperbottom (Ewan McGregor), a young, aspiring inventor who opposes the nefarious schemes of Phineas T. Ratchet?

15. The 2010 Disney animated film *Tangled* is loosely based on which fairy story?

1. The Great Pyramid of Giza (aka the Pyramid of Khufu or the Pyramid of Cheops)
2. Grasshopper
3. *Coraline*
4. *Monsters vs Aliens*
5. *Frozen*
6. Metro Man
7. Snow leopard
8. Pigs
9. *Bolt*
10. Chameleon
11. Giraffe
12. *Count Dracula*
13. *Frankenweenie*
14. *Robots*
15. 'Rapunzel'

1. What was Julia Donaldson's 2004 best-selling sequel to *The Gruffalo*?
2. Who created the imagined world of Alagaesia for his *Inheritance Cycle* of novels, basing it on his home in Montana?
3. Under what name did US novelist Daniel Handler write about the Beaudelaire children in the *Series of Unfortunate Events* books, starting with *The Bad Beginning* (1999)?
4. Who wrote the *Mortal Engines* quartet of books and the *Buster Bayliss* series of books for young readers?
5. *Tales of a Fourth Grade Nothing* (1972), *Superfudge* (1980) and *Fudge-a-Mania* (1990) are books in the *Fudge* series of children's novels by which US author?
6. In a series of books by Richmal Crompton, who was . . . *the Outlaw* (1927), . . . *the Conqueror* (1926), . . . *the Explorer* (1960) and . . . *the Lawless* (1970)?
7. *The Atlantis Complex* (2010) was the seventh and *The Last Guardian* (2012) the eighth novel to feature which criminal genius created by Eoin Colfer?
8. Ian Fleming was best known for creating the British agent James Bond but also wrote about which magical car in 1964?
9. Which *Fast Show* actor and comedian has written a series of novels about a young James Bond including *Silverfin* (2005), *Blood Fever* (2006) and *Double or Die* (2007)?
10. Which character, created by Dr Seuss in 1971, was voiced by Danny DeVito in a 2012 animated film of the same name?
11. Which author has written a series of books featuring a little boy Alfie and his sister Annie-Rose?
12. *Dizzy* (2004), *Scarlett* (2006) and *Lucky Star* (2007) are young adult novels by which Coventry-born author?
13. Which creator of the Alex Ryder novels also wrote an authorised Sherlock Holmes sequel, *House of Silk* (2011)?
14. *Mockingjay* (2010) was the third book in which trilogy of books by Suzanne Collins?
15. Which author of the young adult novels series *Noughts and Crosses* became UK Children's Laureate in June 2013?

1. *The Gruffalo's Child*
2. Christopher Paolini
3. Lemony Snicket
4. Phillip Reeve
5. Judy Blume
6. William (Brown) – in the *Just William* series
7. Artemis Fowl
8. *Chitty-Chitty-Bang-Bang*
9. Charlie Higson
10. The Lorax
11. Shirley Hughes
12. Cathy Cassidy
13. Anthony Horowitz
14. The *Hunger Games* trilogy
15. Malorie Blackman

1. Betty G. Birney has written a series of books about which hamster?

2. In Jill Murphy's *The Worst Witch*, Mildred Hubble is the worst student at whose Academy for Witches?

3. In *The Secret Garden* (1911), the prospects of which weak, sickly and petulant wheelchair-bound boy are transformed through gardening with his cousin Mary and her friend Dickon?

4. What is the occupation of Noddy, created by Enid Blyton?

5. Which character created by Astrid Lindgren shares her house with a monkey called Mr Nilsson?

6. Author of the Artemis Fowl series of books, who was named Ireland's new Children's Laureate in May 2014?

7. In which 2004 Meg Rosoff novel does the outbreak of a third world war result in New Yorker Elizabeth (aka Daisy) being relocated to live with her cousins on a remote farm in England?

8. In *Storm Breaker* by Anthony Horowitz, what creature does the villainous Herod Sayle keep as a pet?

9. Which team, supported by Henry, is drawn against Manchester United in the Cup in the story *Horrid Henry and the Football Fiend*?

10. In which book by Louis Sachar is Stanley Yelnats unjustly sent to Camp Green Lake, a boys' juvenile detention camp?

11. What mushroom-like silent creatures wander around the world of the Moomins in boat convoys, forever trying to reach the horizon?

12. Who wrote the *Rover Adventures* series, which includes *The Giggler Treatment* (2000), *Rover Saves Christmas* (2001) and *The Meanwhile Adventures* (2004)?

13. Derek Landy created which skeleton detective who, with a teenage girl Stephanie Edgley, features in a series of children's novels?

14. *A Week with Willi Worm*, featuring a bookworm named Willi, eventually became which well-loved book by Eric Carle?

15. Also the name of this 1989 book, which line starts the regularly repeated refrain '_____ / We're going to catch a big one / What a beautiful day! / We're not scared'?

1. Humphrey
2. Miss Cackle's
3. Colin Craven
4. Taxi driver
5. Pippi Longstocking
6. Eoin Colfer
7. *How I Live Now*
8. Portuguese man of war
9. Ashton United
10. *Holes*
11. Hattifatteners
12. Roddy Doyle
13. Skulduggery Pleasant
14. *The Very Hungry Caterpillar*
15. 'We're going on a bear hunt'

1. In US slang, what are you giving a person if you rub their head hard with your knuckles?
2. Which books by Tony DiTerlizzi and Holly Black are about the adventures of the Grace children: twins Simon and Jared, and older sister Mallory, who move to the estate of the title and discover a world of faeries?
3. Which US actress and singer, who played Cat on the Nickelodeon show *Victorious*, released the 2014 single 'Problem' (featuring Iggy Azalea)?
4. In Europe and America, the most common use of vanilla flavouring is for which food?
5. A family theme park in the New Forest, Hampshire, is devoted to which children's TV character, the very best friend of Suzy Sheep?
6. Rouge the Bat, Miles 'Tails' Prower the two-tailed Fox, Amy Rose, Knuckles the Echidna, Cream the Rabbit, Nack the Weasel and Blaze the Cat are friends of which video game character?
7. Who was 'gold slimed' along with two of his sons at the first ever Nickelodeon Kids' Choice sports awards in 2014?
8. Which former Liverpool footballer's nicknames include 'the Cannibal of Ajax', 'Lucho', 'El Conejo' (the Rabbit) and 'El Pistolero'?
9. Based on books by Christine L'Heureux, which Canadian animated TV show is about a bald four-year-old 'Prince of the Imagination' who lives with his family in a blue house on 17 Pine Street?
10. Which Scottish uncle of Donald Duck is the richest person in the Disney universe?
11. What is Tinie Tempah's actual first name?
12. Which claymation penguin often gets into trouble with his best friend Robby the Seal?
13. The *High School Musical* character Troy Bolton (Zac Efron) is the captain of which sports team?
14. Which book series by Ricky Gervais features the Flemping Bunt-Himmler, the Clunge Ambler, the Underblenge and Munty Flumple?
15. Which Canadian identical twins featuring The Lonely Island released the *Lego Movie* song 'Everything is AWESOME!!!'?

1. Noogies
2. *The Spiderwick Chronicles*
3. Ariana Grande
4. Ice cream
5. Peppa Pig
6. Sonic the Hedgehog
7. David Beckham, with sons Cruz and Romero
8. Luis Suarez
9. *Caillou*
10. Scrooge McDuck
11. Patrick – full name: Patrick Chukwuemeka Okogwu
12. Pingu
13. East High School basketball team (in Albuquerque)
14. *Flanimals*
15. Tegan and Sara (aka Tegan Rain Quin and Sara Kiersten Quin)

1. In 2014, which author of *Hollow Pike* became the first male winner of the Queen of Teen award for *Cruel Summer*?

2. Complete the title of the 1970 novel by Judy Blume: *Are You There God? It's Me, . . . ?*

3. *Where She Went* is the 2013 sequel to which novel by Gayle Forman, about 17-year-old cellist Mia Hall and the out-of-body experience she undergoes thanks to a car crash?

4. Who was 15 years old when she started writing the coming-of-age novel *The Outsiders* (1967)?

5. Who is the author of *The Maze Runner*, its sequels *The Scorch Trials* and *The Death Cure* and prequel *The Kill Order*?

6. Which 1993 novel starts off and gives its title to the sci-fi quartet by Lois Lowry that includes *Gathering Blue* (2000), *Messenger* (2004) and *Son* (2012)?

7. Winner of the 2013 Carnegie Medal, which novel by Sally Gardner is narrated by its hero Standish Treadwell, who stands up to the oppression of the Motherland?

8. In *The Fault in Our Stars* by John Green, Hazel and Augustus have their first kiss in which museum?

9. After *Divergent* and *Insurgent*, which novel completes the *Divergent* trilogy by Veronica Roth?

10. Canada's Marie-Sophie Nélisse played the teenage title role of Liesel Meminger in which 2013 film, adapted from a best-selling book by Markus Zusak?

11. Ruled by Mia Thermopolis's grandfather, Prince Philippe Renaldo (rather than Queen Clarisse Renaldo in the movies), which fictional country in *The Princess Diaries* is located between France and Italy?

12. Declaring 'I'll always be a geek', who is the nerd heroine of the novels *Geek Girl* and *Model Misfit* by Holly Smale?

13. In which novel by Rachel Hawkins is the 16-year-old witch Sophia sent to a school, nicknamed 'Freak High', for witches, faeries and wizards?

14. Executed at the end of the first *Hunger Games* book, Seneca Crane is replaced by which man in the role of Head Gamemaker?

15. Which 2012 novel by R.J. Palacio is the moving and uplifting tale of August 'Auggie' Pullman, a boy born with a terrible facial deformity that results in him having 27 operations?

1. James Dawson
2. *Margaret*
3. *If I Stay*
4. S.E. Hinton
5. James Dashner
6. *The Giver*
7. *Maggot Moon*
8. Anne Frank House, Amsterdam
9. *Allegiant*
10. *The Book Thief*
11. Genovia which is ruled by Queen Clarisse Renaldo in the movies
12. Harriet Manners
13. *Hex Hall* (Hecate Hall)
14. Plutarch Heavensbee
15. *Wonder* (Palacio is the pen name of New York-based graphic designer Raquel Jaramillo)

1. Which singer, who released her first album *Don't Forget* in 2008, made her debut as a child actress in *Barney and Friends*?

2. Which Aussie band, formed in 2011 by students at Norwest Christian College topped the singles chart in April 2014 with *She Looks Perfect*?

3. 'Maybe it's the way she walked / Straight into my heart and stole it' are the opening lines of which One Direction hit?

4. In 2010, the Wanted topped the singles chart with which debut release?

5. Which British musician featured on Taylor Swift's 2013 hit single 'Everything Has Changed'?

6. Which 2014 no. 1 has a chorus that begins 'If you gave me a chance I would take it / It's a shot in the dark but I'll make it'?

7. Topping the charts with their debut single 'Me and My Broken Heart', the group Rixton is fronted by which son of Shane Richie and Coleen Nolan?

8. In 2013, which boy band had top ten hits with 'Carry You' and 'Beautiful Life'?

9. Born in 1993, who is the youngest member of Little Mix? She got engaged to One Direction member Zayn Malik in August 2013.

10. In July 2013, which band uploaded their first original song, 'Wildheart' (later retitled 'Wild Heart'), onto their YouTube account?

11. At the 2013 MTV Video Music Awards, which teenage US singer won the Artist to Watch award for his song 'What About Love'?

12. During the 2010–11 TV season, which then teenage pop star played the role of serial killer Jason McCann in two episodes of *CSI: Crime Scene Investigation*?

13. In June 2014, which finalist on *The X Factor* went straight to no. 1 with her debut single 'Ghost'?

14. Which singer, who released her debut album in 2012, has the middle name Sahatçiu?

15. Which group was created for an US TV show about four ice hockey players from Minnesota – Carlos, Logan, Kendall and James – who are selected to form a boy band?

1. Demi Lovato
2. Five Seconds of Summer
3. 'Best Song Ever'
4. 'All Time Low'
5. Ed Sheeran
6. 'Rather Be' – Clean Bandit, featuring Jess Glynne
7. Jake Roche
8. Union J
9. Perrie Edwards
10. The Vamps
11. Austin Mahone
12. Justin Bieber
13. Ella Henderson
14. Rita Ora
15. Big Time Rush

1. In which film does a Stone Age cavewoman named Eep live with her father Grug, mother Ugga, grandmother Gran and younger siblings Thunk and Sandy?

2. El Macho, also known as Salsa & Salsa Mexican restaurant owner Eduardo Perez, is the villain in which 2013 film?

3. Dean Abigail Hardscrabble is the English-accented chair of the Scarer programme at which place of higher learning?

4. 'What have we done?', spoken by Bilbo Baggins, is the last line of which 2013 film?

5. Dusty Crophopper, Skipper Riley, the forklift Sparky and the fuel truck Chug are characters in which 2013 film?

6. Who played Dominic Badguy, the sidekick of Constantine, the *Muppets Most Wanted* villain and dead ringer for Kermit the Frog?

7. Which series has featured Raz the Procoptodon and Captain Gutt the Gigantopithecus, as well as Smilodon Chamitataurus and Palaeolagus characters?

8. In *Oz The Great and Powerful*, Finley is a winged type of which creature?

9. The inventor Flint Lockwood returned in which 2013 movie?

10. The movie *Maleficent* retells the story of which Disney film from the viewpoint of its villain?

11. Which film featured the villains Electro, Rhino and the Green Goblin?

12. In *Rio 2*, the parrots Blu and Jewel have their three children, music lover Carla (the oldest), book-loving Bia and which mischievous son, their youngest kid?

13. Partners with the rat Buddy, which purple squirrel is the hero of the film *The Nut Job*?

14. Which 2014 film is about a talking dog who is the smartest being in the world and the orphan he found and legally adopted?

15. Which character in the movie *Frozen* sings 'Let It Go'?

1. *The Croods*
2. *Despicable Me 2*
3. Monsters University
4. *The Hobbit: The Desolation of Smaug*
5. *Planes*
6. Ricky Gervais
7. *Ice Age* – (they are, respectively, a giant short-faced kangaroo and a giant ape; the other names refer to terms for a sabre-toothed cat, a prehistoric badger and 'ancient hare')
8. Monkey
9. *Cloudy with a Chance of Meatballs 2*
10. *Sleeping Beauty*
11. *The Amazing Spider-Man 2*
12. Tiago
13. Surly
14. *Mr Peabody and Sherman*
15. Queen Elsa

1. Dinosaurs first appeared on earth during which geological period, the first of the Mesozoic era?

2. The word 'dinosaur' comes from the Ancient Greek meaning what?

3. What name is given to someone who looks at fossils to study past forms of life such as dinosaurs?

4. Which Englishman coined the word 'dinosaur'?

5. What was the first dinosaur to be described scientifically?

6. Dinosaurs can be divided into two main groups – Saurischians, or 'lizard-hipped', and Ornithischians, with hips like what kind of creatures?

7. Not technically dinosaurs, which group of winged lizards were the first vertebrates to develop the ability to fly (as opposed to just gliding)?

8. Which dinosaur's reputation as a vicious killer was enhanced by its depiction in the novel and film *Jurassic Park*?

9. Which dinosaur that lived in the late Cretaceous period was known for the thick armoured plates which coated its body, and its tail with a club on the end?

10. What type of dinosaur is the childen's television character Barney?

11. By what name was the large dinosaur apatosaurus formerly and better known?

12. Named for the amount of specimens found there in the early 20th century, Dinosaur National Monument is located in which country?

13. What dinosaur's name means 'roofed lizard', a reference to the triangular bony plates running down its back and tail?

14. Brachiosaurus and diplodocus were members of which group of dinosaurs, which contained the longest and heaviest of all the dinosaurs?

15. Which carnivorous bird-like dinosaur has a name meaning 'wounding tooth' and is known for its unusually large brain?

Answers to Dinosaurs: Children's Quiz 10

1. Triassic
2. 'Terrible lizard' or 'terrible reptile'
3. Palaeontologist
4. Richard Owen
5. Megalosaurus
6. Birds
7. Pterosaurs
8. Velociraptor (although the dinosaurs depicted in the film were more similar to Deinonychus)
9. Ankylosaurus
10. Tyrannosaurus
11. Brontosaurus
12. United States of America
13. Stegosaurus
14. Sauropoda or Sauropods
15. Troodon

1. What is the name of the forgetful tabby cat in the children's books by Judith Kerr?

2. Which two types of food does the narrator tell Sam-I-Am he does not like in the Dr Seuss children's book?

3. A frog, a dog, a cat and a bird are the four animals looking for room on what object in the title of a children's book by Julia Donaldson?

4. Who has twenty-five cats, a houseful, in the book by Alyssa Satin Capuchilli?

5. Which brother and sister, who also appear on television, appear in the book *I Will Not Never Ever Eat a Tomato* by Lauren Child?

6. What is the name of Spot the dog's mum in the books by Eric Hill?

7. Which Janet and Allan Ahlberg book ends with characters like Tom Thumb, Mother Hubbard and the Three Bears having a picnic?

8. How does the Gruffalo like to eat owl, according to the mouse?

9. What animal isn't sent back to the zoo in *Dear Zoo* by Rod Campbell?

10. Boris and Barbara Bear, Poppy Pig and Snuffy are friends with which rabbit in a series of children's books?

11. In a book by David Mckee, which child tried to warn his parents a monster wanted to eat him, but kept getting told 'Not now'?

12. Which creature has stolen the bear's hat in Jon Klassen's *I Want My Hat Back*?

13. In the book by Julia Donaldson, which creature travels round the world on the back of a whale?

14. What type of small beetle was bad-tempered in a children's book by Eric Carle?

15. In which book by Jill Murphy does Mr Bear look for lots of places to sleep, eventually returning to his own bed?

Answers to Younger Children's Books:
Children's Quiz 11

1. Mog
2. Green eggs and ham
3. The broom
4. Mrs McTats
5. Charlie and Lola
6. Sally
7. *Each Peach Pear Plum*
8. As owl ice cream
9. A puppy
10. Miffy
11. Bernard
12. A rabbit
13. A snail
14. A ladybird or ladybug
15. *Peace at Last*

1. Which panto usually features Fleshcreep and Daisy the Cow?

2. In *Matilda the Musical*, what is the name of the tiny cupboard lined with sharp objects that Miss Trunchball locks disobedient schoolchildren in for hours?

3. The Polka Theatre put on the puppet show *Moominsummer Madness*, based on a book by which writer? The 100th anniversary of her birthday was celebrated in 2014.

4. Which play for young people by Alan Ayckbourn is about a book-loving kid named Kevin, whose library comes to life, along with the mysterious underworld baddie the Green Shark?

5. Widow Twankey is which pantomime title character's mother?

6. Based on a book by Ross Collins, which show is about a little girl who finds out that she is living in a house with a rather large ghost-animal?

7. In *Angelina Ballerina – the Mousical*, the tiny rodent ballerinas must create a winning routine for which TV show?

8. The show *The Tiger Who Came to Tea*, based on the picture book by Judith Kerr, has a tiger visit a girl and her mummy. What is the girl's name?

9. Which TV programme's live version has come in two shows: *Pinky Ponky Show: Makka Pakka Washes Faces* and *Ninky Nonk Show: Igglepiggle Loses His Blanket*?

10. What do *Aliens Love . . .* according to the title of a show that made its West End debut in the summer of 2014?

11. A one-woman show starring Danyah Miller when it arrived in the West End in August 2014, *I Believe in Unicorns* is based on a book by which writer?

12. Which novel by Jacqueline Wilson, about a girl who escapes from her children's home and joins a travelling circus, has been made into a West End show?

13. ZooNation's 'dance-theatre-fun mash-up' *Groove on Down the Road* is based on which movie musical?

14. Which German composer's epic story of gods, dwarves and a powerful ring was made into an outdoor summer show for families without all the singing?

15. Which musical features the songs 'Almost Nearly Perfect', 'The Double Bubble Duchess', 'Strike That', 'Reverse It!' and 'Pure Imagination'?

1. *Jack and the Beanstalk*
2. The Chokey
3. Tove Jansson
4. *The Boy Who Fell into a Book*
5. Aladdin
6. *The Elephantom*
7. *Dancing with Mice*
8. Sophie
9. *In the Night Garden*
10. *. . . Underpants*
11. Michael Morpurgo
12. *Hetty Feather*
13. *The Wizard of Oz*
14. Richard Wagner
15. *Charlie and the Chocolate Factory*

1. Which minifigure comes in nine variants, all made up of combinations of two torso designs, a cape and four heads (with variations in the eye colour, eyebrows and scar patterns), but just one trademark helmet piece?
2. Who comes in Farmboy of Tatooine, Stormtrooper Disguise, Medal Winner, Hoth Rebel Commander, Injured at the Infirmary, Cloud City, Jedi Knight and Camouflage on Endor variants?
3. Biggs Darklighter, Wedge Antilles, Zev Senesca and Dak Ralter are all classified as which type of pilot?
4. Which infamous 'goofy Gungan' broke the Lego mould as the first minifigure ever to have a unique head sculpt?
5. Which 'dangerous Dug' is the arch rival of child Anakin Skywalker and one of the most successful podracers on Tatooine?
6. Which elite pilots of the Imperial Navy are referred to as 'bucketheads' by Rebel pilots because of their bulky black helmets?
7. The Ewok Wicket Wystri Warrick lives on which moon?
8. Appearing in only one Lego set, which Mon Calamari minifigure commanded the Rebel Alliance's assault on the second Death Star from his flagship *Home One*?
9. Which secret apprentice of Darth Vader from the Expanded Universe is the pilot of *Rogue Shadow*, making her the only female Imperial minifigure to make an appearance?
10. Which Governor of the Imperial Outland Regions has appeared in two Lego *Star Wars* sets since 2006 – Imperial Star Destroyer and Death Star?
11. In which set (no. 4501) do Han Solo and Greedo have their deadly (for the latter) chat about the unpaid debts that Han owes Jabba the Hutt?
12. Which bounty hunter is exclusive to 2002s *Slave 1* set (no. 7153)?
13. On a covert mission for the Rebel Alliance, the 'ill-fated' Captain Antilles commands which consular cruiser? It is boarded by Darth Vader, who ends up strangling the captain.
14. Admiral Firmus Piett makes his only Lego appearance in a 2011 set, commanding which giant Star Dreadnought warship?
15. Dressed in brown trousers and a white shirt, the Han Solo delivered to Jabba the Hutt is frozen inside a block of what?

1. Darth Vader
2. Luke Skywalker
3. X-wing pilot
4. Jar Jar Binks
5. Sebulba
6. TIE pilots
7. Endor
8. Admiral Ackbar, Rebel Supreme Commander
9. Juno Eclipse
10. Grand Moff Tarkin
11. Mos Eisley Cantina
12. Jango Fett
13. *Tantive IV*
14. *Executor*
15. Carbonite

1. Which New Zealander became a global star thanks to the release of her debut album *Pure Heroine* and its lead single 'Royals'?

2. Born in South Korea in 1997, New Zealand's Lydia Ko is one of the world's top players in which sport?

3. Who is the youngest daughter of Bruce and Kris Jenner, and youngest half-sister of Kim Kardashian?

4. In March 2013, 17-year-old Londoner Nick D'Aloisio sold which app to Yahoo for $30 million?

5. Then 17-year-old American Missy Franklin won four gold medals at the London Olympics in which sport?

6. Partly thanks to his outstanding Afro, Dante de Blasio became a fashion icon when his father Bill was elected mayor of which US city in 2013?

7. The US child actress Kiernan Shipka's most famous role is that of Sally Draper in which TV drama?

8. Best known for playing Hit-Girl in the two *Kick-Ass* movies, which US actress became a leading lady for the first time in the 2013 remake of *Carrie*?

9. Which daughter of Barack Obama shares her name with a holiday resort on Crete?

10. Which 15-year-old US author rose to fame for keeping a diary to help her become popular, following old-fashioned tips from the 1950s self-help book *Betty Cornell's Glamour Guide for Teens*?

11. Miley Cyrus was only 19 when she announced her engagement to which Australian *Hunger Games* star?

12. Shereen Cutkelvin, Amira McCarthy and Asami Zdrenka are the teenage members of which British girl group, who released their debut single 'Trouble' in August 2013?

13. Which member of *Britain's Got Talent*-winning dance troupe Diversity won the second series of *Splash!*, in 2014?

14. Which *Outnumbered* actor has gone on to present a BBC Three documentary series in which he *Takes On* . . . subjects like 'The Perfect Body' and 'Love'?

15. Which Australian was the top-placed teen musician (at no. 33) in *Heat* magazine's 101 Hottest Hunks of 2014?

1. Lorde/real name Ella Marija Lani Yelich-O'Connor
2. Golf
3. Kylie Kristen Jenner
4. Summly
5. Swimming
6. New York
7. *Mad Men*
8. Chloë Grace Moretz
9. Malia
10. Maya Van Wagenen
11. Liam Hemsworth
12. Neon Jungle – Jess Plummer (born 1992) is the oldest member of the four-piece
13. Perri Kiely
14. Tyger Drew-Honey
15. Luke Hemmings, frontman of 5 Seconds of Summer

1. On which planet was Superman born as Kal-El?
2. In which country did Wolverine fight the Silver Samurai in *The Wolverine*?
3. In Iron Man 3, a Stars 'n' Stripes paint job came with the new name 'Iron Patriot', what name does Lieutenant-Colonel James Rhodes use when he wears the Mark II prototype Iron Man armour?
4. Which director of S.H.I.E.L.D. is played by Samuel L. Jackson?
5. What was the name of the alien race that invaded New York during the final part of *Avengers Assemble*, also titled *The Avengers*?
6. Played by Scarlett Johansson, what is Black Widow's real name?
7. In *The Dark Knight Rises*, Miranda Tate is revealed to be the daughter of which other villain?
8. Who is the father of Thor and ruler of the realm known as Asgard?
9. Which newly elected District Attorney in *The Dark Knight* says: 'You either die a hero or you live long enough to see yourself become the villain'?
10. In *The Incredibles*, what is the superhero identity of Helen Parr, the wife of Mr Incredible (Bob Parr)?
11. What is the name of the terrorist group that kidnaps an injured Tony Stark at the start of the first *Iron Man* film?
12. Steve Rogers is the real name of which Super Soldier who fought the Red Skull during World War II?
13. Which demon-superhero has been played in two films by Ron Perlman?
14. Which *X-Men* character, played most recently by Jennifer Lawrence, is also known as Raven Darkhölme?
15. What is the name of the aunt that Peter Parker lives with in the *Spider-Man* movies?

1. Krypton
2. Japan
3. War Machine
4. Nick Fury
5. The Chitauri
6. Natasha Romanoff
7. Ras al Ghul – Tate's real name is Talia al Ghul
8. Odin
9. Harvey Dent – who becomes the villain Two-Face
10. Elastigirl
11. The Ten Rings
12. Captain America
13. Hellboy
14. Mystique
15. Aunt May/May Parker

1. Which actress, who later played a main character, appeared as a soothsayer in 'The Fires of Pompeii'?
2. Which red hat, named after a Moroccan city, was sometimes worn by the Eleventh Doctor (Matt Smith)?
3. Which actor played the Doctor when it returned to TV in 2005?
4. Which race of alien villains become 'quantum-locked', occupying a single position in space and becoming stone, when people observe them?
5. What is the name of the race that the Doctor belongs to and lives on the planet Gallifrey?
6. Which villain is known as the creator of the Daleks?
7. Which enemies of the Doctor were originally a race of human-like beings who lived on earth's twin planet Mondas?
8. Which gadget does not work on wood, with the Doctor saying: 'I've got to invent a setting for wood. It's embarrassing!'?
9. Designed to hold the most fearsome being in the whole universe, the fabled prison known as the Pandorica is located underneath which famous English landmark?
10. What was the name of Amy Pond's boyfriend, who becomes her husband?
11. Which companion made her first appearance in the episode 'The Runaway Bride' and is given the knowledge of a Time Lord when she touches the Doctor's regeneration-energy-infused severed hand in 'Journey's End'?
12. Which *Doctor Who* villain disguised himself as Professor Yana and Prime Minister Harold Saxon?
13. Which Scottish actor replaced Matt Smith as the Doctor?
14. Which character was born Melody Pond?
15. What does TARDIS stand for?

Answers to *Doctor Who*: Children's Quiz 16

1. Karen Gillan, who later played companion Amy Pond
2. Fez
3. Christopher Eccleston
4. The Weeping Angels
5. The Time Lords
6. Davros
7. Cybermen
8. Sonic screwdriver
9. Stonehenge
10. Rory Williams
11. Donna Noble
12. The Master
13. Peter Capaldi
14. River Song
15. Time And Relative Dimension In Space

1. Which film and subsequent musical is set in a fictional mining town in the north-east of England and follows a young boy's dreams of becoming a ballet dancer?

2. Based on a comic strip, which musical follows the adventures of the 11-year-old title girl and features songs including 'Tomorrow' and 'Hard-Knock Life'?

3. Which US cartoon series featured the children Tommy, Chucky, Phil, Lil and Angelika?

4. In 2012, in her boat *Guppy*, Laura Dekker became, at the age of 16, the youngest person to do what?

5. Yulia Lipnitskaya was, at 15, the youngest Russian winner of a gold medal at the Sochi Olympics. In which sport did she win?

6. Which very famous tennis player became father to identical twin daughters Myla Rose and Charlene Riva in 2009 and then twin sons Leo and Lennart in 2014?

7. In the nursery rhyme, if Monday's child is 'fair of face', which day's child is 'loving and giving'?

8. Set in the Norfolk Broads, in which 1930 book do we meet the Walker and Plackett children?

9. Jim Hawkins is the narrator of which 1883 novel by Scottish author Robert Louis Stevenson?

10. What is the surname of Peter Pan's friend Wendy and her brothers John and Michael?

11. In the book *Heidi*, Heidi befriends which goatherd while staying with her grandfather in the mountains?

12. Which girl, living on the fictional Isle of Struay, off the west coast of Scotland, is the title character of a series of children's picture books written and illustrated by Mairi Hedderwick?

13. Whose famous diary was first published in English in 1952 as *Diary of a Young Girl*?

14. Set in Prohibition-era Chicago, which 1976 British musical gangster film boasts a cast of children including Jodie Foster and Scott Baio?

15. In a series of films, which title character is taught martial arts by Mr Miyagi?

1. *Billy Elliot*
2. *Annie*
3. *The Rugrats*
4. Sail solo around the world (with stops)
5. Figure skating/ice skating (the team event)
6. Roger Federer
7. Friday
8. *Swallows and Amazons*
9. *Treasure Island*
10. Darling
11. Peter
12. Katy Morag
13. Anne Frank
14. *Bugsy Malone*
15. *The Karate Kid*

1. Which cartoon cat first appeared as Jasper in *Puss Gets the Boot*?
2. With friends including Benny the Ball, Fancy-Fancy, Spook and Choo Choo, which Manhattan alley cat regularly outwitted Officer Dibble?
3. Which *Looney Tunes* cat repeatedly chased Tweety Bird?
4. How was Emily's large, saggy, pink and white striped cat named in a much-loved BBC children's series?
5. What is the name of Bob the Builder's cat?
6. In which children's animated TV series does Joe Pasquale voice Nine, a cat whose best friend is the little girl Lottie?
7. Living in Springfield, which animated TV family have owned a succession of cats named Snowball?
8. According to the nursery rhyme, where had the pussycat been?
9. Which character in the *Harry Potter* books has a pet called Crookshanks?
10. Which cat in *Alice's Adventures in Wonderland* was able to disappear from view until only his wide grin remained?
11. Which 1970 Disney animated film featured cats named Thomas O'Malley and Duchess with her three kittens Toulouse, Marie and Berlioz?
12. In 1957, who wrote the children's book *The Cat in the Hat*?
13. The cat Sergeant Tibbs helps kidnapped pups to escape from Cruella de Vil in which 1961 Disney film?
14. Actor Antonio Banderas voiced which fairy-tale cat in various *Shrek* films and then in the character's own 2011 film?
15. In T.S. Eliot's *Old Possum's Book of Practical Cats*, which feline is known as the Napoleon of Crime?

Answers to Fictional Cats: Children's Quiz 18

1. Tom Cat (of Tom and Jerry)
2. Top Cat (aka *Boss Cat*)
3. Sylvester
4. Bagpuss
5. Pilchard
6. *Frankenstein's Cat*
7. *The Simpsons*
8. London (to look at the Queen)
9. Hermione Grainger
10. The Cheshire Cat
11. *The Aristocats*
12. Dr Seuss (aka Theodor Geisel)
13. *One Hundred and One Dalmations*
14. Puss in Boots
15. Macavity (the Mystery Cat)

1. In which Pixar film did Paul Newman voice Doc Hudson? It was his last feature film role and proved to be the highest-grossing film of his career.

2. In *A Bug's Life*, Flick uses a rolled-up blade of grass and a bead of dew to make what for Princess Atta?

3. The grasshopper bar in *A Bug's Life* lies under what tatty item at the base of a cactus?

4. Why does Jerry, the floor supervisor in *Monsters, Inc.*, count down from seven?

5. In *Toy Story*, what is the name of Sid's dog?

6. What, in *Ratatouille*, is remarkable about the car registration 820 NJK 77?

7. In *Wall-E*, what is the name of the giant spacecraft in which humanity has been exiled for 700 years?

8. Wall-E loves to listen to an old video recording of 'Put on Your Sunday Clothes' from which musical?

9. Name either of the two grim options for Bo Peep's death offered by Dr Pork Chop in *Toy Story 2*?

10. In a possible reference to the Bond film *Goldfinger*, what does Mr Potato Head use to stop the apartment building doors from shutting as the toys pursue Al in *Toy Story 2*?

11. In *Toy Story 2*, whose small arms make him unable to press the fire and jump buttons at the same time when using a computer game controller?

12. When we first meet Russell in *Up*, which Wilderness Explorer badge is he missing?

13. In *Up*, who had smuggled an arsinoitherium out of Ethiopia disguised as dental equipment?

14. Mr Incredible finds what important single word carved into the cave wall by Gazerbeam?

15. Which French-accented villain from *The Incredibles* makes a fleeting cameo appearance as a street mime in *Ratatouille*?

1. *Cars*
2. A telescope
3. A sombrero (Mexican hat)
4. He has six fingers and a thumb!
5. Scud
6. It is shared by two cars which crash into each other – visible in just one single frame!
7. *Axiom*
8. *Hello, Dolly!*
9. Shark or death by monkeys
10. His (bowler) hat (he throws it into the gap)
11. Rex (the dinosaur)
12. Assisting the Elderly badge
13. Charles Muntz
14. Kronos – the computer system's password
15. Bomb Voyage

1. Occasionally spotted in rock pools, what sort of creature is Patrick, SpongeBob SquarePants's best friend?

2. Sometimes found at seaside resorts, which entertainment features characters such as a baby, a constable, a clown, a crocodile and a skeleton?

3. What treat, that can sometimes be enjoyed at the seaside, is known as cotton candy in the United States?

4. Available at many seaside resorts, what hard stick-shaped boiled sugar confectionery, most usually flavoured with peppermint or spearmint, may have lettering running lengthways through it?

5. What name has been given to a stretch of coastline in Devon and Dorset noted for the numerous fossil finds in its cliffs?

6. A combination of the earth's rotation and the gravitational pull of which objects on the earth's oceans leads to the tides?

7. Because they look like plants, which tentacled animals, frequently seen in rock pools, take their common general name from a terrestrial flower?

8. The largest seabird in the North Atlantic, which large white bird, which makes spectacular dives into the sea hunting fish, can be seen on certain islands off the British coast?

9. The shore, velvet swimming, hermit and edible are types of which creature found in British seaside waters?

10. The blue, barrel, compass and lion's mane are different types of which creatures sometimes seen stranded on the sand at the seaside?

11. Found on the seashore, what two-word name can be given to egg cases holding the fertilised eggs of certain rays, skates and sharks?

12. Found at the seaside, carragheen, laver and dulse are edible types of what?

13. Four examples of what structure have, in turn, been built on the dangerous Eddystone Rocks, nine miles off south-west England?

14. Blackpool, Southport, Brighton, Southend and Weston-super-Mare all boast examples of which seaside feature?

15. A speciality of Scotland and parts of England, what word describes golf courses located near the sea on sandy, quick-draining soils?

Answers to the Seaside: Children's Quiz 20

1. Starfish
2. Punch and Judy shows
3. Candy floss
4. Rock (e.g. Blackpool rock)
5. Jurassic Coast
6. Moon or Sun
7. Sea anemone
8. Gannet
9. Crab
10. Jellyfish
11. Mermaid's purse or devil's purse
12. Seaweed/algae
13. Lighthouse
14. (Pleasure) pier
15. Links